(Canada) Ltd.
The Political Economy of Dependency

(Canada) Ltd.
The Political Economy of Dependency
Edited by Robert Laxer

McClelland and Stewart Limited
The Canadian Publishers
25 Hollinger Road, Toronto

ISBN 7710-4980-3

Contents

Foreword

(Canada) Ltd., the Political Economy of Dependency is at once an analysis and a strategy. As a scholarly work, the book is distinguished not only by its cogent analysis of Canadian society in crisis, as a dependency moving towards colonial status in the American Empire, but by its strategy to change that society towards independence and liberation.

While other scholars may lend their talents to the esthetics and the rigour of an argument or to the internal consistency of their models, this book concentrates on the real world of political economy, on the struggles of working people for jobs, a higher quality of life and independence for their country. The logic and method of the authors derives from the contention that to understand the world is to be involved in changing the world.

In contrast to the view that the social sciences should examine society with detachment and stand above the world of political conflict, political economy analyses the world dynamically in the context of practical experience and creates a strategy to transform the world. In this discipline, analysis and strategy are closely linked – for not only is strategy based on analysis, but the test of strategy in practice is at the same time a test of the analysis and the need for its modification with experience.

Thus political economy, as a discipline devoted to changing as well as explaining the world, is a challenge to current views of the role of the social sciences in Canadian universities. From the standpoint of political economy it is wrong for Canadian university departments of social sciences to treat Canadian dependency as if it were a happening in outer space. It is wrong not simply on the ground that Canadian universities should guard the interests, culture, and promise of the nation which nurtures them. It is also wrong because the failure to deal with the Canadian reality leads to poor scholarship. The favoured practice in most departments is to import inappropriate models from the metropolis. The consequence is that much of the academic work on Canada falls short of explaining the Canadian social structure and its status of a U.S. dependency. What is even more important from the standpoint of political economy is that most studies do not begin to produce a strategy designed to overcome that dependency. And therein lies the weakness of the academic social sciences – divorced as they are from the world where people and social forces confront each other in the real political economy, in the struggle to discover social alternatives which Academe has not even begun to consider.

Structure of the Book

The structure of this book on Canada's political economy is therefore based on a method and an explicit logic. The first six chapters focus on contemporary and historical aspects of the dynamics of the economy, while the last six take up questions broadly political relating to ideas and institutions which contend for supremacy in Canada.

The opening chapter provides a broad historical perspective. It also contributes a new hypothesis, in discovering the historical roots within the Canadian political economy for the particular form and nature of the trade-union movement in Canada – a thesis which is likely to stir new arguments in the running dialogue over Canadian vs. U.S. unions in Canada. The financial-commercial business class in Canada is displayed under the glare of historic scandals and its checkered career as sales agent of Canada's resources to the highest bidder. The chapter on the role of social classes in Canadian society subjects the viewpoint of Porter in his Vertical Mosaic to critical review, and demonstrates the validity of the concept of class in all social analysis. The role of women in Canadian history and contemporary society receives novel treatment by rooting the analysis in the context of a study of the political economy and by examining women's position in the work place as the ground from which to launch their full liberation. Resources as the chief reason for three empires' exploitations of Canada are presented as the chief issue around which may be fought the struggle for Canadian independence. The decline of Canadian manufacturing in terms of its weight in the GNP and the work force – the thesis of de-industrialization –

receives its first treatment in this volume, within the broader context of a developed anti-imperialist analysis.

From these six chapters the book moves into the area of the state and other broad ideological and class-laden issues. There is a promising beginning in the attempt at a precise definition of the role and nature of the Canadian state, as a state – neither colonial nor imperial, but controlled by American corporations as seniors and Canadian financiers as juniors – a dependent capitalist state in the American empire. Serious study of the labour movement has just recently begun in Canada; an historic approach rooted in a study of the political economy promises to lay bare the roots of American and business unionism in this country. The history of the CCF-NDP – of social democracy in Canada – needs far greater study than can be given justice in one chapter. The role of liberal culture in a dependent, colonial-minded society takes a new departure in a chapter which suggests the need for several volumes. Quebec nationalism as a phenomenon of contradiction and inner class conflict begets an historical-developmental approach which emphasizes objective analysis, rather than the favourite English-Canadian pattern of prescription for Quebec.

As made explicit earlier, the alternatives facing Canada flow logically from the chapters on its political economy and an examination of the ideas and institutions which are in contention in Canadian society. The concluding chapter gives the reader a summation of the streams of arguments and then presses for a choice.

In the twelve chapters of this volume, the authors examine the alternative analyses and consequent strategies for Canada's future.

The most fundamental issue for scrutiny is that of the spreading presence of the U.S. corporations in Canada. All the authors in this volume start with the assumption that there is a sharp dividing line between two basic approaches which will increasingly contend for public support in Canada. On the one side – and this broadly includes the Liberals, Conservatives and the NDP – are those who feel they can live with the multi-nationals. They would prescribe good corporate citizenship, government regulation and screening of foreign companies and pluralist checks and balances in a well ordered liberal-reformist or welfare society. On the other side are those who confront the American empire with a basic socialist critique and a far-reaching strategy of public ownership.

The consequences of each analysis and related strategy are far from the vapid academic exercise of building an aesthetically pleasing model to explain the data. A liberal-reformist analysis grants merit points as well as demerits to the integration of Canada into the technologically most advanced economy in the world. It offers steady, although begrudging, support to the continental drift. It leads logically to a hinterland mentality of bartering resources for the finished goods of the advanced metropolis, with the hope that assembly-line manufacturing and supply depots will remain profitable to the U.S. companies and leave some jobs in Canada.

An anti-imperial analysis, on the other hand, views continentalism as a crushing blow to the Canadian people and the promising potential of an alternative society free from the exploitation and decay of the empire of Standard Oil and the I.T.T. It projects a society to open opportunities through an expanding economy in which resources create employment in Canadian manufacturing instead of serving as unprocessed raw materials for export abroad.

De-Industrialization as a Major Thesis

Probably the most crucial aspect of the analysis presented in this volume is the thesis of de-industrialization. The drive to de-industrialize Canada is not only a strategic aim of U.S. government policy as it tries to solve the crisis of over-production, now aggravated by its inter-imperialist rivalries with Japan and Western Europe. Such a policy to shift manufacturing and jobs to the U.S. has received official support from the top leadership of American labour.

If the proposition is upheld, that de-industrialization is the most important result to Canada of integration in the American empire, the consequences are frightening. But they are more than just frightening. The thesis can become a tool, a rallying cry for Canadians to join the movement for independence through socialism and socialism through independence.

This thesis may prove the best answer to those who would decry theoretical analysis of modern imperialist systems as the idle exercise of impractical academics. It is our contention that the theory of de-industrialization as a consequence of imperial dominance will have more practical consequences for the future jobs, economic security, and quality of life for Canadians than any single explanatory concept on the Canadian horizon. The debate

9

between its protagonists and opponents will engage Canadians in a highly practical dialogue on the country's economic alternatives. This particular debate represents a new stage in an older dialogue on Canada's future which George Grant opened up in his *Lament for a Nation.*

Grant's lament for Canada's early demise as an independent nation was born of a despair that Canadians were too deeply colonialized within the American empire to opt for a socialist alternative to satellite status. Public ownership and planning of the Canadian economy – the only alternative to continentalism which seemed workable to Grant – was a price Canadians would not readily pay for their sovereignty. It followed, therefore, that Canada-da's ruling elite, chief Canadian beneficiaries of integration, would sustain the drift to a final surrender. That was 1965.

Four years later, in the spring of 1969, a group of Canadians defied the logic of continental inevitability and gathered to write a hopeful call to Canadians for an independent socialist Canada. In the Waffle Manifesto, there was a challenge to the myth that Canadians are so fixedly anti-socialist that they would abandon their country's sovereignty rather than choose public ownership and control of resource industries, large-scale manufacturing and financial institutions.

Some journalists who saw this as a threat to their myth-making soon rose to do battle. Several days after the Waffle Manifesto had been unveiled at an Ottawa press conference in September, 1969, Douglas Fisher predicted in his syndicated column that the group who planned to take the document to the Winnipeg federal convention of the NDP in October, 1969, would be fortunate if they mustered 15 votes at that convention. As it turned out, the NDP establishment headed by David Lewis, Dennis McDermott, Tommy Douglas, John Harney, and Ed Broadbent failed to crush this new declaration of Canadian independence through socialism. The Waffle Manifesto garnered 288 ballots, 36 per cent of the votes cast. The Waffle group, continuing as an organized group went on to challenge the established NDP view of foreign ownership and nationalization for the next three years.

The debate within the NDP ended in Ontario in June, 1972, at the Provincial Council meeting in Orillia with the expulsion of the Waffle as an organized group. It revealed more than a difference over tactical formulations. Lynn Williams, now director of District

6 of the United Steelworkers of America, the most powerful union within the NDP, put his finger on the basic differences. At the Orillia Meeting he declared that there were "two ideologies" within the NDP and that there was room for only one in the party. Whatever the merits of his argument that the NDP should not tolerate two basically different viewpoints within its ranks, his reference to two ideologies contributed to clarity. Williams' formulation of two ideologies had the merit of defining the set of views and the program supported by the dominant wing of the NDP and the trade unions as a full-blown political and economic ideology. In contrast to some would-be pragmatists who claim that what guides the NDP are current existential experiences, Williams' designation pointed squarely to the underlying differences in the national debate.

As later chapters prove, Canada is in the grip of the economics and politics of dependency. The large American companies and Canadian financial institutions command not only the strategic heights of the economy – they are also masters of the Liberal and Conservative parties and the state institutions over which they preside. Increasingly, Canadians turn a skeptical eye to the gyrations of these two business parties. For while Canadian sovereignty evaporates they continue to appoint endless commissions on the national economy, on energy requirements or regional development. Many Canadians feel loss of control over their futures. They are uneasy about the squandering of non-renewable resources to corporations south of the border when hundreds of thousands of Canadians search vainly for rewarding jobs. Their dreams of rising incomes within an expanding economy have been dashed by inflation, rising costs of food and rents, and an insecurity that has not been known since the 1930s.

At the intuitive level they grow distrustful of the Liberal party, whose continentalist history includes the reciprocity election of 1911, the post-1945 agreements with the U.S.A. such as NORAD and Defence sharing, the Auto Pact of 1965 and the vast handovers of Canadian resources to U.S. enterprises. They are equally suspicious of the Conservative Party, whose unseemly haste in helping to sell Canada to their U.S. seniors has not distinguished them under Diefenbaker or Davis from the brokerage of Pearson, Trudeau or Bourassa.

If it is also demonstrated (as it is in this book) that the NDP, too, is wedded to a variant of continentalism, then the array of forces which originally led to Grant's pessimism in 1965 may appear unconquerable. Yet these continentalist forces, from right to left, are afflicted with one fatal flaw, which may be their undoing. Much of this volume is devoted to demonstrating the growing contradictions which bedevil the American empire and the world imperial system and the direct consequences which such contradictions will bear for Canada.

Is the NDP An Alternative to Continentalism?

Although all parties in Canada ignored the multi-national corporations and their role in the federal election campaign of October, 1972, the corporations did not disappear. The issues for Canada became more acute than ever during the "energy crisis" of 1973 with the prospect of a full-blown continental energy scheme. Even as the rate of Canadian export of oil to the U.S. reached over a million barrels a day in February and March 1973 – half of our total production – Donald MacDonald, federal Minister of Energy, Mines and Resources, continued to deny that rising oil exports and plans for a Mackenzie Valley Pipeline constituted *de facto* Canadian integration into a continental energy arrangement.

In the winter and spring of 1973 there were also predictions that the Canada-U.S. Auto Pact would either be abrogated or its safeguard provisions allowed to lapse. What some protagonists saw as a boon to Canada in its trade talks with the U.S., that is, bartering the Auto Pact safeguards in exchange for a guarantee of large U.S. markets for our gas and oil, others viewed as a dual disaster for Canada, as an acceleration of the de-industrialization process and Canada's devolution into a resource hinterland for the U.S.

In various parts of the book, analysis of the NDP leads to conclusions about its role which might be designated as the left-wing of continentalism. Such a designation of the NDP arises inherently from the study of the Canadian political economy, from the logic which leads to a socialist-independence strategy for changing Canadian society. Since the Liberal and Conservative parties are the chief buttresses of the *status quo*, one would not expect such an analysis and socialist strategy for independence to engage its supporters to the degree that one would predict for the NDP.

For the CCF-NDP has enjoyed hegemony over progressive politics and radical thought in Canada for several decades. It has been the centre of the debates and hopes of people committed to rebuilding Canadian society. It follows, therefore, that a critique of the Canadian political economy with socialist solutions as the only alternative to Canadian dependency would have particular meaning for the NDP and its trade union affiliates.

Although there are several references to the role of the NDP and the trade union leadership in Canada throughout the book, it seems useful to make explicit and to elaborate the findings of the authors at the outset. The NDP is central to the debate because many Canadians who are committed to radical social change have pinned their hopes on that party. The effect of the book's analysis of the political economy will be to sharpen the debate among those who desire social change in Canada. An important result of the book will then be to focus attention on the role of the NDP historically, and on its ability to analyse the significance of American imperial domination of Canada. An even more important test is its potential to undertake a tough strategy to counter such imperial dominance.

To illustrate the extent of the sharp divisions in the two sets of analyses, two groupings of inter-related statements are presented. The first questions: "Is there an organic link between: (a) the hesitancy of the NDP and trade union leadership in Canada to confront the American empire, (b) their opposition to large-scale nationalization as a solution to U.S. suzerainty, (c) their support for American-dominated unions in Canada and (d), the control by these same American-dominated unions, through their officers, of the federal and Ontario NDP leadership?"

Conversely, the second question is: "Is there a logical connection between: (a) the view that an effective confrontation of American imperialism in Canada requires public ownership of resource and other major industries and the banks, (b) that a mass challenge to the corporations requires fully independent Canadian unions and, (c) that the Canadian people need a socialist party that stands forthrightly for Canadian independence and independent Canadian unions?"

Authors of the book contend that each set of these elements constitutes a chain, the organic unity of an analysis and a political strategy – an ideology, if you will. The reader may question the validity of some of the statements presented as links in each of the two chains. If he does, the reader is urged to scrutinize the evidence and to return at the end of the book for a re-examination of the claim that the case is logically consistent.

Palpably, there are views and platforms which appear to stand somewhere between the two poles of liberal continentalism and socialist independentism. This, however, does not gainsay the proposition that there are basically two options, and that the intermediate positions are really variants of either one or the other of the two ultimate polarities – axes around which future Canadian politics are likely to rotate. Although an analysis and a strategy are basic components of either of the two polar positions, one could conceivably suggest a separation of any proposed strategy from the analysis which precedes it. Thus, some supporters of the Committee for an Independent Canada might argue that theirs is a variation of an anti-imperialist theme, but that they cannot accept socialism as the answer to U.S. dominance either on grounds of principle or on George Grant's earlier grounds of a lack of popular support. The point, then is to challenge those who reject an independent, socialist Canada to chart an alternative route to Canadian sovereignity. This forbidding task they have yet to perform. It is a task which George Grant thought impossible eight years ago when he despaired of winning Canadians to the one and only alternative to U.S. control – massive public ownership of Canada's economy.

What has changed since 1965 is not the validity of Grant's description; the trend to de-industrialization has added further weight to the anti-imperialist critique. The main change since 1965 in the search for a practical alternative is the basic shift in public opinion towards public ownership as a solution.

A recent Gallup poll (March 1973) asked Canadians: "Do you think that – the Canadian government should nationalize our oil and gas – that is, own and operate them, or do you think private enterprise should still control them as at present?" Results showed that 48 per cent opted for nationalization, as compared to 36 per cent who supported "private enterprise." More Liberal and Conservative supporters backed nationalization than free enterprise. In the case of NDP supporters, the backing of nationalization was over three times as large as for free enterprise (69 per cent to 22 per cent).

First reactions of Liberal Donald Macdonald of the Federal Government and Conservative Darcy McKeough of the Ontario

Government were to attribute this Canada-wide opinion to ignorance of the issues involved. If only people knew better, they would embrace the continentalism of corporate private enterprise with unreserved affection – using Canada's resources as the ace in the game of profitable barter.

For the NDP this poll has destroyed the favourite argument that the Canadian people abhor nationalization and that for electoral advantage it is unwise to press for public ownership. The 48 per cent of Canadians who apparently support nationalization of energy resource industries do, after all, constitute two-and-one-half times as many people as those who voted for the NDP federally in October 1972.

But at least two further steps are needed to extract the meaning of the poll's results. First, on the background of de-industrialization and the evolving continental energy scheme, the logical exercise proposed is to ponder the reversal in the December, 1972 convention of the Ontario NDP of a policy of public ownership of energy resource industries. This policy had been adopted by an overwhelming majority at the October, 1970 convention of the Ontario NDP when the Waffle was still in the party as an organized group. From this evidence it is difficult to avoid the conclusion that there has existed a systematic pattern of resistance by the NDP and trade union leadership to an anti-imperialist analysis and strategy. The question then arises: since the nationalization of energy resource industries and perhaps even nationalization of other resource industries now have popular backing in Canada, will the NDP now move to write these into its platform? Will the NDP reverse its 1971 federal convention opposition to public ownership of resource industries?

This is by no means excluded from their *realpolitik*. Social democratic parties like the NDP, such as the Labour Party of Great Britain, have often included a degree of nationalization in their platforms. It should be added, of course, that in practice they have generally placed the least profitable sections of the economy under public ownership – those capitalist enterprises which required bailing out by the public purse (like the CNR in Canada) and which did not in the end benefit the working people. Inclusion of some nationalization in an NDP platform would not cause surprise nor dismay for those who want to get on with nationalization as a solution, because such a *demarche* would mean that the people had readied themselves for the next stage of the struggle for independence.

Will Co-Option Work?

Experience shows that when a telling analysis about economics and politics has been accepted by the people, it becomes a material reality and that all political forces have to try to deal with it. Efforts to co-opt issues are perennial. They are evidence of a growing understanding of the need for radical changes. The example of what happened in Quebec in the 1960s is instructive. This was a time of important political change, in which traditional forces and parties such as the Liberals and the Union Nationale co-opted issues to stem the tide to radicalism. Thus did Quebec Hydro come under public ownership with Lévesque as a minister in the Lesage cabinet. Educational reforms brought thousands of youth into colleges and universities and created a new social force. This group began to press for greater opportunities for the French language in Quebec and for a radical reorganization of Quebec society. Trade unions gained strength by taking advantage of reformed labour laws designed to contain them within a liberal purview. A new mood of militancy and a class-consciousness emerged. In the last few years they have begun to move from business to social unionism, to union policy which challenges the very system within which the new collective bargaining laws were to co-opt them. The consequences of this classical effort at co-option of popular ideas was to promote those very issues and in due course to encourage involvement of new social groupings among working people and students. Since then the popular mood in Quebec has overflowed the traditional channels and has opened new ones outside the Liberal and Conservative parties, and even outside the P.Q. and the Creditistes. Apparently, co-option of radical issues does not necessarily lead to their impotence, because co-option does not usually resolve the issues themselves but often moves people from traditional to radical political expressions.

Co-option may work if the demands for change cover limited social objectives. This has been true of specific educational or civic reform movements, or the attempt to stop expressways. William Davis of Ontario did that with the Spadina expressway prior to the Ontario election of 1971. This has happened to the civic reform movement in Toronto, when Conservatives and Liberals led the movement into blind alleys.

But the dynamics of co-option can play tricks with its manipulators, if the popular mood is for social changes across the board. For example, resources and resource industries affect Canada in a whole variety of ways. The range covers jobs for skilled and unskilled, research opportunities, investment policy, inflation, the price of energy and other products, ecology, planning for manufacturing and regional development, building a broader base for financing of public endeavours such as education, and indeed Canada's overall future. Touch one, touch all! While some people move on one front, others move on other fronts! The movements interpenetrate, deepen each other and raise popular confidence. Co-opting one issue may not work, therefore, because other issues demand attention. Co-opting the ecology movement, for example, or the movement of the native peoples on the Mackenzie Valley Pipeline would not stop the movement for nationalization of energy resource industries, because the Mackenzie Valley is only the tip of the iceberg.

The growing movement on energy resources has in it industrial workers who demand jobs and future energy supplies at low prices; there are socialists who press for nationalization as an overall solution to independence; there are auto workers who watch the antics of a government ready to trade their jobs (Auto Pact safeguards) for guarantees of bigger U.S. markets for oil. It is now a problem of the dam springing leaks everywhere. Co-opting one issue only points to other issues that need attention; and when co-option begins to fail, liberalism and social welfarism are in historic trouble. Co-option is like a split personality which seduces but which does not deliver; instead of the desired action it produces only unrelieved frustration. The built-in weakness in the co-option technique is that the appetite roused by traditional forces in raising the issues cannot be assuaged by the established means of sending the electorate to vote for alternate establishment parties every four years.

The NDP might adopt some modicum of nationalization in its electoral platform: the objective result of which would be to further move peoples' thinking to the socialist alternative. For the NDP as a party this poses a contradiction which will eventually push its supporters far beyond its leaders. Such a flawed contradiction is unavoidable in the life of those who presumably espouse the cause of working people while supporting or critically tolerating a continentalist drift.

If then, the NDP tries to co-opt the nationalization issue – for example, by advocating a Crown corporation in the energy field to compete with Imperial Oil, Texaco or Shell – will that stop the Canadian movement for nationalization of all energy resource industries? Quite the opposite, for such an attempt is likely to show the inadequacies of limited public ownership. If public ownership of some oil and gas industries is possible, then why not of all energy resource industries?

And now for one further step in the sequence. If, perchance, nationalization of all Canadian resource industries were to become a major platform of the NDP and of the unions affiliated to it, could nationalization of Canadian unions be far behind? Lynn Williams and his colleagues in trade union officialdom would then be required to move from an "ideology" of tolerating U.S. domination and opposition to large-scale nationalization toward the policy which they rejected at Orillia in June, 1972. Stranger things have happened in history, as witness the radicalization of the three top labour leaders in Quebec and their call for "breaking the system." But this new reversal would require a direct confrontation with the issue of American domination of unions in Canada. Such domination is the Achilles heel of Canada's official labour movement – for no movement towards Canadian independence can be half-shackled and half-free.

The change in public opinion since 1965 and 1969 is not a epiphenomenon whose explanation lies in a discovery of the elusive Canadian identity, or in an ephemeral mood of anti-Americanism. Nor is it to be explained as primarily the result of the skillful articulation of the public ownership position by a group of persuasive socialist independentists, although their part has been important. It is the contention of the authors that this change is rooted in the change in Canada's economy – the main source of changes in political institutions and political thinking. Canadians have become much more aware of American domination because this domination has not only increased in scale and intensity, but because it has had a more direct impact on the lives of working people. Plant shut-downs, unemployment (even among university graduates and teachers), visible crises and potential disasters in Canada's energy and resources policy, particularly in relation to manufacturing – these and other factors such as steeply rising prices have begun to threaten people's security.

It is in the context of the actual changes and dislocations in the political economy, in the direct effect it has had on the economic position of working people, that the alternative of public owner-ship finds fertile ground. Without such a change in the economy, advocacy of public ownership would fall on deaf ears.

Herein lies a source of difference in analysis with the approach of George Grant or of Abe Rotstein – who have contended that public ownership of basic industries and banks is a utopian idea that has no roots among the people. Our viewpoint here derives from the proposition that predictions about the potential move-ment of people towards or against an idea must start with devel-opments in the political economy. Grant and Rotstein have per-ceived the pervasiveness of the multi-national corporation and have exposed its threat to Canadian sovereignty. What has been lacking is an understanding that the thrust of de-industrialization and plant shut-downs, combined with resource sell-outs, would not only rouse the anger of a few sentimental nationalists but would set millions of Canadians into political motion to challenge the disaster which faces them. It is this underestimation of the potential of the working people to rally to Canada's defence which leads to Grant's or Rotstein's pessimism about the socialist option.

Pessimism about Canada's future is thus rooted in an incom-plete analysis of the political economy, an analysis which necessar-ily includes the reaction of people to changes within that econ-omy. This returns us to the earlier contention about the separation of strategy from analysis. The conclusion of those who would separate an anti-imperialist analysis from a socialist strategy by arguing for the first but rejecting the second is now patently impractical. The point being added is that the faulty strategy proposed by the c.i.c. flows from a faulty analysis, an analysis which is at best incomplete.

It is not the idea of public ownership, attractive in some abstract humanist sense, which has given it the force of broad public support. It is the conditions of economic life which are pressing the people towards independence through socialism.

Therein lies the optimism or more exactly the confidence of

those who argue for the strategy suggested in the concluding chapter. The confidence does not arise from the optimistic personalities of the writers; the confidence arises from the perception that large historical forces in Canada are joining the battle of independence against continentalism.

The authors, several of whom wrote the original draft of the Waffle Manifesto, derive confidence in their analysis from the now evident movement of people towards the public ownership position. It is a confirmation of their thesis and prediction that changes within the Canadian political economy would move people towards public ownership. Social sciences are not noted for accuracy of prediction. The fact that the 1969 Waffle thesis has been borne out (*e.g.*, by the Gallup poll on public ownership of energy resources of March, 1973) in the face of such widespread pessimism lends additional weight to the soundness of their hypothesis.

The Rule of the Disinherited – A Second Thesis
Along with the major thesis of de-industrialization and the companion strategy of public ownership to counter it, a second major thesis forms a cornerstone for much of the argumentation in this book. The thesis is that there exists in Canada one potential social power to counter de-industrialization and win Canadian independence. This social power consists of those 75 per cent of Canadians who work for private capitalists or state-controlled bodies in non-managerial jobs – the working class. This second major thesis of the book likewise derives from an examination of the dynamics and contradictions of Canada's political economy, and not from a sentimental attachment to the moral superiority of those who live by their sweat instead of their dividends.

In several chapters, the authors present the historical evidence that the Canadian business class were never predominantly industrial in their orientation, and that the main source of their income and power has always been their financial and commercial enterprises. In this role they have acted out the typical part of dependent capitalists, not that of entrepreneurial captains of industry – such as those who led the business classes in England or the U.S., Japan or Germany to heights of imperial power. For the Canadian business class, who never developed an independent industrial base in Canada, de-industrialization is not a particularly disturbing prospect. As long as the Canadian financiers can continue to be the "honest" brokers in the sale of Canada's resources to U.S. enterprises and secondarily serve as merchants for Canadian imports from abroad, so long will they plan to share with their senior foreign partners in the bounteous life which Canada has offered them during the past two centuries.

Within the confines of their world of political economy there is truly no alternative to Canada's integration into the American empire. Nor is there an alternative to the dominant position in the Canadian economy and the Canadian state of such U.S. giants as Imperial Oil, General Motors, or International Nickel. If private profit is the source of all the expansionist adventures which befall a "free" country, then it makes little sense to bother about an alternative to Canada's continentalist course. For truly there is no greater income for those Canadians whose lot it is to live thereby than through partnership with the most advanced, computerized and automated enterprises. Fully 75 per cent of Canada's GNP is currently produced through these foreign corporations. What basic alternative exists for Canadian capitalists, who play by the same capitalist rules as these American corporations, even if they were to heed the pleas of a few nationalist businessmen in their midst? The two-way process of their integration into the American empire and the U.S. corporations' integration into the core of the Canadian economy and the Canadian state has gone too far for them, even if they have occasion to regret their historic follies. This group cannot now reverse the continentalist tide of de-industrialization of Canada.

Furthermore, their favourite argument that an independent Canada would mean a loss of income has a ring of truth or at least of partial truth. For certainly the only course that could lead to Canadian independence would mean a loss of income to the financier class, the class which has specialized in selling Canada abroad.

The issue to be examined, therefore, is whether a loss of income to the 5 per cent (only 10 per cent of all Canadians own shares in corporations and most of these are small shareholders) who benefit from the sale of Canada abroad would necessarily mean a loss to the other 95 per cent of Canadians. For most of the 95 per cent have naievely accepted the proposition of the continentalists that everybody benefits from Canada's primary role as resource base for the U.S., that the faster we sell our resources the better for business and therefore for all Canadians.

Again that argument once possessed limited validity, as long as "special status" provided Canada with a branch-plant manufacturing base. But with the end of "special status," with the Nixonomics of 1971, and its likely 1973 to 1974 successor, that argument folds.

But even if the old argument folds, those who hold the old benefits of continentalism do not fold. They are the very people who need not weep over de-industrialization, because their livelihood does not depend primarily on Canadian manufacturing. They now share economic and political power in Canada with their seniors in the U.S. And if only the rest of us could live without working, or if we could exist without a manufacturing base, the position of the Canadian elite would be secure. But we cannot live that way, and we would hardly accept a minimal guaranteed annual wage as a substitute. This economic reality is the basic root of the new Canadian nationalism.

For where are the jobs and opportunities to come from, for skilled and semi-skilled industrial workers, clerical staff, technicians, technologists, researchers and teachers? Without widely-based manufacturing there is an ever-narrowing foundation for people with specialized skills, and for government financing of the public sector – an area which affects the jobs and conditions of teachers, nurses and other professional, semi-professional and skilled groups in the public service. The continentalists appear to have no answer to this conundrum as the American empire returns manufacturing and jobs to the metropolis.

If de-industrialization is the Achilles heel of continentalism, as it is the Achilles heel of American continental unions in Canada, then those social forces in whose interest it is to stop continentalism have gained firm ground from which to launch a new strategy for independence. For although resource extraction as the concomitant of de-industrialization produces large profits, it creates few jobs.

Those who need and want the jobs are those who work, a group known in the older days – although dismissed in behaviourist, statistical, U.S.-inspired sociology – as the "working class." For working people it is not sentimental or utopian nationalism which is the impelling force, it is the unavoidable contradiction that the private enterprise system fails many of those whom it needs to produce the surplus labour on which it thrives. That includes industrial workers, technologists, researchers, and even teachers. Even the easily-grasped goal of expanding Canada's home production for internal consumption of manufactured goods to the percentage level of that attained in the U.S.A. would currently mean an increase of seven billion dollars per year in Canadian manufacturing. Such a step alone could solve Canada's unemployment problems for the skilled and unskilled, for technologists and teachers. But that is impossible under the present rules and the business class holds current rules to be sacrosanct. And while the business group believes that there is no rational alternative to individualist private profit, there are people who as workers, produce goods and services in a milieu which is entirely social and collective. It is therefore within the range of their social experience to search for social or collective solutions to their future. If private ownership does not meet their needs, perhaps public or social ownership can. Once they are socialized by collective bargaining, workers may not find the idea of collective ownership as abhorrent as it is to their would-be mentors.

Are People Ready For Social Power?

What is more problematic, however, is the realization that Canadian independence requires a basic change in relations of social power. This idea, much more than public ownership, requires a revolution in people's thinking. It may sound simplistic to those who think that new rules are unthinkable, but those who need the jobs to survive, those who have no alternative to working for a living, may now be ready to change the rules and to undertake a fundamental change in power relations. If they have been socialized for socialized production, can they now make the leap to socialized ownership and social power – to an independent socialist Canada?

That is one of the major questions of this book; and therein may lie the secret of Canada's independent future. When a sizeable section of working people in Canada have decided that they can find it within themselves to accept responsibility as a new social power to lead society, as the dispossessed who shall inherit Canada's earth, then perhaps the movement to independence will have entered its highest stage.

The authors of this book argue that such a development appears likely because the prospect of Canada as a resource hinterland for the U.S. is not an acceptable alternative. Great historical events presumably happen when people have little choice but to change the rules under which they live. The working people may perforce have to change the rules. They are objectively in a position in social production where their future is threatened and where their interests are diametrically opposed to Canada's integration into the American empire.

The second major thesis of the book is that it is because of their current relations to resources, production and ownership that working people can now begin to think about the task of fashioning a new society and a new state in Canada based on social ownership of large resource, industrial and financial institutions. They share a common status, in that they are collectively part of the 90 per cent of Canadians who do not own shares or enterprises, who do not live by profits and who do not currently decide economic or political policy. In unions they act collectively in negotiations over contracts; often they vote 98 per cent collectively to go on strike and usually to stay on strike together to the successful or bitter end. They have been socialized by the collectivity of their work and are potentially capable of creating a society in which there is social ownership. Indeed, there is no society that working people of Canada can fashion in their own image, other than an independent socialist society and state.

They may now be ready in English Canada, as they have become more obviously so in Quebec, to take the historic leap to a new role in society. It is perhaps no accident that the group which gave strongest support in the recent Gallup poll to nationalization of energy resources industries was the "middle income" group – the very group which includes most trade unionists in Canada. For while to the business class nationalism seems a luxury they can ill afford except as an after-dinner speech, for the working class nationalism and anti-imperialism may now be a necessity for survival.

The authors' strategy for Canada is based on an analysis which reveals the working people as the cohesive and reliable social force to lead the nation to socialist independence, with revitalized Canadian unions, and a new type of socialist independentist party as their chief instruments for liberation. Authors of the book make no apology for their bias towards an independent socialist Canada. For most of them, political-economic analysis and theorizing must be rooted in practical struggle if the theories are to serve as accurate predictors and guides to action.

Furthermore, as already argued there can be only a mechanical separation of strategy from the basic analysis. A sound plan of action can arise only from a sound analysis and cannot be logically separated from it. Conversely, a political economic analysis which has no strategic consequences makes no contribution either to developing understanding or towards action.

Such explicit partisanship enhances the book's value. An avowed rejection of neutrality in the social sciences is preferable to the pretence of detached objectivity. The reader's awareness of the authors' assumptions will help in following the analysis; the analysis itself will receive the acid test during the 1970s and 1980s, the decades when Canada's future will be pointed either towards continentalism and a final lament or toward socialist independentism and a new birth.

Bob Laxer
June 21, 1973.

Introduction to the Political Economy of Canada
Jim Laxer

A central contemporary dilemma conditions the questions Canadians want answered when they study their history. How can Canada be so rich and at the same time so dependent on an outside country – the United States? Or to ask the obverse question: if Canada is so dependent on the United States, why is it so well off compared to other countries in the American empire?

A decade ago these would have been non-questions for Canadians, most of whom assumed that it was American investment and American technology that accounted for Canadian prosperity. Today, a new round of trade rivalry among the imperialist blocs, the United States, Japan and western Europe and a general crisis of over-production in the capitalist world challenges the comfortable Canadian assumptions of the early sixties. Canadians are now aware that it is the dependent features of Canada's relationship to the United States that are increasing. An uncomfortable realization is taking hold that this dependency is responsible for fundamental and worsening structural problems in the Canadian economy.

How then did Canada get so rich and so dependent and where is its social structure taking it today?

Canada was first peopled by European societies as a place from which to extract staple products for metropolitan countries. The *raison d'être* of Canada was to be found in the cod fisheries, the fur trade and later in timber, wheat and mineral resources. For historians like Harold Innis and Donald Creighton the quest for the staples of Canada within a commercial communications system based on the St. Lawrence-Great Lakes waterway with its centre at Montreal is the principal fact around which Canadian history is organized.

For Creighton, it was the penetrating vision of the Montreal merchants in understanding the imperatives of the St. Lawrence-Great Lakes system that makes them the heroes of Canadian history. He sets forth the merchant's vision of the St. Lawrence as follows:

> It was the one great river which led from the eastern shore into the heart of the continent. It possessed a geographical monopoly; and it shouted its uniqueness to adventurers. The river meant mobility and distance; it invited journeyings; it promised immense expanses, unfolding, flowing away into remote and changing horizons. The whole west, with all its riches, was the dominion of the river. To the unfettered and ambitious, it offered a pathway to the central mysteries of the continent. The river meant movement, transport, a ceaseless passage west and east, the long procession of river-craft-canoes, bateaux, timber rafts and steamboats which followed each other into history. It seemed the destined pathway of North American trade; and from the river there rose, like an exhalation, the dream of western commercial empire. The river was to be the basis of a great transportation system by which the manufactures of the old world could be exchanged for the staple products of the new. This was the faith of successive generations of northerners. The dream of the commercial empire of the St. Lawrence runs like an obsession through the whole of Canadian history; and men followed each other through life, planning and toiling to achieve it. The river was not only a great actuality: it was the central truth of a religion. Men lived by it, at once consoled and inspired by its promises, its whispered suggestions, and its shouted commands; and it was a force in history, not merely because of its accomplishments, but because of its shining, ever-receding possibilities.[1]

But for Creighton, if the geographic fact of the St. Lawrence was the inspiration of the society, it was also the source of its defeat. And for Creighton defeat is the outcome of the drama of Canadian history, defeat in the quest for independence for the northern half of North America from the United States. And so the following passage, although it deals with the defeat of the merchants of Montreal in their competition with New York in the

1840s, also summarized Creighton's view of the final outcome of Canadian history as a whole. He writes:

> There was, in fact, some primitive defect, some fundamental weakness, in the society of the St. Lawrence, in the resources which it could bring to bear upon its problems, and in the very river itself which had inspired its entire effort. The St. Lawrence was a stream which dashed itself against the rocks and broke the hopes of its supporters; and all the long struggle, which had begun when the first ships of the French sailed up the River of Canada, had served, in the end, to establish a tradition of defeat.
>
> ... All these deeds and struggles took on, in retrospect, the appearance of episodes which had been intended merely to postpone the dénouement of a drama upon the last page of which there would inevitably be written the word defeat.[2]

The Innis-Creighton school of Canadian historians has served as the intellectual basis for the conservative nationalism of George Grant in *Lament for a Nation*.[3] For socialist historians, Innis and Creighton provide an essential starting point for an understanding of Canadian history. But socialist historians are not satisfied that Canada's continuing character as a resource-extractive country dependent on outside imperial powers is to be explained by geographic or technological determinism. Instead they see dependence resulting from the relationship that has existed between the capitalist class in Canada and the capitalist class in the metropolitan countries on which Canada is dependent. As Tom Naylor states in his article, "The Rise and Fall of the Third Commercial Empire of the St. Lawrence":

> Colonial status cannot be explained by technological or geographic determinism, or by 'comparative advantage', but only by reference to the relative stages of capitalist development achieved by both the metropole and the hinterland. The metropole defines the character and extent of economic development in the hinterland area.[4]

Canada's dependency is a function not of geography and technology but of the nature of Canada's capitalist class. The Canadian business class has been dominated historically by financial capitalists who have made their profits on the exchange of Canadian staple products in return for manufactured goods imported from metropolitan countries. At no stage have native Canadian industrialists who profited from the production and sale of manufactured goods dominated Canadian capitalism. This central fact has flowed from the weakness of Canadian capitalism in relation to that of outside imperialist countries. Dependency has shaped the character of Canadian capitalism and has created a capitalist class that has needed continued dependency for its continued well-being.

Between the time of the conquest of New France in 1759 and the dismantling of the British mercantile system in 1846, the dominant business class in Canada was a merchant class that made its money in serving as the middle-men in the fur trade and in the timber trade. Canada's merchant capitalists also made fortunes in land giveaways from the crown and in the buying up of seigneuries in Quebec by English merchants.

During this period the Montreal merchants worked to improve the transportation system of the St. Lawrence. The building of the Erie canal in New York State, the later rise of the railways and the end of preferential treatment for Canadian grain in the British market with the repeal of the Corn laws, as well as Britain's failure to regain territory on the other side of the Great Lakes during the war of 1812 led to the collapse of their hopes. The long battle for commercial hegemony in the trade of the west was won by the New York merchants over those of Montreal.

The merchants in Canada were middlemen in a British imperial system. This British system functioned with the colony supplying the staple such as fur and timber and serving as a market for the manufactures of the mother country. The merchants of Montreal profited from this system. Their own power was dependent on the power of the imperial system and not on its overthrow. Such a bourgeoisie held back rather than enhanced the development of manufacturing within the colony.

During the 1820s and 30s, democratic movements arose in both Upper and Lower Canada to challenge the Family Compact and the Chateau Clique, which were the governments of the merchants. These democratic movements brought together the grievances of the farmers, the French Canadians and the emerging industrial bourgeoisie to achieve democratic national control of the affairs of the colony. The defeat of this first democratic national movement that united the two peoples of Canada against imperialism maintained the merchants in power.

Following the defeat of the Canadian rebellions, British mercantilism finally died in the 1840s with the repeal of the Corn Laws, an event which all but destroyed the commercial system of the Canadian merchants.

This setback, along with the rise to office of the reformers in the province of Canada, led many of the merchants to abandon their fervent loyalty to Britain and instead to throw themselves headlong into the arms of the emerging alternative empire in the United States. Canadian business has never been able to exist apart from dependence on an imperial power and 1849 gave a foretaste of the willingness of Canadian business to replace the British with the American empire in Canada.

In 1854, the tendency of the Canadian system to move from one relationship of dependency on an outside metropolis to another became apparent in the reciprocity agreement with the United States. Under Reciprocity, which existed from 1854 to 1864, a system strikingly parallel to that of the present day prevailed. Reciprocity operated to ensure the flow of Canadian raw materials to the United States and to ensure a market for American manufactured goods in Canada. In much of what is now Ontario, an assault of major proportions was launched on Canadian forests in the export trade with the U.S.

However, U.S. domination of the Canadian economy was not to take hold in the straightforward way implied in the reciprocity agreement. Reciprocity was shattered primarily for political reasons. Britain and Canada experienced immense tension with the United States during the American Civil War due to British support for the cause of the Confederacy. Northern victory in the American Civil War consolidated the development of industrial capitalism in that country. The hostility of Washington towards Britain and its appendages led to American cancellation of the reciprocity agreement. This did not mean that the United States was writing Canada off. In fact, President Grant thought that it would be reasonable for Canada to be ceded to the United States in settlement for the claims of the U.S. against Britain, for providing the South with warships such as the Alabama during the Civil War.[5].

Without reciprocity and with a hostile relationship with the

United States, the British North American colonies were forced to rationalize their situation. Confederation was a popular movement in Canada West for a new agricultural frontier in the distant north-west, in what was to become the prairie provinces. It was part of a strategy for imperial rationalization of all the holdings of the British empire on the northern half of the contnent.

Although the 1850's and 60's had witnessed the emergence of the beginnings of significant Canadian-owned industry that grew up around the building of the railways, the Canadian bourgeoisie remained predominantly a merchant-finance class at the time of Confederation. The strategy of the merchants was to expand the size of their commercial operations by bringing the potential wheat-growing area of the Canadian west into a union with the province of Canada.

In the National Policy begun in 1879 and brought to fruition between the mid-1890s and World War I, the logic of Confederation for the merchants became clear. The National Policy consisted of three basic elements: the building of a transcontinental railway to link the potential breadbasket of the Canadian West to Montreal; the promotion of immigration to people the new internal colony in the Canadian west; and the erection of a tariff to force the farmers of western Canada to purchase their manufactured goods from central Canada. The system, like earlier Canadian economic strategies, was based on the export of a staple product, this time wheat to Britain and Europe. The export of wheat via the CPR to Montreal and thence to Europe was to bring purchasing power to western farmers, who would then buy the manufactured goods of the east again shipped to them on the CPR.

The primary purpose of the tariff then was not to protect Canadian industrialists but to guarantee the monopoly of the trading system of the Canadian merchants and to force American industrialists who wanted part of the Canadian market to establish factories in Canada.[6] Thus, while Canadian-owned manufacturing did grow under the National Policy, by 1913 American direct investment in Canada totalled $520 million.[7] But it was the financial capitalists with their money in railways, grain elevators and merchandising who dominated Canadian policy during this period. The Canadian state was their state and it served well in subsidizing the CPR and in using the powers of the federal government to protect and promote the trading system. The CPR and the Conservative government of Sir John A. Macdonald were so close that it was once observed at the time that "the day the CPR goes bust, the Conservative party goes bust the day after."[8] This is not to say that the link with business was unique at this time to the Conservative party. If it was true that in the golden age of the Conservative party under Sir John A. Macdonald, the party was firmly anchored to the twin pillars of the Bank of Montreal and the Canadian Pacific Railway – then it was equally true that Laurier's great achievement was to move the Liberal party from the shaky foundation of western Ontario farmers to the more durable base of the Bank of Commerce and the Grand Trunk Railway.[9]

Canadian financial capitalists pursued a sub-imperial strategy during the period of the National Policy. One element in the strategy was the promotion of Canada as the place within the British Empire where the Americans would do their manufacturing. As well as gaining entry to the Canadian market through the establishment of branch plants in Canada, American business also gained access to the preferential system of the British Empire.

The modern corporation, amalgamating industrial and finance capital, was invented in the United States in the late 19th century. This new phenomenon of business organization became multinational in its operations almost from the moment of its birth. American corporations, making use of mass production techniques such as assembly-line production and precision tooling, entered Canada to gain access to the markets of the British Empire. It is no accident that American supremacy was immediately established in Canada in the fields of automobiles, chemicals, and the production of machinery and electrical goods, while Canadian businessmen remained strong in textiles and clothing, food processing, farm machinery, brewing, distilling and iron and steel.

A brief look at the automobile industry in Canada illustrates that Canadian firms made an effort to enter fields where the advantages of American production techniques and corporate organization were strong. In 1907 Sam McLaughlin of Oshawa began assembling Buick automobiles on licence. The weakness of his operation was that while he owned it, he was forced to import his engines from Detroit. He did the same thing with Chevrolet after 1914. Then, in 1918 he sold both companies to General Motors and General Motors of Canada was formed.[10]

The behaviour of American automobile companies in Canada

in the 1920s illustrates the importance of Canada's position behind the tariff wall of the British Empire as a key factor in determining the behaviour of the firms. In 1929 Canada's American-owned auto industry produced the second largest number of cars of any country in the world and exported over 100,000 automobiles out of the quarter million produced. These exports were mainly to other British Empire countries. 1929 was, in fact, the high point of the Canadian auto industry in relation to production in other countries.[11]

But the success of the sub-imperial strategy of Canada's merchant-financiers under the National Policy was based on a particular balance between the power of American and British capitalism which proved ephemeral. As Britain declined in power and as the United States moved ahead, Canada's financial capitalists were reduced over time to powerful but subsidiary status.

During World War I, Britain lost its position as a major exporter of capital and Canada could no longer make use of large-scale British portfolio investments. The aftermath of the war and the decline of Canadian wheat markets in Europe struck a blow at the east-west transportation system of the National Policy. During this period the debit charges on the expansion of Canadian agriculture and transportation became very onerous.

The 1920s saw the rise of new staple industries that basically altered Canadian development. Hydro electricity, pulp and paper and the new mineral extractive industries of the north increased in importance. New trade ties developed between the United States and Canada and increasing quantities of Canadian minerals flowed south. Provincial governments which enjoyed the tax revenues of the resource industries became more powerful in the 20's and began to replace the federal government as the level of government closest to business.

During the 1930s, depression further strained the structure of the Canadian National Policy as the market for Canadian wheat collapsed, thereby increasing enormously the burden of fixed interest charges on railway and utility debts payable from Canada to Britain. The answer was to import more direct American investment into Canada.

In 1935, on Remembrance Day, the recently-elected government of Mackenzie King signed a reciprocal trade agreement with Washington. The closer relationship with the United States was symbolized by U.S. President Franklin Roosevelt's statement in 1938 at Queen's University in Kingston, Ontario that the United States would not allow Canada to be dominated by any other empire (than the British).[12] In 1940 Mackenzie King motored down to Ogdensburg, New York with one assistant to meet with Roosevelt. Without prior consultation with his own cabinet, let alone the House of Commons or the Canadian people, he signed a permanent military alliance with the United States and established the permanent joint defence board. In return for entering into the tightest alliance in Canadian history, King demanded and obtained one concession from the Americans – the date of signing was moved one day to fall on the same day of the month as his birthday.[13]

The establishment of the permanent joint defence board on August 17, 1940 marked the political transition of Canada into the American empire. It came just weeks after the fall of France, at a moment when Britain was begging the United States for 50 used destroyers. The establishment of the joint defence board occurred just as the Battle of Britain was getting underway, a battle from which many in North America did not believe that Britain would emerge intact.

Symbolic of Canada's changed relationship to the United States was the fact that in 1942 the Canadian government decided to allow the United States military to build the Alaska highway across Canadian territory to Alaska. In 1938 King had refused an earlier bid to have the Americans build the highway stating in a letter that:

> Grounds of public policy would not permit using the funds of a foreign Government to construct public works in Canada. It would be, as Lapointe phrased it, a matter of financial invasion, or, as I termed it, financial penetration.[14]

While World War II led to an important increase in Canadian-owned manufacturing, it also led to an economy more closely interlocked with that of the United States. The war and Canada's permanent military alliance with the United States marked the end of significant British power in Canada. The balancing act between two empires had ended for Canada's financial capitalists. In 1945, C. D. Howe, the country's Reconstruction Minister, recognized the imperatives of the new era when he established an economic policy based on invitations to U.S. firms to invest in manufacturing and resource extraction in Canada.

In the post-1945 period Canada's financial capitalists were no longer dominant in the running of the Canadian state. They were locked into a junior partnership with American corporations which now securely controlled primary and secondary production in the economy. The relationship between Canadian and American capitalists was a settled one – Canadian merchants and bankers shared in the surplus value generated by the American productive apparatus in Canada.

The informal American imperial control of the Canadian state can be demonstrated in numerous ways for the period since 1940. In economic policy, it can be seen in the fact that the large multi-national corporations pay the lowest levels of taxes of any corporations in Canada – always an indicator of where power lies.

It can be seen in a final sense in the nature of the military "alliance" that Canada has with the United States. In the 1950s Canadian parliamentarians were, on occasion, barred from parts of the Canadian north which were open to U.S. military personnel. During the Cuban missile crisis in 1962 when NORAD put the Canadian forces on alert against the explicit wishes of the Canadian Prime Minister, John Diefenbaker, the location of ultimate power in the Canadian state was demonstrated. There are some, of course, for whom no list of economic, political and military examples of American control of the Canadian state would prove the case that American capitalism is the ultimate power in the Canadian state. For such people, informal empire is simply too difficult to comprehend. Without the imperial flag and the foreign governor, empire cannot exist. Even the fact that 75 per cent of the gross national product is generated within foreign-owned firms in Canada today leaves some people wondering whether foreign capitalists really run the show in this country.

American capitalist control of the Canadian state both directly by American corporations and indirectly through the military and political sway of the U.S. state over Canada did not appear to have any immediate negative effects on Canadian economic development. As long as the American empire was expanding economically, expansion occurred in Canada, both in the manufacturing and especially the resource sector of the economy. During this period of "special status" for Canada in the American empire, far more American investment flowed into Canada than into any other country in the world. Canadian manufacturing was managed more and more from outside the country; pre-packaged foreign technology became the norm in Canadian production; basic production began to be replaced with a trend toward the reduction of Canadian industry to warehouse-assembly operations. But in spite of the increasing structural weaknesses, the manufacturing economy grew during the period from the 1945 to the mid 1960s. In special arrangements like the Defence Sharing Agreement and the Canada-U.S. auto pact, industry in Canada shared in the gravy of the North American market.

In the mid-1960s, Canada began to experience the long term effects of the loss of the Canadian state to American capitalist control. By this date, more profits and dividends were flowing south than were being replaced with new foreign investment from the U.S. American corporations by the end of the 1960's were financing 90 per cent of their investment in Canada through the reinvestment of profits made in Canada and through money borrowed on the Canadian money market. American investment began by the mid-1960s to shift out of Canadian manufacturing and into investments in resource industries in Canada or out of the country altogether and into western Europe. The American empire had passed its zenith economically.

As American rivalry with Western Europe and Japan became insistent by the end of the 60's and as the American economy showed telling signs of weakness, the United States began to face the problem of economic rationalization within its empire. This meant the beginning of a new economic epoch for Canada. The manufacturing sector of the Canadian economy had become an arena of surplus production in a period of shrinking world markets for the U.S.

The growth curves projected by the Economic Council of Canada for Canadian manufacturing were replaced by stagnation in the manufacturing sector of the economy. From 1966 to 1972 virtually no jobs were created in manufacturing in Canada. Plant shut-downs and layoffs occurred on a massive scale, particularly in foreign-owned industries.[15] In August, 1971, when Nixon announced his new economic policies, the end of "special status" for Canada in the American empire was clear.

Nixon and his Treasury Secretary, John Connally, made it clear that Canada was expected to contribute to solving America's trade problems. Since that date, Canada has been pressured to enter into resources agreements with the U.S. and in return to purchase more manufactured goods from the U.S.

Of critical importance is the current energy crisis in the United States and the consequent American pressure for a continental emergy deal with Canada. As Canada's exports of oil and natural gas have increased, discussions with the Americans proceed on mammoth projects like the Mackenzie Valley pipeline. For sale is not only Canadian energy resources, but Canadian sovereignty – the right to control Canadian resources for Canadian development. The Canadian government in its talks with Washington has been stressing the security benefits of the Mackenzie Valley route for American petroleum – thus making clear the implications of an energy deal for the independence of Canada.

A continental energy deal would work this way: American oil companies would ship a much larger amount of oil and natural gas out of Canada to the U.S. Canada's oil and gas prices would rise to meet the American price increases which are expected. The American oil companies would get the profits as well as the oil and gas. Southern Canadian supplies would be depleted more rapidly, thereby necessitating the building of the Mackenzie Valley Pipeline, which would again increase the cost of gas because of the greater distance of transportation. The pipeline would endanger the environment of the Canadian north and would dispossess Canada's original peoples still further. And of course, in return for gaining access to the American energy market, Canada would be expected to buy more manufactured goods from the United States – perhaps automobiles, which would destroy jobs for Canadian autoworkers in southern Ontario.

The cost of the loss of control of the Canadian state to American corporations is now increasingly clear to Canadians; in a period of inter-imperialist rivalry and a crisis of overproduction for the United States, it means de-industrialization for Canada.

Clearly any prospect for Canadian independence depends on a new class coming to power – and today that can only mean the working class through a socialist programme.

People's movements of resistance to the development strategy of Canadian capitalism have grown up in response to the exploitation and human dislocation which have resulted. But while these movements have responded to material conditions, they have also been conditioned in their development to reflect the cultural and institutional framework that has been the legacy of the Canadian people.

When British and European workers and farmers came to Canada they did not come here simply as undifferentiated humanity upon whom the material conditions of capitalism in Canada would act. They brought with them their ideas, their culture, their patterns of trade union and political activity and institutional ties with Britain and Europe.

Especially in the case of British immigrants, Canada's continuing ties with the empire meant that British political and cultural patterns would be transplanted to Canada. It is not surprising, therefore, that the English-Canadian popular culture, particularly the nature of Canadian Protestantism, was affected by this link. It is also understandable that the dominant strain of radical consciousness in the Canadian working class would be the British social democracy of the CCP-NDP variety.

Thus, while working class resistance in Canada has arisen in response to material conditions in Canada, it has done so within the traditions and framework imported from two imperialist countries: Great Britain and the United States. British social democracy and American unionism have provided the tradition and the framework for the politics of the Canadian working class. These phenomena have each developed initially among the more prosperous strata of the working class in Britain and the United States and have been the framework for quiescent politics in these countries.

The origins of the social democracy of the CCF in imperialist ideology is evident from the fact that the CCF supported American imperialism at the zenith of U.S. power in Canada and the world at large. During the Cold War years of the early 50's, the CCF supported the foreign policy of the American empire, including the Korean War, and supported Canada's inclusion in the American military alliance system.[16] During these same years which saw the greatest incursion of American investment into Canada, the CCF waged no campaign against the foreign takeover of Canada. As a result, no mass movement of the Canadian working class was anti-imperialist during the Cold War years.

Today the NDP continues the failure of the CCF to come to grips with imperialism. The NDP gives expression to the view that even if change and progress is not occurring rapidly enough in Canada, nonetheless the society is moving in a generally progressive direction. Seen this way, the problem for progressive citizens is to push things along and to make the gradual transition to a more humane world a little more rapid. The reduction of Canada to dependency within the American empire, with its attendant costs, makes the politics of social democracy in Canada irrelevant not only in degree but in kind.

The importance of the existence of American unions in Canada is directly related to the developing American penetration of the economy. As we have seen, industrialization in central Canada took place during two phases in the evolution of Canadian capitalism: first, in the period of Canadian capitalism's balancing act between the British and American empires from the late 19th century to World War II and second in the period of American control after 1945.

As industrialization proceeded in central Canada, a significant working class employed in manufacturing came into being. Working-class political militancy tended to be located outside this favoured region of Southern Ontario, in the primary producing regions of the country or among manufacturing workers located in regions that were basically primary producing regions. This is true of the socialist and syndicalist movements that flourished in British Columbia after 1900; it is true of the Western Labour Conference, which split off from the more conservative eastern trade unionists at the end of World War I; it is true of the Winnipeg General Strike of 1919; and it is true of the radicalism of the Cape Breton miners in the 1920s.

Southern Ontario, although the scene of many militant strikes was also the rock of political conservatism in the Canadian labour movement, on which the waves of western Canadian labour radicalism were dashed. Although demands for Canadian unionism developed in Southern Ontario as well as in other parts of the country, radical political manifestations of Canadian unionism in opposition to the business unionism of the Trades and Labour Congress (TLC), dominated by the American Federation of Labour (AFL), arose outside Southern Ontario in movements like the One Big Union. It is difficult to find any evidence that in Southern Ontario organizations like the All Canadian Congress of Labour were more militant or more radical than were TLC unions.

During the two phases in the development of Canadian manu-facturing from the late 19th century to World War II and from 1945 to the mid-1960s, American unions served to fragment the Canadian labour movement and to make it difficult for it to pursue its own national objectives. It is difficult to avoid the conclusion, however, that the greater political militancy of workers outside southern Ontario had more to do with the political economy of the regions in which they were located, than with the fact of Canadian or American unions.

In fact, during the period from 1945 to the mid-sixties, it was certainly the relatively well-paid workers in the large capital inten-sive manufacturing plants of southern Ontario, organized into American unions who served as the mass base for the quiescent politics of the Ontario CCF-NDP. During this period, although Canadian workers were not masters of their own trade union movement, the general expansion of the manufacturing economy within the framework of an expanding American empire led to political passivity.

The recurrence of a general crisis of overproduction in the capitalist world, beginning in the late 1960s, changed this position of relative security for unionized Canadian workers in the large manufacturing industries. With Nixonomics in 1971 the commun-ity of interest between the American labour leadership and the Canadian members of their unions was shattered. As American labour leaders fought for protectionist legislation that would max-imize American manufacturing at the expense of other countries, Canadian workers were experiencing plant shutdowns and layoffs on a massive scale in the industrial sector of the economy.

The long-term consequence of American unionism in Canada then became clear: as soon as the interests of Canadian workers were threatened by a changed economic direction in the American empire, the link of Canadian workers with American unions became their greatest encumbrance. As this process proceeded, the demand for completely Canadian unions became more insistent in all parts of Canada.

During the period of special status for Canada within the Ameri-can empire from 1945 to the end of the sixties, this twin legacy of British social democracy and American unionism served as the basis for the quiescent politics of the Canadian working class. Current changes in the Canadian political economy threaten the viability of both British social democracy and American unionism in Canada. The need for Canadian independence to end the exploitation of Canada by the American empire has given birth to new strategies and a new institutional framework for Canadian working class politics.

Notes

[1] Donald Creighton, *The Empire of the St. Lawrence*, (Toronto, 1956), pp.6,7.
[2] *Ibid*., pp. 384, 385.
[3] George Grant, *Lament for a Nation*, (Toronto, 1965).
[4] R. T. Naylor, "The Rise and Fall of the Third Commercial Empire of the St. Lawrence", Gary Teeple (ed.), *Capitalism and the National Question in Canada*, (Toronto, 1972), p. 2.
[5] Donald Creighton, *Dominion of the North*, (Toronto, 1957), p. 314.
[6] R. T. Naylor, *op. cit.*, p. 16.
[7] Kari Levitt, *Silent Surrender*, (Toronto 1970), p. 66.
[8] Frank Underhill, *In Search of Canadian Liberalism*, (Toronto, 1961), p. 35.
[9] *Ibid.*, p. 40.
[10] James Laxer, "Lament for an Industry," *Last Post*, Dec. 1971.
[11] *Ibid.*
[12] James Eayrs, *In Defence of Canada*, (Toronto, 1965), v. 11, p. 183.
[13] *Ibid.*, p. 208.
[14] *Ibid.*, p. 178.
[15] Toronto Wafflers' Deindustrialization Study (unpublished).
[16] W. E. C. Harrison, *Canada in World Affairs, 1949 to 1950*, (Toronto, 1957), p. 285. In his book Harrison states, "Mr. Stanley Knowles reported it [intervention in the Korean situation] had been endorsed by a national convention of the CCF, meeting in Vancouver in July. The main objections were not that the government had gone too far, but that it had neither the troops at its disposal, nor the conviction to persuade it to act as promptly as the case required."

The History of Domestic and Foreign Capital in Canada
Tom Naylor

To examine the evolution of Canadian capitalism one must begin by considering the foundations of the great Canadian fortunes, the basis of social stratification. This is essential because capital, that which is used to employ wage labour in the production of commodities, had its origin in income inequality. Unless there exists an unequal distribution of income, the financial wherewithal for one small class to control the labour of a larger class does not exist.

While a true pioneer economy comprised solely of independent commodity producers with more or less equal income and wealth has never existed, as a theoretical model it is a useful construct, for in the early stages of Canadian history the society did have many pioneer attributes. The first task, then, is to see how Canadian society evolved out of the quasi-pioneer stage, how social differentiation into capitalist and non-capitalist classes occurred. This requires explicit consideration of the sources of the great fortunes – which are basically six in number.

First, arising out of the conquest of New France, the heroes of our history books arrived in Canada in the form of army contractors who followed the British army around the world to feed off the spoils of conquest. Once they arrived in New France they undertook a programme of systematic impoverishment of the French peasants and artisans by currency manipulation or the purchase and sale of commodities to the inhabitants of the war-ravaged colony at ruinous prices – with the willing assistance of the British military authorities.[1] Here is illustrated clearly the process of social differentiation, the impoverishment of the many for the enrichment of the few.

A second important source of the initial accumulation of wealth was a system of extortion known as the "fur trade," operating out of Montreal and out of London, England. The nature of the "bargains" struck is too well known to require repetition here.[2] Under the system of exploitation that evolved, the Indians were kept dependent on the fur trade for gunpowder. Furs were exchanged for gunpowder and other goods and the "terms of trade," the rate of exchange between furs and gunpowder, was made increasingly unfavourable to the Indians. The more furs they brought in, the lower the "price" paid, and the harder they had to search for furs to maintain their supplies of powder. And the harder they searched and the more furs they caught, the richer the merchants became. In this type of swindle one finds the roots of the Bank of Montreal.

In these two forms of initial accumulation, in the fur trade and in the commodity and currency double-dealings such names as Frobisher, McTavish, McGill, Molson, Ogilvie and others could be found, names quite familiar in Canadian history, although the origin of their wealth is generally obscured.

A third important source was piracy in Nova Scotia and to a lesser extent on the Great Lakes. Here the archetypal Canadian entrepreneur was one Enos Collins from New England, a sort of pre-Revolutionary Loyalist in Halifax, who sailed the Seven Seas in search of loot. Once he got too old for such pursuits, he settled down first with an import-export firm dealing in the goods brought back by other pirates, then financed privateering expeditions, and finally into money-changing. It was an attribute of piracy that the participants had little choice in the type of currency in which they were rewarded for their services. Hence a money-changing business played a key role, and out of this evolved the Canadian Imperial Bank of Commerce.[3]

A fourth source was land-jobbing. After the Indians were pushed off, the land was turned over to groups of favoured individuals and in the colony to one large commercial land company. The land companies hoarded land and blocked settlement. The individual land grabbers did help settlement to some degree but kept their tenants in the conditions of medieval serfs, who turned over large amounts of their produce in rent for the land which the land grabbers often did not even legally own. Two of the best known of these figures in Upper Canada were McNab and Thomas Talbot.[4]

Talbot left a memorial behind when, canonising himself in the process, he named the centre of his settlement St. Thomas.

A fifth source of wealth was office jobbing – getting the best government positions through nepotism and favouritism. This illustrates a very important point in the process of capital accumulation – the role of the state. The state in a capitalist society helps foster the accumulation of capital by raising money from the many and giving it to the few. This goes on today in the form of DREE grants and the like with tax money; but in pioneer British North American office jobbing with high salaries paid the privileged few was the important thing.

Lastly, mention should be made of the role of the War of 1812 which had two major effects. With it came the usual bonanza for army contractors, but more important was the emergence of the first permanently impoverished class of settlers in English Canada out of the carnage of the War. Here from the effects of war came the genesis of the Anglo-Canadian working class,[5] supplemented by the import of impoverished and cholera-stricken refugees from Ireland.

It is important to note the distinction between industrial capital accumulation and commercial capital accumulation. An industrialist is involved in the physical production of goods, whereas a commercial capitalist is a merchant who simply intermediates the sale of goods produced elsewhere. Today it is not easy to make a sharp distinction. Big corporations like General Motors Corporation not only produce but also handle their own advertising, financing, and other aspects of the actual final sale of the goods. But until at least World War I in Canadian history the differentiation between the commercial and industrial spheres was very pronounced and absolutely essential to comprehending the process of historical evolution. The most striking characteristic of Canadian development, and that which differentiates it sharply from British and American experience, is the degree to which commercial capital began *and remained* at the top of the socio-economic ladder. Commerce controlled industry – obviously there was a great deal of industrialization. But control of the economy and the state rested largely with the commercial group. This is an attribute of colonial economies. They produce staple goods – fish, furs, wheat, wood and minerals, for export to the imperium and import finished products; and the group who control the export and import, and the relations with the imperium are a mercantile capitalist class.

One other preliminary definition should be kept in mind – the distinction between direct and portfolio investment. Direct investment occurs through the purchase of stock which gives a claim to the ownership of physical assets and a share of profits. With portfolio investment there is a transfer of a bond which gives the holder a claim to a sum of money and interest payments – it does not involve ownership of physical assets.

Keeping these definitions and the origins of Canadian wealth in mind we can examine the creation and development of the Canadian state – Confederation and the venerated National Policy. Confederation united British North American colonies which had nothing in common besides colonialism and debts to the British merchant banking house, the Baring Brothers. Ontario was a rather backward agricultural community, Quebec was more urbanized and somewhat industrialized, the Maritimes were the richest and most flourishing part of British North America – a commercial and industrial community well past the take-off stage of industrial progress. The National Policy can best be analysed as a five-point program, rather than the usual three points, which conventionally omit the two most important facets.

(1) Consider the institutional and class basis of the creation of the Canadian state. That is, examine who gains and who loses and how the winners dictate the institutional patterns. This by itself takes us out of the confines of the apologetic history which regards us as one big happy family where everyone gains from the steady march of progress. Confederation was the work of a few British investors in colonial securities and a handful of Montreal wholesale merchants and financiers who created the Canadian state in their own image. As commercial capitalists they created a commercial state to further their class interests and we are still living with the consequences in terms of American control of the productive apparatus.

Canada in its conception was the most centralized of all the classical federations of the world, with stronger federal control than the U.S., Australia, or Switzerland. Every major commercial and economic power was given to the federal government, that is to say, to the Montreal clique whose creature the federal government was. In many respects the Confederation terms were extremely reactionary. For example, before Confederation, the Senate in the Province of Canada was elected. After Confederation it was appointed by the clique who controlled the House of Commons. Confederation did not mean independence from Britain. All that happened was that a few colonial office functions were re-allocated to the Ottawa clique who in turn were ultimately answerable to Britain. There was no net movement towards independence – quite the reverse. For the individual provinces were much more answerable to Ottawa and therefore indirectly to Britain than they had been directly to Britain before Confederation.

Why did the provinces choose to join? In fact they did not choose, but were coerced. There was no broad franchise. In the case of Prince Edward Island, a bank and a railway company engineered a phony financial crisis just before a vote and told the frightened depositors and taxpayers that the situation would be saved if they voted for Confederation. The railway men and bankers were rewarded for their part in the democratic process by the federal government purchasing from them some unsalable railway securities.[6] This incident appears to have been studied before the "Brinks coup" of the 1970 Quebec election. In Nova Scotia the esteemed Father of Confederation Charles Tupper wrote to the Baring Brothers in 1866 asking them not to try to market provincial securities which would have to be sold at "deep discount prices" – which for securities is not a particularly desirable state of affairs. Instead he told them to hold off until after Confederation was effected, when they could be sure of a good price. After Nova Scotia made its democratic choice and was bulldozed into the union, the securities sold at a large premium.[7]

(2) Land Grabs. Throughout Canadian history there had been a steady process of stealing Indian land and pushing the Indians further west into the waiting clutches of the Hudson's Bay Company, which controlled all of the area west of Ontario and Labrador as well. The Indians were totally subordinated to the whims of the high-ranking officers of what vulgar historians called "the honourable company," as were the Métis and what few white settlers existed in the territory. The "honour" of the company consisted of summary execution of interlopers who might carry news of its resources to the outside world, of execution for private

trading to escape the monopoly exactions of the company, not to mention wholesale destruction of fur-bearing animals in any area where competition threatened. Labrador, another part of the fiefdom, was the place where Lord Strathcona made his initial "killing," the consequences of which were the destruction of half of the Nascopie nation and his Lordship becoming a leading stockholder in the Bank of Montreal.[8]

However, the Hudson's Bay Company was eventually taken over by a handful of British and Canadian commercial and financial capitalists, among them this same Lord Strathcona. By then it was no longer a fur-trading company but had become instead a land speculation company. After the land-grab was over and the lands had been sold, the Hudson's Bay Company became a retail store chain, serving initially the same area it had pillaged with the fur trade and robbed in bank sales. This illustrates the remarkable adaptive power of commercial capitalism and also illustrates well how the initial accumulation of capital in the fur trade managed to evolve and grow.

The Hudson's Bay was not the sole beneficiary of the initial rip-offs in the fur trade. The Canadian Pacific Railway received most of the lands that were taken away from the Hudson's Bay Company. But when you examine the list of the share-holders and directors of the two institutions, you discover that this great exercise of national sovereignty, revered in our textbooks, really was a minor re-shuffling of corporate assets. Lord Strathcona, the head of the Hudson's Bay Company, was also by no great surprise, the head of the Canadian Pacific Railway, and the man who drove the last spike.

What happened next? The Canadian Pacific Railway now had all these lands that had been stolen from the Indians indirectly by the Hudson's Bay Company and brought in white settlers. It had an excellent system of land sales. It would sell a settler one plot and hold the adjoining plots. The harder the settler worked his plot, the more he would raise the commercial value of the surrounding plots. At the same time, the harder he worked his own plot, the greater was going to be the need for him to expand and buy up the adjoining plots. It was "Catch 22" with a vengeance.

(3) Policy to encourage foreign investment. A number of policies were worked out by the federal government with a view to

encouraging the inflow of foreign, especially American, but also British investment. The tariff was the most important of these. It is generally regarded as a sort of declaration of industrial independence from the U.S., but on closer view it becomes a matter of inviting American capitalists to shift the locus of their production northward. Canada was the pioneer of the process of industrialization by invitation and this was a conscious policy. *Canadian Manufacturer*, the oracle of the Canadian Manufacturers' Association before the turn of the century, declared that "whenever a man comes to Canada to live and contribute in any way to the material success of the country he may very properly be considered a Canadian. His birthplace may be Europe, Asia, Africa, an Isle of the Sea, or even the Land of the Yankee and protectionists will be ready and willing to acknowledge him a Canadian. There will be no objection whatsoever because of the place of his nativity, and the same as regards his money."

This tariff strategy in several respects was harmful to existing industry. First it produced an inflow of branch plants which had access to superior financing via their American parent and whose competitive position was therefore stronger than existing firms. Second, a heavy tax was put on industrial raw materials, which raised production costs. In many cases industry received less protection from foreign competition from the National Policy of high tariffs than it did from the preceding lower tariff.

Who benefited from this structure? First, a handful of coal mine owners and the owners of a steel plant in Nova Scotia, who were largely British. Second, Canadian railway owners and bankers, who got fat on the charges they could exact from industry for freight and credit. The tariff operated in a curious way. With the tariff the consumer paid high prices to industry which in turn paid high charges to the railway lords. When tariff rates went up the railway rates went up, thus producing a transfer of income from the consumer to the railway owners. Even after the last spike was in place it cost more to ship general merchandise from Winnipeg to Montreal than from Chicago to Liverpool.

The tariff was not the only policy to promote an inflow of American direct investment. Another rather technical one was a system of patent protection, whereby an inventor or a firm owning a patent had to produce it in Canada for the patent to maintain its validity. Another astonishing policy was the Bonusing system, a sort of vicious intercommunal warfare in which Canadian munici-palities competed to drive each other into bankruptcy by escalat-ing the amount of bribes they would pay to branch plant industry to locate within their sphere of authority. This, of course, was the direct ancestor of the DREE grant system. Standard gifts were; free site, twenty year tax exemptions, cash gifts, a free or low utility rate, and municipal building of railroad spurs. If a firm were especially lucky, the municipality might guarantee its bonds and even buy some stock which was usually pure water. The system got so bad that Yankee Sam Slicks were wandering about Ontario, conning municipalities out of bonuses, pocketing the cash, and skipping town. The burden fell heavily on already established firms who had to pay higher taxes to support the give-aways to the newcomers.

(4) Railway Policy. Every school child is taught the romantic story of how the CPR was built atop the carcasses of buffalo and Indian rights with the aid of gargantuan sums from the public purse – an operation that ensured that the costs of making a sizeable group of millionnaires would fall on Canadians at large for several generations. Railway owners, as we have seen, formed the top stratum of the Canadian socio-economic hierarchy, and the rail-ways were a constant drain on the farm population and on industry. The tale of the struggle of organized farmers against the railroads is well known. A parallel fight existed between the railroads and organ-ized manufacturers, who always lost. The CPR was the first, and the Conservative Party was its political tool. Subsequently the Liberal Party, to break the CPR monopoly of political and economic power, sponsored the Canadian Northern Railway and the Grand Trunk transcontinental ambitions. If such a situation repeated itself today, one would expect the Canadian Manufacturers' Association to rec-ognize where its true friends were and support the New Democratic Party.

The Canadian railways were geared to long distance traffic and discriminated in favour of the international movement of staples against the local marketing of finished products. Discrimination also existed between regions. The rates in Nova Scotia on coal and raw materials were lower than the rate on its finished prod-ucts which blocked shipment of manufacturers into Ontario. On the other hand, raw materials could move to Ontario and be used in processing industries there, and finished products sent back. The rate discrimination worked in reverse as well, making it easy for central Canadian industry to ship finished products to the Maritimes. Maritime industries could not fight back. A demand for the secession of Nova Scotia resulted in part from destruction of several of its industries. To ward off this separatism, the Laurier government gave it a primary iron and steel industry in the biggest handout policy since the CPR construction.

(5) Monetary Policy. Monetary policy is usually neglected in discussions of the National Policy, although it may well be the most important single facet of it. Under the terms of Confederation the federal government was given absolute control over banking and currency, *i.e.,* the banking cartel through the federal government was given absolute control. The bankers were able to get together in Ottawa every ten years to write the bank act that was supposed to regulate them. On the same principle, thieves and extortionists should have been permitted to draft the criminal code.

The banking system in Canada is extremely powerful and it is important to understand its character. It is what is called a commercial banking system, which means it won't make any sort of long-term, risky investments. It invests in short-term, very liquid types of assets. It will invest in moving commodities from one place to another. It won't invest in actually producing them. Again, we are back to the distinction between mercantile or commercial, and industrial capital; and Canadian banks, just as the Canadian railways, are definitely a commercial type of operation. Now this, of course, has the effect of draining funds away from the industrial and into the commercial sphere. For example, Canadian chartered banks moved into the Maritime provinces where there were a lot of small local banks which had been building up a fair amount of industry in the Maritimes. These were systematically wiped out and all the savings from the Maritimes were then shipped out to the Canadian west. The Maritimes were drained of any sort of industrial funds and this capital from the Maritimes was converted into short-term commercial capital and used to keep the farmers in the west permanently in debt to the banking cartel. This is the real root of the Maritime underdevelopment, the process of takeover by central Canadian financial institutions which drain all the potential industrial funds out of the area. The Maritime provinces once had the most thriving industrial base, the most active entrepreneurial class in Canada. The only reason for the current predicament is a lack of access to capital which is only explicable by the activities of the Central Canadian financial institutions.

There is a great myth about the stability of the Canadian banking system which is promoted by the Canadian Banker's Association itself. Before the first world war in particular, countless eulogies were written by its members extolling the virtues of the system, while bank after bank was coming down around their ears. In fact, the Canadian banking system has an appalling record of swindles and failures. There were dozens of cases of absconding with funds and of jail terms. There was a steady flow of bank managers from Canada to the United States following the pathway already blazed by the political refugees from the rebellions of 1837. They were the ones who were caught in the act; think of the ones who got away!

Now a final aspect of this monetary policy is the extent of monetary centralization. This was extremely important for borrowing portfolio capital from Britain. One of the main objectives of Confederation was to integrate the North American colonies in order to make British investors more secure. Canada became increasingly dependent on Great Britain. In 1900 the British government introduced a piece of legislation called the Colonial Stocks Act whereby in order to borrow in Britain, the Dominion Government had to agree that it would repeal any pieces of legislation that British investors thought might detract from the security of their investment. This was the independence policy pursued by Macdonald and Laurier.

Now let's look briefly at the process of capital accumulation within the framework of the National Policy. There were three main sources of capital for the Canadian economy. One was portfolio investments from Britain, a second was direct investment from the United States and the third was domestic accumulation. Consider first the portfolio investments. Using these portfolio investments by the British financiers, Canadian commercial capitalists managed to build an elaborate banking and financial system, a huge, over-extended system of railroads (more railroads per capita than any other country in the world – most of them useless), and of course, a series of public utilities. The linkage runs from British financiers into the commercial sectors of the Canadian economy. The British were paid back many times over. For example, when the British goldmine investors decided to take over the South African republics, Lord Strathcona raised a troop of private horsemen at his own expense to go over and fight in the Boer War. Many of the recruits were former Mounties who were well experienced in the art of dealing with restless colonials.

The second source of capital was American direct investment. Now this is a very different process because direct investment involves a flow of funds directly into the productive system. With portfolio investment, there is no loss of ownership. Portfolio investment is simply a debt contracted, but when foreign direct investment occurs ownership over assets is alienated.

There were three main ways in which the Americans became involved in production in Canada. The best known was via branch plants, but there were two additional methods. One was by a licensing system, whereby an American patent was rented and American goods were produced in Canada under licence. The other way involved joint ventures, where the Americans might hold only 20 per cent of the stock (for example) and Canadians 80 per cent. But all these methods created a technological dependence on the United States. Thus ownership is not the only factor in dependency, because a licensed venture is just as much a sort of branch plant of American technology and American capital as is a full-fledged branch plant that is 100 per cent American owned. What this means, of course, is that one cannot really measure the amount of American control over the economy just by looking at the amount of American ownership, because licensed ventures and joint ventures were also derivatives from American technology and American capitalism. They result from and perpetuate a technological gap that has always existed between Canada and the United States.

The technological gap exists because of what is called the National Policy, or more aptly, the MacDonald-Strathcona underdevelopment policy. First, the tariff. It promoted a group of over-coddled branch plants, and the bonusing system helped a great deal as well. It made Canadian industry totally derivative, even when it was ostensibly independent. Secondly, the financial establishment avoided investments in Canadian industry and preferred to invest in U.S. industry and U.S. railroads. This was not because of any anti-nationalist conspiracy but simply because the American ventures were much more stable, being bigger and safer. Capitalists always behave that way. They don't worship flags, they worship dollars – as long as the exchange rates are fixed! Third, transportation policy. Again the same process of draining funds from industry and systematic discrimination against areas where Canadian industry was strong, in favour of areas where American industry was strong and becoming stronger. The immigration policy also helped a great deal in this process of building up a technical dependence. All of Canada's skills were imported and there was no effort to build them up at home.

Education policy was also an important consideration. Education was a function given to the provincial governments, but the federal government took over all the sources of revenue and the provinces lacked the funds with which to invest in a technical education system. There is a rather obvious contrast to the United States here. In the U.S. a system of what were called "land grant colleges" to promote technical education were built up. In Canada we had a system of "land grab colleges," whereby McGill University and the University of Toronto would get fat on their investments of money that had been derived from alienation of prairie lands. Even as early as the 1880s the Canadian Manufacturers' Association was complaining about the lack of technical education in Canada because the commercial elite who controlled the Canadian economy were not interested in that field.

The third source of capital was domestic accumulation. The sources of domestic accumulation are essentially two in number. Commerce, which has already been described, and industry. Industry in Canada even though it was subordinate to commerce, nonetheless was a potent force. A fair amount of capital was accumulated the way any capital ultimately is, that is through appropriating the product of unpaid labour. (See Chapter 3 of this book). A large number of examples could be given. There was one flagrant case of exploitation in the 1890s in the textile industry where the total weekly wage for a 60-hour week was eighty cents. In the boot and shoe industry a case came to light where workers were paid one cent for each sole made. There was a four cent fine for each defective one and the fines were so staggered that the manufacturer made a clear profit of one cent on every sole he could condemn as defective. In one textile firm the total amount of fines that were levied came to 25 per cent of the total dividend payments. And in that firm the dividends were running at something like 12 to 14 per cent per year. Private police forces in the factories were very common and piece-work rates were geared to super-human levels.[9]

On top of the factories came the sweating system, which was so flagrant that even the Canadian Manufacturers' Association had to condemn it. The sweating system is a sub-contracting system and ideal for commercial capitalism. Merchants do not want to invest in a physical plant and equipment, so they let the work out to some contractors, who in turn may let it out to a family. This is very prevalent in the garment industry, even now: the family doing all the work at home. It is an effective way of dodging minimum wage legislation and restrictions in child labor. Entire families would be economically, socially, and even geographically trapped by the sweating system, working eighteen and twenty hours a day. And there is no way, of course, of enforcing the law, even if any governments wanted to. But remember, these measures were just icing on the capitalist cake. The major part of the appropriation came through the wage system itself.

One thing that should be mentioned here is the relationship between Canadian capitalists and the British Empire. Until World War II, they had a peculiar "northern vision." They thought of themselves as being Americans in Britain, producing goods inside Canada for export to the British market. And this system worked, as long as the British Empire worked; that is, as long as the British Empire was there to provide portfolio investment to maintain the Canadian banking and railroad structure and as long as the British markets existed to which they could send the products of American branch plants. After World War I and increasingly until the 1930's when the whole system collapsed, this vision came under attack. The British Empire started to die, and there was no more flow of portfolio investments into Canada. The over-extended railway and banking system started to contract, leading to railway nationalization in Canada, the biggest give-away of them all. Once the growth of the British Empire stopped, there was more room, of course, for the expansion of the American Empire. There was also no longer any need for joint ventures, for licensing arrangements and for Canadian capitalists performing a secondary or subordinate role in the productive apparatus. During the 1920s and 1930s, there occurred a steady freeze-out of Canadian capital as the American firms got rid of the redundant Canadian ownership.

After World War II the role of Canadian capital changed. Not much was left of the British Empire. Now the Canadian capitalists' relationships were mainly with the United States. Canadian capital's roles became tributary. The railroads and the transportation network formed a commercial artery preoccupied with the flow of goods between American corporations on both sides of the border, because there was no longer any "all red route" servicing the British Empire. The banks and the insurance companies preferred to invest in American firms and, by so doing, they abetted the process of take-over. The raw material producers had a very clear stake in the American system. Even when the resource industries were not owned outright by the United States, they were usually tied by long-term contracts to American industry. As for the branch plants, they experienced a very rapid growth because licensed ventures and joint ventures were no longer significant. As Canadian capital was increasingly squeezed out of the realm of production, it increasingly moved into the commercial sphere. It started in the commercial sphere and made a few minor movements into the industrial sphere and then was forced back out again and into commerce.

There is a tendency in all modern economies for the cost of production of commodities to fall steadily. But a problem arises in marketing these commodities because the producer has to convince people that they want the goods with which they are increasingly satiated. This requires an escalation of the amount of money that is spent in marketing and that is where Canadian capitalists come in. The so-called independent sectors of Canadian capital are very important in marketing American goods in Canada, and they are just as interlocked with the American system as the branch plant managers. In fact, they are in their glory now, because as the costs of circulating and of marketing rise, they have a claim to an increasingly large slice of the pie. There is now, however, a tendency for American firms to try to take over the sphere of circulation to capture all the profits from circulation themselves. This may explain the attempts at the take-over of the banking system.

It is the role of bourgeois nationalism to try and defend Canadian capitalism. Thus, when Canadian capital is threatened in the sphere of circulation, its control of the commercial sphere, one hears nationalist sounds. Canadian capitalists don't want to be redundant; they would rather retain their freedom to be subordinate.

Notes

[1] Adam Shortt (ed.) *Documents Relating to Currency Exchange, and Finance During the French Period* vol. 2, Ottawa, 1925, p. 765 *passim*.

[2] United Kingdom House of Commons, Select Committee on Hudson's Bay Company, *Report*, London, 1857.

[3] V. Ross, *History of the Bank of Commerce*, Vol. I, Toronto, 1920.

[4] N. Macdonald, *Canada 1763-1841*, Immigration and Settlement, Toronto, 1939.

[5] A. Shortt, "Economic Effects of the War of 1812 on Upper Canada," Ontario Historical Society, Papers and Records, Vol. 10, Toronto, 1913.

[6] A. Macphail, *History of Prince Edward Island*, Toronto, 1914.

[7] E. M. Saunders, *Life and Letters of the Hon. Sir Charles Tupper*, London, 1916.

[8] Gustavus Myers, *A History of Canadian Wealth*, Toronto, 1972.

[9] Royal Commision on the Relations of Labour and Capital, *Report*, Ottawa, 1889.

Class and Income Distribution in Canada
John Hutcheson

One view of Canada which is widely disseminated, and perhaps even widely believed, holds that this country is tolerant, broadly egalitarian, by and large affluent, and above all classless. The purveyors of this view argue that Canada is essentially classless because we are all more or less "middle class" by virtue of a high-level, standardized consumption of automobiles, television sets, various household appliances, clothing, vacations and sporting facilities. The "more or less" qualification allows for the fact that some are a little less "middle class" because they consume a little less of these things, while some are a little more "middle class" because they consume a little more of them.

Not surprisingly, those who hold this view also tend to believe that Canada is obviously well along the way to the "American way of life." As one example, consider the following passage from a Canadian historian and politician, William Kilbourn:

> Everywhere in the twentieth century man is becoming American, or to put it another way, is moving in some way towards a condition of high industrialization, affluence and leisure, instant communication, an urban man-made environment, and a mingling of cultures and traditions in a mobile, classless, global society. There is no country in the world, except the United States, which has gone further in this direction than Canada. . . . [1]

In fact, the same historian takes up the argument that Canada is in some respects a more successful version of the American dream, since Canada has managed to avoid the lawlessness, violence and terror of the U.S.A. He suggests that "this Canada of ours might be a guide to other peoples who seek a path to the peaceable kingdom."[2]

Of course, not all Canadians share this facile view of their society. Many studies of Canadian society have suggested considerable modifications of this approach. But it is worth considering some of these studies in order to discover the extent to which they do help us to a better understanding of our society and the way in which it has been changing and is likely to change in the future.

In 1965 there appeared a study which was generally hailed as a milestone in social studies and which was considered by many to have provided a basic interpretation of Canadian society, one which could not be neglected by those who wished to understand the nature of this country. John Porter's *The Vertical Mosaic*[3] was considered to be a milestone because it dealt with the subjects of social class and power in Canada. Because it has been so enthusiastically acclaimed it is worth devoting a section of this chapter to a discussion of it, before going on to consider further studies of Canada.

In *The Vertical Mosaic* Porter demonstrated that the "classless" or "middle-class society" view of Canada was false, and that Canadian society was marked by fundamental inequalities. Canada, he concluded "has a long way to go to become in any sense a thoroughgoing democracy."[4] The book contains a substantial body of information to support this argument.

The main thrust of *The Vertical Mosaic*, however, was that the educational system was the mechanism that perpetuated inequality and was thus the mechanism that could be used to produce a democratic Canada. Porter argued that there were class barriers to individual achievement since the educational system was not yet democratized through to the university level. Even at lower levels, he suggested, education was only formally democratized, since there was a combination of barriers which biased schooling in favour of the upper classes. Income, family size, regional differences in facilities, religious attitudes and also psychological barriers are the factors which he identified.[5]

In Porter's view it is inequalities in education that lead to inequalities in social position, since educational and occupational levels are highly correlated. "People who have little education are not likely to have a high class position as measured by occupation."[6] In fact, Porter's main indictment of Canadian society is that it fails to provide maximum opportunity for individual achievement of a "high class position."

> Canadian society is not mobility oriented and has not made mobility values the underpinnings of its educational systems.[7]

The failure of the educational system has two further consequences for Porter. The first concerns a division within the society and the second concerns the whole society in relation to other societies. First, in addition to providing a means for social selection, the educational system provides a basis for genuine citizenship:

> A further aspect of educational achievement is the ability to partake in the cultural achievements of the society. In the contemporary world knowledge is increasingly required to realize the good life. There is, so to speak, a culturally depressed status resulting from educational deprivation.[8]

Secondly, Porter argues that an "industrial society" must be one of "upward mobility" and "high levels of skill are essential to future development." He suggests that Canada has relied too much on immigration to upgrade its labour force and because of internal barriers to mobility is falling behind other "democratic, industrial societies":

> The richness of its educational system will determine an industrial society's chances of growth and survival.[9]

To argue that Canada's survival as an "industrial society" depends on the "richness of its educational system" is to make a fundamental judgment about Canada which needs further examination. Among other things, the argument fails to consider the nature of the international framework within which "industrial societies" operate. In particular it fails to consider the fact that Canada's past development has been conditioned by its dependent status within a succession of empires and that its future development will also be conditioned by its relationship to a changing U.S. empire.

Furthermore, when Porter argues both that the full participation in society by each individual rests on the success of the educational system and also that "mobility values" must be made the basis of the educational system, he is making a fundamental judgment about the nature of democracy. This also must be further analyzed. In order to look at this question, it is necessary to consider the framework within which Porter carries out his analysis.

What Porter does in *The Vertical Mosaic* is to develop an analysis of political power in Canada by the introduction of the sociological analysis of "elites." Porter rejects both the pluralist argument (discussed in this book in Chapter 7), and the tradition in political theory which argues that the state is an "all embracing coercive apparatus" because it neglects the power which inheres in other "sub-systems":

> In the modern complex society there is a very clear breaking up of . . . power functions into separate but interrelated systems or sub-systems. These sub-systems . . . are the economic, the political, the administrative, the defensive, and the ideological.[10]

According to this theory then, power is exercised by a series of elites, or leaders, each of which stands at the head of a "sub-system" of the total social system. That is, within each "sub-system" there is a hierarchy, those at the top being the elite which exercises power throughout the particular "sub-system".

The hierarchy within any "sub-system", however, is linked to divisions within the society as a whole:

> The structure of power reflects the structure of class, for class determines the routes and barriers to advancement up our institutional hierarchies. Power is used to perpetuate a given structure of class.[11]

What Porter is arguing then, is not that power is exercised by a ruling class, but that it is exercised by a series of elites. He does argue, however, both that a class structure determines the formation of the elite and that the elites use their power to reinforce this class structure. At this point it becomes necessary to ask what Porter means by "power" and what he means by "class."

On the first point, Porter states simply that "power arises because of the general social need for order," and in one place he defines power as "the recognized right to make effective decisions on behalf of a group of people." That Porter does not, however, see power as something delegated by the majority to its representatives emerges at many places. For example, where Porter discusses the enjoyment of power by those who occupy high positions:

The rewards lie in the right to control the resources and facilities of the society, and in the receipt of deference from those without power, rather than in the enjoyment of prestige. Deference, moreover, becomes the appropriate attitude within bureaucratic hierarchies in which the values of docility and servility are more important than achievement.[12]

It may be true that all societies have a social need for order, but to accept that such order requires control on the one hand and deference, docility and servility on the other, is to abandon belief in the possibility of democracy. That Porter has in essence rejected the possibility of any genuine democracy is suggested by his conclusions:

If power and decision-making must always rest with elite groups, there can at least be open recruitment from all classes into the elites.[13]

Thus Porter's arguments for educational reform are part of an argument that simply defines democracy as an opening of the opportunities to control others.

Porter himself states that the analysis of society in terms of elite groups grows out of a literature which has argued against the possibility of creating "industrial societies in which reason and humanitarian values are the principal characteristics."[14] To be more precise, the basic literature developing the theory of elites has been part of a violently anti-democratic and anti-socialist doctrine. Vilfredo Pareto, who played an important role in developing the theory, was an anti-democratic, authoritarian critic of a "decadent bourgeoisie" which had lost sight of the need to use force in maintaining its power. Porter's discussion of Pareto and his use of elite theory should be considered in this context.[15]

Porter also reveals an underlying aspect of his book when he suggests that an analysis of the power of elites enables one to establish a polarity between "western" societies and "totalitarian" or "soviet" types of society. In the "totalitarian" type of society the elites are united through a centralized institution, or through allegiance to a leader or to a "quasi-religious ideology." In the "western" type of society, however, "except perhaps in times of war," the elites are not unified, but instead "compete for power, with the result that such co-ordination and control as there are come about by a floating equilibrium of compromise."[16] The validity of this polarity obviously turns on the question of whether the elites in "western" type societies do or do not constitute a class. It is, in fact, when one turns to the analysis of class that a pronounced inclination to Cold-War rhetoric becomes a dominant feature of Porter's discussions.

As we have seen, Porter argues that the structure of power reflects the structure of class. But the classes which he employs in his analysis are merely "artificial statistical groups which do not have any life of their own or any coherence."[17] They are classes as defined by Porter, by his own process of classification. They are not distinguished by any "readily available visible criteria" and, since there are "no clear dividing lines, no one can be sure how many classes there are."[18] Porter appears to draw back slightly from these statements when he also suggests that "class is something which is experienced in everyday life and hence becomes real. . . . Class becomes real as people experience it." But this "reality" is reduced by Porter to a question of subjective assessments of other members of the society on the basis of the prestige of various occupations. It can then be ignored on grounds of lack of information and the likelihood that "occupational ranks thus derived" are not "markedly different from occupational ranks based on the objective criteria of skill and responsibility."[19] These latter "objective criteria" are correlated with income and education, which serve as the basis for the researcher's assignation of class.

Obviously this concept of class is very different from the Marxist theory of class which argues that the classes which exist in capitalist society are defined objectively in relation to the means of production, and that there are two major classes which are in conflict with each other as each class pursues its own class interests.

Porter claims that the Marxist theory of a class conflict which leads to social change has been "abandoned by contemporary theorists for the good reason that the facts do not fit the theory." (Porter uses "modern" and "contemporary" in the style of Madison Avenue.) Marx, he says, did not foresee the "main drift of twentieth century industrialization," and the concept of a social revolution transforming the entire society is merely "ideology, a set of quasi-religious ideas foretelling a millenium of equality, co-operation, and the kingdom of freedom":

The capitalism that Marx wrote about has passed out of existence in a much less violent fashion than he thought it would ... [and] in the present day ... classes are statistical categories and nothing more.[20]

What, according to Porter, are the characteristics of the "Post-Marxian Industrial World"? There are three main arguments. The first suggests that for the proletariat the "world of work has not been one of increasing drudgery" but instead has become "a hierarchy of skill and responsibility, and also, no doubt, prestige." This, he says, has destroyed class solidarity and many workers, especially non-manual workers, do not see themselves as working class.[21] This argument will be discussed later in the chapter, but it can be said here that the fact that the whole Canadian working class has not unified itself as a class for itself to establish socialism, does not negate the Marxist definition of class. Also, there is considerable evidence that non-manual workers are increasingly becoming aware that they are part of the working class.

The second line of Porter's argument is that the bourgeoisie, the owners of capital, have been replaced by professional and salaried managers who "run the internal machinery of the modern corporation." Porter begins by saying that this is "not disputed,"[22] though he then says that the "exact location of control" is not clear and the separation of ownership and control "has not gone nearly as far in Canada as it supposedly has in the United States."[23] In fact, when one pursues Porter's own discussion of this argument[24] it becomes clear that it is a genuine example of the "quasi-religious ideology" to which Porter frequently refers. His argument, then, falls back on the claim that while there has been a concentration of economic power, there have also been "structural changes" in "modern" societies which prevent the power of the "economic elite" from "spilling over" to other institutions. He says that it is an empirical question whether the "modern corporate elite" have "successfully mastered" the other institutions, but he suggests that, even if they do form coalitions with other elites, it would be on the basis of shared power. This in fact becomes the key question in Porter's dismissal of the Marxist analysis of class. If the various elites which Porter identifies are not independent but are unified on the basis of the ownership of, and the defence of, capitalist property, then they can be identified as the bourgeoisie of Marxist analysis and capitalist society is still, inevitably, characterized by class conflict.

Porter's own evidence on this point is curiously uneven. The overwhelming weight of the evidence of Part II suggests that there is indeed a unified ruling class in Canada. With the significant exception of his "labour elite," which even in Porter's description is clearly not an elite like the others, there is integration through kinship, schooling, personal contact, institutional contact and through a legal framework. There is, moreover, a common interest created by the fact that "the power of all elite groups rests on the social institutions which capitalism has created."[25] It is trivial to argue, in the face of all this evidence, that "economic power in any society at any time may be dominant, but it is not dominant everywhere."[26] It is absurd to argue that there is no conflict between those with power and those without because it is "difficult to draw the line between those in power and those excluded."[27] It is necessary to conclude that *The Vertical Mosaic* is in fact a defence of capitalism:

> It could be said that in the "western" system the values of capitalism, particularly those of private property and profit making, unify the elites, because capitalism is one form of rational behaviour and must therefore ultimately, in the real world, win out over the other two principal sources of values, nationalism and Christianity, which are irrational.[28]

Ultimately, however, *The Vertical Mosaic* is a failure because it cannot explain the development of the Canadian political economy. When Porter states that the "historical source of the image of a classless Canada is the equality among pioneers in the frontier environment of the last century,"[29] he is accepting as fact for Canada what is only a myth for the United States. More important he reveals that he has not understood the significance of the work of Innis and Creighton. When he suggests that it was the educational system in Quebec that prevented "French Canadians from making their full contribution to Canadian society,"[30] he shows little understanding of the nature of national domination. When he states that the Winnipeg General Strike was "the one outstanding example of 'class struggle' in Canada,"[31] he joins hands with those who talk of a "peaceable kingdom" and reveals that he cares little about the experience of the working class in this country. Porter's analysis of class and power cannot explain our present situation and it can only mislead us as to the future.

It is worth considering, briefly, a few other studies which destroy the myth of the affluent, egalitarian society.

A series of recent studies of incomes in Canada have left no doubt that Canada is not an egalitarian society. Not only is income distribution unequal but many Canadians actually live in what can only be described as poverty. From the Report of the Special Senate Committee on Poverty we can learn that, even after transfer payments such as welfare benefits have been received, almost 40 per cent of non-farm family income goes to only 20 per cent of the total number of families, while an equal number of families at the other end of the scale receive only about 7 per cent of the total income. And this pattern of unequal distribution has been almost constant for the last two decades.[32] In fact, a recent study by Leo Johnson shows that transfer payments have masked a growing disparity of incomes net of transfer payments.[33]

The problem of establishing an adequate standard for the measurement of poverty is discussed in *The Real Poverty Report* and in the 1968 Annual Review of the Economic Council of Canada.[34] A rough dividing line would be an income of $2,000 per year for an unattached individual and $5,300 per year for a family of five. Even conservative estimates suggest that at least one-quarter of the population of this country are living in poverty.

The Economic Council of Canada disposes of many of the myths concerning poverty in Canada:

> Many Canadians may assume that the problem of poverty is close to identical with the problem of low average incomes in the Atlantic Provinces and Eastern Quebec (especially their rural areas) and among the Indian and Eskimo populations. But this is an inaccurate impression. The *incidence* of poverty – the chance of a given person being poor – is certainly much higher in the areas and among the groups just mentioned. But in terms of absolute numbers, between a third and a half of total poverty in Canada is to be found among the white population of cities and towns west of Three Rivers.[35]

The Economic Council also provides some figures to combat the notion that poverty is simply the consequence of misfortune, lack of effort, or personal inadequacy. In 68 per cent of low-income non-farm families there were adults who were in the labour force for at least part of the year. In 76 per cent of the group there were *one or more* income earners in the family, and 66 per cent of the families obtained most of their income from wage, salary and self-employment earnings. In 77 per cent of the families there were adults under 65 years of age. And in 87 per cent of the families in the group there were adult men.[36]

The conclusion that emerges is that many Canadians are poor *despite* the fact that they work. The Economic Council also warns us against the assumption that bad wages are found only in a small number of occupations. It is true that the incidence of low incomes is high for farm workers, loggers and fishermen, but families including farm workers, loggers and fishermen account for only about 10 per cent of low income families.[37]

There is a further study that should be just mentioned here, since many Canadians assume that the tax structure redistributes income away from higher incomes towards lower income receivers. In fact, as the 1966 Report of the Royal Commission on Taxation (the Carter Commission) showed, Canadians suffer from a regressive tax structure. That is, taxes take away a higher proportion of income from the low-income receivers than from the high-income receivers. In other words, individuals are not taxed according to their ability to pay.

But none of these studies, from Porter to the poverty reports, explain *why* there is so much inequality and poverty in a country as rich as Canada. They do not explain why there is so much unemployment in a country where there is still so much poverty, and where the basic needs of so many Canadians are not being satisfied. They do not explain why so many people's wages are so low.

The argument that follows is an introduction to the Marxist analysis of class. It may be fashionable in academic circles to regard the Marxist theory of surplus value or the theory of exploitation as passé. Some academics may concede that Marx may have been right in analyzing the economic conditions of early 19th century England, where wages paid to men, women and children were clearly at or below the bare subsistence level. But presumably now that has all changed, with more civilized capitalists and more civilized capitalist laws to protect the poor.

This idyllic presentation of the present in contrast to the horrific past, ignores the current reports on poverty in Canada. As we have seen these show that one-quarter to one-third of the Canadian population lives at the bare subsistence level and even below that level. Think of a worker's daily efforts to reproduce his or her ability to work on a deficient diet. The minimum wage of $1.80 in Ontario is clearly below the subsistence level for any worker who supports more than one person, and even the minimum is often ignored. We have seen that even with several wage earners in the family there is often difficulty in maintaining even minimum standards for family survival. The cost of housing has become a major part of the family budget, so that for many working-class families what is left after payment of rent is insufficient for a minimally adequate diet. It is hard to. ignore the conclusion that even now a sizeable portion of the work force lives below what could be called a decent level of subsistence.

Furthermore, the Marxist analysis of class can be developed to explain the specific nature of the Canadian economy. It can explain what is happening in Canada as part of the U.S. empire.

Some of these questions will be answered in other chapters in this book. But to begin with it is necessary to provide a basic framework for an analysis of Canada which can explain the situation which Canadians face. This framework will explain why it is important to understand who owns the factories and the machinery, the mines and the oil wells, and thus controls the development of Canada and the conditions in which we live.

Capitalism is a society of commodity production in which labour-power is a commodity and in which capitalists accumulate property through the purchase of the labour-power of workers. Workers are forced to sell their labour-power to the capitalists because the capitalists own all the means of production, such as raw materials, machinery and plant.[38]

We have to look at a few of the terms in this definition to understand its full meaning. When we say that capitalism is a society of commodity production, we mean that it is a society in which objects generally are produced for the market, that is for sale to others, and not just for consumption by those who actually produce the objects. If you make something at home for your own use it is not commodity production. When you work in a factory producing thousands of objects for sale wherever there is a market it is commodity production.

If all commodities are produced for the market there must be some means of determining their value in the market so that they can be exchanged for one another. Of course when you go to buy something it has a price on it and you either pay the price or you don't get it. But how are these prices determined? Essentially they are determined by the exchange-value of the commodity and the only basis on which exchange-value can be calculated is the amount of labour that has to be used to produce the commodity. That is why a car costs more than a TV set and a TV set costs more than a pair of shoes. Exchange-value is in fact a social relationship between the owners of commodities although it appears to be a relationship between the commodities themselves.[39] Although air is essential to life it does not have an exchange-value, or price, because it is not the product of labour and is not owned by anyone. When oil is owned by someone and has to be pumped from a well it does have exchange-value. The amount of labour that is relevant for determining exchange-value is the socially necessary labour time,[40] that is roughly the amount of time using the most efficient method of production.

So commodities have an exchange-value which is based on the amount of necessary labour that goes into their production. Commodities also have a use-value which is what the purchaser of the commodity is interested in. In a capitalist economy, food, for example, is produced as a series of commodities and each type of food has an exchange-value based on the amount of labour necessary for its production. The use-value of food in general is obvious since you need it in order to stay alive. However, it is clear that, whereas the exchange-value of any one kind of food is objectively determined, its use-value is subjective since people want different kinds of food and the use-value of each kind of food varies from one consumer to another.

Let us go back to the definition of capitalism as a society of commodity production in which labour-power is a commodity. This does not mean that the worker is bought and sold like a slave, but the labour, or more precisely the labour-power, of the worker is bought and sold on the market. And labour-power, like any other commodity, has both an exchange-value and a use-value.[41] The exchange-value, or very roughly the price, of labour-power is determined by the amount of labour-time that is required to produce and reproduce the commodity. That is, by the amount of total social labour time that is required to produce the food, clothing, housing and other commodities consumed by the worker. So the exchange-value of labour-power is represented by the wage with which the worker purchases these goods.

The use-value of labour-power is what the capitalist wishes to consume. The capitalist consumes the worker's labour-power by putting the worker to work to produce commodities for the market. Each worker provides a specific use-value for each capitalist. But just as all of us need food, capitalists have to consume labour-power in order to stay alive as capitalists. From the point of view of the capitalists there is only one reason to buy labour-power to produce commodities for the market and that is to make a profit by the process.

But how is it possible for the capitalist to make a profit if he has to pay for all the commodities he needs for the production process? The important thing to remember here is that the capitalist does *not* have to "cheat" in order to make a profit. That is, even if he pays the full exchange value to other capitalists for the raw materials and the full exchange-value to workers for their labour-power, he can still make a profit. Profit is not the result of "cheating" in a capitalist economy. Profit is the very basis of capitalist society. The consequence of production within a capitalist society *must* be the division of total product into profits and wages.

But profit is the result of exploitation. That is, it is acquired through the control of the labour of the working class. To say that profits are not the result of "cheating" is only to say that the production of a surplus, which results from unpaid labour, can not be stopped by better regulation of capitalism. The production of surplus-value can be brought to an end only when the working class produces in a social manner, for itself and in the interest of society, rather than for the capitalist class.

The purpose of Marx's analysis of capitalism is to explain why "capital" exists, that is why the means of production are owned as capital by a class whose interests differ from those of the workers.

We tend to take the existence of "capital" for granted and habitually talk of "capital" and "labour" rather than machinery and men and women. In fact, many assume that "capital" is necessary to maintain modern standards of production. Of course, it is the development of technology that makes possible the present high levels of productivity of workers. But that does not mean that the machinery, buildings and raw materials must always be "capital" in the sense of being owned by capitalists for the purpose of making profits. The machinery, buildings and raw materials were not created by the capitalists. They were produced by workers and appropriated by capitalists because of the laws of capitalist production. This type of society has not always existed and it is not an inevitable "fact of life." It may be true that capitalist ownership played an historically important role in raising productivity, but the costs have always been high and they are now becoming much higher. In fact, as the studies of the Science Council of Canada show, "capital," which in Canada predominantly takes the form of the U.S. corporation, has become a hindrance to technological development.

In order to understand the development of "capital" it is necessary to understand the source of profit, since profit is the means by which capital is accumulated to be used, not in the interests of social production, and to help the worker, but as a means for still further accumulation. Capitalists continue to accumulate the product of past labour to be used to control present labour. Profit is not the result of manoeuvres in the market place, after the product has left the factory, in the world of buying and selling. It results from the conditions of labour in capitalist society, that is, from the fact that the worker is exploited.

It is, then, important to develop the theory of exploitation, or of surplus-value, for several reasons. First, because profit is simply a form of surplus-value, after the total surplus-value has been distributed amongst all the capitalists, through the sale of all the commodities on the market. Secondly, because it is the drive for profits which is the motive force of the capitalist system, and which leads to the boom-and-slump nature of capitalist production. It is because profit maximization comes first that unemployment occurs even when needs are unsatisfied. The drive for profit maximization is also the source of capitalist expansion throughout the world, as the capitalists seek control of resources and labour everywhere. Imperialism is a concomitant of capitalist production. The whole world becomes either a source of raw materials or a market for the most powerful capitalists. The consequences of this will be seen in later chapters on resources and manufacturing.

Also, without this theory of surplus-value, it is not possible to understand the struggles of the labour movement. In fact, with the

70

theory of surplus-value, we can see that the concepts of class and class struggle possess important explanatory and predictive powers. A static view of society which emphasizes equilibrium, checks and balances, and postulates six or seven statistical categories for social class may seem to explain some of the data, but it fails to contend with the dynamics, with the explosive dislocations, clashes, and breakdowns in society. A static theory may satisfy most people when capitalism is in a period of stabilization but it falls apart when crises, trade wars, and massive class struggles erupt. For example, the liberal theory which explained the FLQ crisis in Quebec in October, 1970, simply as a battle between law and order on one hand and a group of terrorists on the other was accepted by the overwhelming majority of Canadians. One year later the strike at *La Presse* showed that the discontent in Quebec went far deeper than that. A huge demonstration in Montreal pitted the forces of law and order, the police, against many thousands of working people in the streets. Then the liberal explanation of class appeared inadequate and it finally fell apart six months later in May 1972 when the Common Front organized a general strike of 210,000 workers, civil servants and teachers. The class struggle then had a reality which the liberal textbooks could not explain.

Of what value is the division of the working class into "middle-middle" class if they are teachers or computer programmers, "lower-middle" if they are senior clerks, "upper-lower" if they drive a truck or "lower-lower" if they clean government offices? All of these artificial statistical categories fall like cards in the face of the social explosion which broke in Quebec society and sent the social scientists scurrying for new explanations, for new sand bags to plug the gaping holes in their broken dams.

The theory of classes which propounds the existence of two basic classes in the modern Canadian capitalist society carries the burden of explanation and prediction far better. The theory asserts that, in spite of fragmentation of working people, either because they are in separate unions or more often unorganized, the very conditions of facing capitalist exploitation of profit-making by the corporations forces them to unite to defend their interests. Their increasing unity as a class has its roots in the common exploitation which they undergo at work.

The class struggle which results from exploitation is not to be seen every day in the dramatic form of the May events in Quebec in 1972 or in France in May, 1968, because if such events had continued as regular affairs capitalism would be long gone.

Within capitalist limits almost everything possible is done to mitigate the class struggle, as we shall see in chapter 7. But underneath the surface calm of negotiated settlements and new reform legislation in a welfare state, there is the occasional burst of the strike, the wildcats, the demonstration of workers, teachers and students. Sometimes these events reach the high explosive point of a Winnipeg General Strike, or the strike at General Motors in Oshawa in 1937, or the Big Strike movement of 1945, or the events of 1946 in Hamilton, Toronto, Montreal, Valleyfield, British Columbia, or in Asbestos in 1949 or at Murdochville in 1957, or the Common Front in Quebec in 1972. At such moments there is revealed beneath the smooth surface a smouldering volcano of class differences and conflict.

The essential point of the socialist theory of class struggle is that it is dynamic and historical. It serves as a very broad explanatory theme, which explains history on a large canvas. It asserts that through many twists and turns, through periods of quiescence and turbulence, there is a continuous gathering, and breaking up and regrouping of the political forces of the two basic classes of capitalism. And the classes are based on their position in production and their relation to the ownership of the means of production.

Let us return to the analysis of the source of profits. The reason why profits are the result of capitalist production is that in a day's work the worker can produce more than he consumes. That is, the special fact about the use-value of labour-power is that the exchange-value of the commodities which it creates is greater than the exchange-value of the labour-power. After allowing for the reproduction of the raw materials and machinery used up, the difference between the new value and the value that the worker consumes is called the *surplus-value*. The surplus-value belongs to the capitalist because he has bought control of the worker and the means of production and thus of the product.

One could say that there are two immediate consequences of capitalist production. The first is that the labourer works under the control of the capitalist and the product of his labour belongs to the capitalists. Thus, for the worker, his work is a commodity which he has to make over to another. Marx described the consequences of this:

> What [the labourer] produces for himself is not the silk that he weaves, not the gold that he draws from the mine, not the palace that he builds. What he produces for himself is [simply wages that enable him to exist] . . . And the worker who for twelve hours weaves, spins, drills, turns, builds, shovels, breaks stones, carries loads, etc. – does he consider this twelve hours weaving, spinning, drilling turning, building, shovelling, stonebreaking as a manifestation of his life, as life? On the contrary, life begins for him where this activity ceases, at table, in the public house, in bed.[42]

The second immediate consequence of capitalist production is that the value of the product must be divided between wages and surplus-value, profit being one form of surplus-value. Together these two consequences mean that class conflict is an inevitable everyday fact of capitalist society. To argue that Canada is a "peaceable kingdom," is to deny the everyday experience of the majority of Canadians.

Since it is one of the central factors in the class conflict it is important to know what determines the division of the product, or what amounts to the same thing, what determines the ratio of surplus-value to wages, also known as the rate of exploitation.

First of all, the capitalist owns the factories and the raw materials, so the initiative lies with him. But he also needs the labour force, so there is a class bargaining situation. The exchange-value of labour-power, wages, can be increased by collective action on the part of workers. Thus the most obvious importance of unions.

The total product, wages plus surplus-value, is determined by the level of productivity of labour, thus by technological development and historical progress. Increases in the total output make possible increases in both surplus-value and wages. It is, however, always in the interests of capitalists to increase the rate of surplus-value. Capitalists thus make innovations according to their own interests, thus making technological development an issue in the class struggle, distorting development and preventing technological advance from serving the interests of a truly human society.

The ability of capitalists to increase surplus-value depends on:

1) the profitability of investment in new machinery that will increase the productivity of labour,
2) the extent to which increases in surplus-value are opposed by an organized working class.

It is worth considering the second of these points in greater detail. With the benefit of the theory of surplus-value, it can be seen that struggles over wages and hours of work are an aspect of class struggle. To say that wage increases or reductions in hours of work should not be struggled for, is to argue for the right of capitalists to the extraction of surplus-value from workers. To argue that it is anti-social to struggle for increased wages, is to argue that "social" behaviour is defined by the needs of the capitalist.

"Liberals" or reformists who reject the theory of surplus-value are unable to see the nature of the class struggle. They try to reconcile two opposing forces by estimating what is a "fair" wage increase. But they cannot see that, no matter what wage the worker gets, he is being exploited as long as there is capitalist profit. And there can be no "fair" wage in such a situation, because there can be no compromise between justice and exploitation.

There are even trade union leaders who accept the "liberal" or reformist view and who reject the theory of surplus-value. But to do so is to give up the struggle against exploitation which has been the strength of the labour movjement.

The rejection of the Marxist theory of surplus-value by social democratic parties, such as the NDP in Canada, means that these parties are attempting to make a compromise between two opposing forces. To argue that capitalism can be made just by regulation is to become a victim of the needs of capitalists for ever more surplus-value. The vicious spiral of ever more destructive developments within capitalism can only be stopped by removing the capitalists' source of power; that is, their ownership and control of the means of production.

It is apparent from the above discussion that class conflict in capitalist society involves two central classes and it is now necessary to turn to a discussion of the class structure in Canada.[43]

There are two central classes. One is the class which owns the means of production and is called the capitalist class or bourgeoisie. The other is the class which does not own means of production and which can keep itself alive only by selling its labourpower to the bourgeoisie. This class is the working class, or proletariat. There is also in Canada another class which both owns and operates a small amount of the means of production. This is the petty, or petite, bourgeoisie, and the members of this class are typically farmers, craftsmen and small shopkeepers. As Johnson[44] shows, this latter class is declining in numbers and in 1968 represented only about 10 per cent of income earners.

Since the bourgeoisie is defined as the class which owns the means of production, it is necessary to point out that participation in this ownership does not, of itself, turn a person into a member of the bourgeoisie. The development of capitalism has brought an expansion of share ownership so that some people save out of their wages by purchasing a few shares. There is, however, a clear difference between those who own a few shares as a means of saving and those who exercise control over the means of production through substantial ownership or those who can receive a substantial income from ownership without working. The distribution of share ownership is not, in fact, as widespread as many think.[45] In 1968 the top 1 per cent of income earners owned as much as 42 per cent of all shares and the top 10 per cent of all income earners owned 72 per cent of all shares. In fact only 10 per cent of income earners in Canada owned any shares at all.

Capitalists can be divided into two major groups: into industrial capitalists on the one hand, and merchant and financial capitalists on the other. The industrial capitalists stand at the head of the production process and accumulate surplus-value through their control of the means of production. In order to provide for means of concentrating capital and products, this surplus has to be shared with merchant and finance capitalists. The historical development of capitalism has in general led to the merging of these groups of capitalists. (This I take to be the most useful meaning of the term "finance-capital").[46] In Canada, however, the distinction has been historically extremely important (as Tom Naylor shows in Chapter 2) and the two groups are still to some extent separate, by virtue of the fact that the industrial capitalists are predominantly foreign, while the financial capitalists are Canadian citizens.

The financial capitalists of Canada are organized in the banks, the trust companies, and the insurance companies which remain under the ownership of Canadian citizens. This does not mean that the Canadian bourgeoisie is in any sense independent. Its position has always been one of dependency within the dominant empire, though it has benefited by having been allowed to play a "sub-imperial" role within other areas of the empire. It is worth noting, furthermore, that while the financial capitalists are important to the development of capitalism and are thus in a position to demand a share of the surplus-value, the actual production of surplus-value is controlled by the industrial capitalist. In *Theories of Surplus-Value*, Marx pointed out that economics made an advance when it was realized that industrial profit was the form in which surplus-value is originally appropriated by capital and that interest and rent were "mere offshoots of industrial profit... distributed by the industrial capitalists to various classes, who are co-owners of surplus-value."[47] This suggests that the dependent nature of the Canadian bourgeoisie is a consequence of the fact that they themselves do not control the major part of the means of production. They thus receive their share of the surplus-value only to the extent that they have the strength to demand it from the industrial capitalists in return for services to the latter. They have no means of ensuring the continued production of surplus-value against the wishes of the industrial capitalists. If some industrial capitalists move production outside of Canada there is that much less surplus-value to share.

Now, turning to a discussion of the working class, it is necessary to deal with some preliminary complications. According to the definition given above, it is a class which does not own means of production. Thus the members of this class can keep themselves alive only by selling their labour-power. That is, they have to work for wages. But some members of the population who fit this description refer to their incomes as a salary rather than as a wage and, largely because of the type of work they do and the conditions under which they work, think of themselves as being "middle-class," rather than working-class.

The question of the middle class is complicated by the fact that it is hard to find a precise definition and also by the fact that conditions of work change historically. Many so-called "professional" occupations are considered to be middle-class, and in some cases this is a reasonable classification. Obviously, it does not make much sense to refer to the average lawyer as working-class, even though most lawyers have to live by selling their skilled labour. In fact the most successful lawyers, and in particular those who become judges, are often considered to be part of the bourgeoisie, as are some politicians, who also are not always capitalists. One could say that at one end the middle class extends into the bourgeoisie, which is made up of those who, together with the capitalists, constitute the ruling class. The middle class is not, however, the same thing as the bourgeoisie.[48]

Consider teachers, who generally have struggled to be recognized as middle-class professionals. For many working class men and women, teaching was considered a means of social mobility. It has, however, become increasingly unrealistic to consider teachers to be distinct from the working class. The example of Quebec teachers is particularly instructive here, although this phenomenon is not restricted to Quebec and teachers in Ontario are also beginning to recognize their true class position. In fact, there has been a reduction of status, accompanied by changing conditions of work, in many "professional" occupations. The case of secretaries and clerks is an example of a change which took place earlier in the development of capitalism.[49]

The blue-collar, white-collar distinction is becoming less important as more and more workers find themselves in the position of having little or no control over their conditions of work and the product of their work, a situation that typifies proletarianization. Thus, contrary to many assertions, the category that constitutes the working class is expanding, while the indeterminate sector of the population which can be called middle-class is diminishing. A middle-class false consciousness cannot explain the position in which many people find themselves and, what is more important, many of these people are becoming aware of this fact.

Some readers may think that this kind of class analysis is too simple to explain the variety of the Canadian social structure. But it only appears too simplified because the overwhelmingly largest class, the working class, has usually been too fragmented to present the appearance of a unified class. It is easier to recognize the bourgeoisie as a class because it recognizes itself as a class and acts as a class to maintain its domination. It is important to realize that a class only fully becomes a class, in the sense of a class "for itself" when it recognizes its own class interests. The bourgeoisie, both on a national and on an international scale, developed that class consciousness in the course of its struggle for dominance and now reinforces it through its control of property and the institutions of the state.

In terms of an aggressive class consciousness, the middle class is also highly developed. In fact, one could say over-developed, since illusion often outweighs reality. It is not an accident that the phrase "keeping-up" is frequently used, and the aggressiveness of the middle class consciousness is one born of insecurity. It is on this ground that it meets with the class consciousness of the petty-bourgeoisie, thus leading to a considerable confusion between these two classes.

It has, however, been argued in this chapter that a class is defined by its relation to the process of production. The majority of the Canadian population do not own means of production and they thus work under the control of those who do. The majority thus work to perpetuate the domination of the few. As long as this situation continues the majority of the population of this country will form a working class, whatever its "subjective" class-consciouness.

It has also been argued in this chapter that wages are determined in the process of the class struggle. Most production in this country takes place in large-scale capitalist enterprises. The division of the product is the result of the struggle between the workers and the bosses. After allowing for the cost of raw materials and the machinery used up, what the workers do not take home in the form of wages, the boss gets as profit. Most factory workers can see this. They can see that if they get paid less the boss gets more. They can see that if they work harder without more pay, the boss gets more profit. It is, however, harder for many workers to see the nature of the wage system because they do not work directly in the process of production.

It is possible in a capitalist economy to make a distinction between "productive labour" and "non-productive labour." This has nothing to do with the difficulty of the work or the social usefulness of the work, since it is possible for the same job to be "productive" or "non-productive" according to the particular conditions under which the work is done.[50] "Productive labour" refers to work that produces surplus-value directly. The traditional term "blue-colar worker" covers most "productive" workers. "Non-productive labour" refers to labour that does not directly produce surplus-value, but rather is paid for out of surplus-value. This does not mean that such work is not necessary, even for the production of surplus-value. For example, capitalist production cannot do without large numbers of office workers who represent an expense for the capitalist which reduces profits. Government employees are also "unproductive" workers, and the term "white-collar worker" covers a large portion, though not all, of the "unproductive" labour force. Other examples of "unproductive" workers are domestic workers, maintenance workers, teachers and nurses. Many workers in the "service" sector are "unproductive" workers. In fact, the development of capitalism has led to an increase in the number of "unproductive" workers relative to "productive" workers. This has been possible because of the growth of productivity in the economy, but it has also been made necessary by the nature of capitalist development.

It is possible that this uneven growth of the "unproductive" labour force is a factor in the development of the inflationary pressures which are now characteristic of capitalist economies. It is worth discussing inflation briefly since it has become an important factor in the determination of real wage levels. Also, the capitalists' explanations of inflation have served to obscure the underlying nature of the process of income distribution.[51]

The first point to note is that inflation is intrinsic to the contemporary capitalist economy. In fact, modern inflation in capitalist economies dates back to the competitive rearmament spending which immediately preceded World War II. Thus inflation is the result of a new economic strategy which restored the rate of surplus-value following years of depression.

Secondly, there is evidence for a fairly steady pattern of inflation in the advanced capitalist economies averaging about 3-4 per cent per year. There are also a few countries which have experienced a constant inflation of about 30 per cent per year, called "strato-inflation." It appears that in these countries class conflict centres on the basic distribution of income between wages and profits, whereas in the 3-4 per cent countries class conflict has been restricted to the division of the yearly additions to national product.[52]

Although distribution of income is an important factor, the rate of inflation can be affected by a large number of factors. These include the capacity for production of certain goods, such as capital goods, agricultural products and housing. Other factors at work in specific instances may be the existence of "election cycles"[53] and effects of international trade.

Another point is that, in general, the more *equal* are the rates of wage increases in different industries, the higher is the national rate of inflation. It is not true to say that inflation is caused by disproportionate wage increases gained by some "privileged" workers. In fact, what tends to happen is that wages rise faster in capital-intensive "oligopolistic" industries – that is, industries dominated by a few large corporations – because wage increases are offset by high rates of productivity increase. It is not simply a question of these industries passing on wage increases in higher prices. This is important because these pace-setting wage increases are dependent upon the ability of the industries to obtain increased productivity both by new technology and by speed-up. These wage increases are then followed by pressure from workers in other industries, where productivity may not be increasing, and in fact wage demands may come increasingly from "unproductive" workers.

Finally, since the 1950s another factor has entered into the determination of retained real wages – and that is the growing incidence of direct income taxation as money wages have risen to completely alter the effects of income tax structures. This new tax situation means that even if wage claims are limited to productivity increases, there would still be inflation and a redistribution of income away from workers.

In the end, all attempts to analyze income distribution in capitalist societies must come back to the analysis of class and class struggles. The bourgeoisie recognizes this and uses all its power, including its control of the state (see Chapter 7), to maintain its profits and thus its domination of society. That many in the working class do not recognize this is the result of the fragmentation of the working class. Capitalism promotes this fragmentation by creating general insecurity and fear. Capitalism pits low-paid workers against high-paid workers, men against women, Canadian-born against immigrants, employed against unemployed, unorganized against organized. It is the capitalists who rejoice in these struggles. When economists and sociologists take this fragmentation to mean that the working class does not exist as a class, they play into the hands of the capitalists – ultimately, in this country, into the hands of the owners of U.S. corporations, who are now the dominant section of the ruling class in Canada.

All who work in Canada are aware of the *economic* struggle, of that daily struggle to achieve or maintain a decent standard of living. All are aware of the threat of unemployment. All workers are aware of the power which others exercise over them. But many feel defeated in these struggles. As Marx noted, in the "merely economic action capital is the stronger side."[54] The awareness of class solidarity, the recognition of the class nature of the economic struggle adds a *political* dimension to the struggle. It brings the recognition that inequalities cannot be overcome within capitalism. It brings an understanding of Marx's exhortation:

> The working class ought to understand that, with all the miseries it imposes upon them, the present system simultaneously engenders the *material conditions* and the *social* forms necessary for an economical reconstruction of society. Instead of the *conservative* motto, "A fair day's wages for a fair day's work!" they ought to inscribe on their banner the *revolutionary* watchword, "Abolition of the wages system!"

Marx's theory of surplus value, which is the foundation of his political economy and of his analysis of the class struggle in capitalist society, meets the final test in its ability to explain capitalist contradictions and crises. In the 1950s and early 1960s it was the boast of capitalist economists that with the development of Keynesian policies the bitter experience of crises had become a thing of the past. Today, such a claim sounds hollow in the face of unemployment, inflation and the world-wide monetary crises which have ended the international monetary system created by the U.S. in the 1940s. The attack on the position of the U.S. dollar is a symptom of growing capitalist rivalries. Marx's hypothesis was that the secret of capitalism is the production of surplus value, that production of goods on a social, world-wide basis repeatedly comes into conflict with the narrow foundation of private appropriation. This inevitably produces vast surpluses that the world markets cannot absorb. The contradiction between social production and private appropriation is the ultimate source of capitalist crises and over-production leading to mass unemployment, to trade and financial wars and ultimately to violent attempts to re-organize markets.

Revival of interest in Marxist theory in many countries including Canada, is a direct result of the international crises, the inter-imperialist rivalries and the economic stagnation even in the leading imperialist power, the U.S., where 20 per cent of the people are employed in sectors related directly or indirectly to military expenditures, and well over 5 per cent are unemployed. Since social consciousness is primarily determined by "social existence," social consciousness in Canada today has been readied for a study of Marxism by the crises of imperialism and de-industrialization we are now experiencing. The origins of these developments are to be found in the operations of the law of surplus value, the laws of concentration and centralization of capital.

It is for this reason that a creative elaboration and application of the theory of surplus value and the laws which flow from it has today all the power of explanation that it had in the 1850s when it was first propounded. The use of Marxist economics in a study of the Canadian political economy promises to become widespread during the 1970s.

Notes

[1] William Kilbourn in his introduction to W. Kilbourn (ed.). *Canada: A Guide to the Peaceable Kingdom,* Macmillan. Toronto 1970, p. xiii. [2]*Ibid.*, p. xi. [3] John Porter, *The Vertical Mosaic,* University of Toronto Press, Toronto, 1965. [4] *Ibid.*, p. 557. [5] *Ibid.*, p. 557 and pp. 168-73. [6] *Ibid.*, p. 155. [7] *Ibid.*, p. 54. [8] *Ibid.*, p. 155. [9] *Ibid.*, p. 8, p. 6, p. 43, p. 558, p. 166. [10] *Ibid.*, p. 205. See also p. 556. [11] *Ibid.*, p. 6. [12] *Ibid.*, p. 202, p. 201, p. 17. [13] *Ibid.*, p. 558. [14] *Ibid.*, p. 556.
[15] See pages 552-57. For a further discussion of elite theory, see T. B. Bottomore, *Elites and Society,* Penguin. Harmondsworth, 1970. [16] *Ibid.*, p. 210, p. 215. [17] *Ibid.*, p. 11. [18] *Ibid.*, p. 9. [19] *Ibid.*, p. 11-15. [20] *Ibid.*, p. 18-20. [21] *Ibid.*, p. 20. [22] *Ibid.*, p. 21. [23] *Ibid.*, p. 22. [24] *Ibid.*, p. 242, p. 245, p. 252, p. 255. [25] *Ibid.*, p. 212. [26] *Ibid.*, p. 206. [27] *Ibid.*, p. 25. [28] *Ibid.*, p. 212. [29] *Ibid.*, p. 3. [30] *Ibid.*, p. 171. [31] *Ibid.*, p. 316.
[32] Report of the Special Senate Committee on Poverty, *Poverty in Canada*, Information Canada, Ottawa, 1971, p. 15.
[33] Leo Johnson, *Incomes, Disparity and Impoverishment in Canada Since World War II*, New Hogtown Press, Toronto, 1973, Table VI.
[34] Ian Adams and others, *The Real Poverty Report*, Hurtig, Edmonton, 1971.
[35] Economic Council, 1968, p. 104.
[36] *Ibid.*, p. 113. The evidence is based on the 1961 census.

[37] Ibid., Table 6-4, p. 115. [38] See K. Marx, *Capital*, vol. 1, ch. 1-7. [39] *Ibid.*, ch. 1, sec. 4. [40] *Ibid.*, ch. 1, sec. 1. [41] *Ibid.*, ch. 6.

[42] K. Marx, *Wage Labour and Capital*, Progress Publishers, Moscow, 1952, p. 20-21.

[43] This discussion will draw on statistics from an important article by Leo Johnson, "The Development of Class in Canada in the 20th Century," in G. Teeple, *Capitalism and the National Question in Canada*, University of Toronto Press, Toronto, 1972. [44] *Ibid.*, p. 145-153. [45] *Ibid.*, p. 156.

[46] Lenin used the term "finance-capital" to refer to the "bank capital of a few very big monopolist banks, *merged* with the capital of the monopolist associations of industrialists." The concept of financial capitalist, however, refers to capitalists operating from banks, trust companies and insurance companies who may obtain their share of surplus-value simply by portfolio investment, rather than by direct participation in the control of production. Thus while the term "finance-capital" suggests a fusion of banking and industry, the role of the financial capitalist suggests that there may still be a distinction between banks and industry. The financial capitalists, rather than investing for the sake of control of production, are likely to invest for the optimum return on production controlled by others.

[47] K. Marx, *Theories of Surplus Value*, Part I, ch. 2, Foreign Languages Publishing House, Moscow, n.d. (1964), p. 47.

[48] The literature of class analysis can cause confusion on this point because, in countries where there is, or has been, an aristocracy, the term "middle class" sometimes refers to the bourgeoisie.

[49] See Marx's discussion of office workers in *Capital*, Vol. III, Progress Publishers, Moscow, 1966, p. 300.

[50] For a useful introduction to this complicated subject, see Ian Gough, "Marx's Theory of Productive and Unproductive Labour," New Left Review, No. 76, Nov. – Dec., 1972.

[51] An important contribution to the study of inflation is *Do Trade Unions Cause Inflation*, by D. Jackson, H. A. Turner and F. Wilkinson, University of Cambridge, Department of Applied Economics, Occasional Papers no. 36, Cambridge University Press, Cambridge, 1972.

[52] For an argument that there has been a basic redistribution in Britain, one of the 3-4 per cent countries, see A. Glyn and B. Sutcliffe, *British Capitalism, Workers and The Profits Squeeze*, Penguin Special, Harmondsworth, 1972.

[53] See M. Kalecki, "Political Aspects of Full Employment," reprinted in *The Last Phase in the Transformation of Capitalism*, Monthly Review Press, N.Y. 1972.

[54] Karl Marx, *Wages, Price and Profit*, Foreign Languages Press, Peking, 1965, p. 74. The quotation just below is from p. 78 of the same work.

Women in the Canadian Economy
Christina Maria Hill

This chapter contains a sketch of the historical situation of working women in Canada, a discussion of their present economic
status, and some speculation as to what the future holds in store.
There is a wide range of material I could have covered that I
haven't, including many of the activities of the early suffragist
movement and of the women's movement in the 1960s. I've had
to make choices, the central one being that I would put the major
emphasis on the roles that working class women have played in
the development of Canada, and what we can learn from their
experiences. There will no roster of famous or heroic figures.
There are many such, and they will in future years become
well-known, as women popularize their own history. What I seek
to accomplish in this brief introduction to women's concerns is, I
think, more essential at this point. In order that we may understand what is happening to working women now and in coming
years, we must search for lessons in the social and economic
history of the millions of women who have laboured on the land,
in factories, in offices and in homes, the women whose names will
never be recorded.

The first part of the chapter, early history, I have written in
the form of a dramatic monologue, first person.[1] The character I
am presenting is the working women of Canada, and the story
begins in New France in the late 1600s, the colonial era of the
French King, Louis the XIV.

There was terrible starvation and hardship in Normandy when I
left to sail to New France. The voyage was a frightening, terrify-
ing experience. But it was also an adventure. The French king
had been *asked* to send "carefully chosen girls". I had been

chosen, and my destination was marriage. We were all to be brides and mothers. Was I born of gentle people, or was I a prostitute and a criminal? My elusive origins will be debated by male historians in the future, each using me to serve his own cause. But in the present, whatever I am, my destiny is clear.

Now I live in Canada. Now I die in Canada, joining many sisters now gone . . . Sister Anne Hébert, married September 1617, Canada's first bride . . . Sister Marguérite Sedilot, married September 1654, at the age of 11 years, 5 months, in Three Rivers.

I have children. The fathers of large families get a pension from the King of France, and honour. Canada needs people to work the land. I have children, again and again. I must have children. I die having children. My husband marries, again and again.

I work the land. I sustain the home. My youth disappears with the work, and my skin withers with the elements. But I am a woman of merit and virtue. I do not transgress.

But then, again, I do. I am 16. I am a woman. I steal. I am a thief, and I am punished in the public square. I am executed. In 1649, I am the first person to be executed in Canada. Another criminal escaped death by acting as my executioner. The first person to be executed. But then, am I really a person? Is a woman a person? That question, which troubles me, is not legally settled in Canada until 1929.

I am a slave, a black female slave, and I can be bought for $200 and my son for $150, "payable in three months, one-fourth less for ready money." My assets are many. I wash, I cook and I make fine soap and candles to serve my lady. I am a slave long after the import of slaves is outlawed in Lower Canada in 1793. Two decades past that date, there are still many slaves in Lower Canada, hundreds. But I am a woman of merit and virtue. I do not transgress.

But then, again, I do. I am a dissolute woman, of low virtue, in Montreal in 1809. The judge orders 25 lashes on my bare back. I am a dissolute woman, I am whipped. I am subject to whipping until the year 1886, when the law abolishes whipping of women.

I am a working woman in Nova Scotia in 1852. My husband is a working man. He earns $1.59 a week as a junior clerk, and my son, who is nine years old, earns 19 cents a week as a clerical worker. I have produced many workers to support our home. I die with the birth of my seventh, 10 years after the birth of my first. But I die with *two* sons earning 19 cents a week. I hear that ladies of wealth in Upper Canada pay eight and ten dollars a yard for their gowns of silk, and they like to wear little lace point collars from abroad, costing $20 and more. My sons each earn $9.88 a year as clerical workers. But God is with us, and our rewards are in heaven, surely.

So ends the dramatic monologue, but it isn't the end of the drama.

Let's move on to the 1880's, a period which saw the growth of large-scale industrial production in Quebec. During this period also, one of the female's most important economic roles is the production of children. Children for work on the land, as was the case earlier, but now, as well, children for factory work, to meet the demands for industrial cheap labour . . . demands that were so pressing that pauper children were imported from Britain to work in Canada's factories.[2] These were children, 8, 9, 10, 11 years old, for many of whom the future was bleak, for as soon as they ceased to be "apprentices" and became entitled to slightly less meagre adult wages, they could easily be fired.[3]

These children laboured along with women, for a pittance, in cotton mills, tobacco factories, glass factories, for as long as 6 a.m. to 6 p.m. and longer, sometimes through the night, around unprotected machinery, with few or no breaks, signing agreements to work holidays, earning around 25 cents a day . . . women earning more than children, but much less than men.[4] And from these below subsistence earnings, there were deductions, not for social benefits but for fines, which were attributed to offenses as severe as talking on the job. Entire families trudged off to work in the early hours of the morning, came back late at night, and exhausted themselves further in a restless sleep in rat-infested shacks.

It was from this kind of exploitation that the textile millionaires of Canada, direct ancestors of today's Dominion Textile Company, made their millions, as Charles Lipton illustrates so well in his book, *The Trade Union Movement of Canada.*

There were two royal commissions of inquiry into labour conditions in the 1880's (1881 and 1887). Their documentation of what some call "industrial discipline" is worth reading. Little girls whipped for talking, girls and boys beaten regularly with planks and imprisoned for punishment in hot rooms where tobacco was placed to sweat, or in a coal box, as was the case in the tobacco factory of J. L. Fortier in Montreal. Children were dragged off by factory constables to appear before the Montreal city recorder, the law at the service of industry, who told the Royal Commission that "the Master has the right of correction by 'positive law,' 'civil law,' 'natural law' and 'divine law.' "[5]

The ancestors of today's textile entrepreneurs had what one might call almost uncanny instincts for how to get the most for their money: get the largest number of people possible into the smallest spaces; avoid frivolous expenditures on ventilation (for labour is cheaper to replace than to protect); cut wages in the winter when there is surplus labour; and employ women and children whenever possible, for they are dirt cheap. *And* extoll the virtue of large families, of course.

The contrast between the daily lives and working conditions of most women and the pompous and virtuous statements of the well-heeled regarding "womankind" would make a major study in itself for anyone who would want to take on such a momentous task. It is not a frivolous one, for it tells us how the propaganda of the oppressors both encourages and disguises a multitude of injustices.

Just as an illustration, let us contrast one day in the life of a young woman worker in the Fortier tobacco factory with the views of a Quebec MP of the same period.

Georgiana Loiselle tells the second Royal Commission:

> 'Mr. Fortier asked me to make one hundred cigars. I refused and he beat me with the mould cover. I was sitting, he seized me by the arm, threw me to the ground and beat me with the mould cover.'[6]

Guillaume Amot, Quebec MP, impresses upon his public the notion that woman is "the point of connection between earth and heaven. They assume something of the angel. Let us leave them their moral purity, their bashfulness, their sweetness, which gave them in our minds so much charm."[7]

I'm not sure which women he was talking about, but presumably it was the same class of ladies as those who attended the vice-regal balls in a slightly earlier period, with the discriminatory stipulation that they should "wear low-necked dresses, without

Court Trains.... Ladies whose health will not admit of their wearing low-necked dresses, may, on forwarding to the A.D.C. in waiting a medical certificate to that effect, wear square cut dresses."[8]

Throughout the history of this country, the exaltation of the modest and deliciously immodest virtues of womankind has masked the brutal and bestial attitudes towards working women that underlie their continuing exploitation in the labour force. It was ladies of the Hon. Monsieur Amot's class who were described by one of the rare women academics of the time as having interests somewhat different from their toiling sisters in the millinery and dressmaking establishments in Ontario, who worked long hours and overtime, sometimes without evening meals, to meet "urgent" requests.

Jean Thomson Scott writes in a paper published by the University of Toronto in 1892:

> Conversation with those in the business reveals the fact that it is not orders for dresses for weddings or funerals which cause overtime – but for balls and parties ... The general desire again on the part of many to have a new gown or bonnet for Sunday makes Saturday the busiest day for dressmakers and milliners. In England no woman can be employed in such establishments after 4 P.M. on Saturdays. It is not customary to pay for such overtime in Toronto.[9]

The pressure for change during this Dickensian period of Canadian history came from two main sources. One was a slowly emerging, almost totally male labour movement, organized initially around the crafts and trades, but gradually picking up the issues and support of industrial workers who were threatened and weakened by cheap labour in the form of children, women and Orientals. I don't want to exaggerate the size or the strength of this movement, and I can't in the course of this short chapter deal with all its variations by provinces and politics, but I will say that the prolonged and painful battles of the labour movement were central to the eventual passage of legislation protecting workers to a limited extent from the unlimited appetites of their bosses for profits. I would also say, however, that these same pressures for *general* protection of workers, contributed to changes already underway which would exclude women *and* Orientals from jobs in what was to become the most powerful and well-protected sector of the labour force.

Organized workers were of two minds during the pre-1900 period with respect to solutions for the problems of female cheap labour. One is presented in this quote from the Ontario Workman, a labour publication: "Women can no more do men's special work, than men can do women's."[10] The other was represented in the discussion of and the demand for equal pay for equal work, and suffrage for women. These two perspectives merged, however, in a common pressure for "special" protective legislation for women. The underlying concept here was that women comprised a labour force separate and different, which had to be protected from the demands of men's work. This concept was quite compatible with the capitalists' recognition that women could be used in ways different from men. Despite the goodwill that accompanied some of labour's demands for better treatment of women workers, the agitation of the movement did not lead to a rise in the status of women workers. Instead, there was the creation of totally female ghettos of employment which, to this day, maintain the status of female labour as cheap labour, easily exploited and readily available, and concentrated in unskilled and semi-skilled, low-paying jobs.

While the working man's attitude to working women in the 1880s was ambiguous enough to leave relatively few scars on our consciousness, that was not the case with Orientals, who became victims of the most bitter feelings against cheap labour. Chinese women were not accepted as immigrants in this country, but Chinese men were imported in large numbers, much to the dismay of the B.C. labour movement. The latter eventually organized a boycott against bosses who had anything to do with the Chinese, whether they were accepting them as workers or as customers.[11] This boycott was so powerful that the city of Vancouver had to open a labour bureau to import female cheap labour from Eastern Canada to replace the Chinese workers.[12]

The Toronto Globe had problems at the time understanding working men's hostility to cheap labour. The newspaper tried to appeal to the artisans, the labour aristocracy, by suggesting that cheap labour, presumably female, could be used to relieve the burdens of their wives:

The artisan's home life is happier, his life more cheery, his primary wants are better satisfied if his wife can leave a portion of the harder work to another. . . . [13]

Other pressures for change in the situation of working women came from the women's suffrage movement that emerged as an organized force in the 1880s and continued until after the First World War. The movement focussed its concerns and most of its energies on getting the vote, which was denied to women along with children, idiots, lunatics, paupers, and criminals. The sentiments of that struggle were well expressed in a poem in the Toronto Globe, September 28, 1912:

You may be our close companion
  Share our troubles, ease our pain,
You may bear the servant's burden
  (But without the servant's gain);
You may scrub and cook and iron
  Sew the buttons on our coat,
But as men we must protect you –
  You are far too frail to vote.

You may toil behind our counters,
  In our factories you may slave
You are welcome to the sweatshop
  From the cradle to the grave.
If you err, altho' a woman
  You may dangle by the throat
But our chivalry is outraged
  If you soil your hands to vote.[14]

Although the movement in Ontario, certainly, was dominated by women of comfortable means, the problem was not that it was insensitive to the suffering of most working women. It was that it posed the solution in terms of petitions and agitations for legislative changes, seeing the vote as a source of power and ignoring the central source of workers' power . . . collective organizing in the workplace. This was its essential naiveté and the root of its inadequacies – and this was the heritage passed on to the women's movement of the sixties, which spent so much of its energies on legislative appeal and so little on building power in the workplace.

It is interesting for those who wish to pursue a study of the suffrage struggles to examine the split in Quebec between the

English-speaking wealthier women and the French-speaking, more working-class and militant women. It is also interesting to look at the West, where women, who were playing a central role in the mainstream rural economy as farm workers, received widespread support from farm and labour organizations, and, in Saskatchewan, for example, developed a grass-roots movement with broader demands ranging over a multitude of issues, including nationalization of natural resources.[15] Finally, it is important to study the major influence of Temperance activities within the suffrage movement, and to examine closely some of our latter-day prejudices against this phenomenon, for it cannot be denied that the widespread abuses of alcohol and the consequent disabling of working men and diffusion of their militance was of major concern to working class women in a period in which divorce was almost non-existent and women had no legal rights over their own children.

For the purposes of this chapter, I will conclude my discussion of the suffrage movement with the same basic point that I made regarding the labour movement. Despite the goodwill that accompanied the demands for better treatment of women workers, the agitation of the movement did not lead to a rise in the relative status of women workers. Instead, there was the continuing creation of totally female ghettos of employment which, to this day, maintain the status of female labour as cheap labour, easily exploited and readily available, and concentrated in unskilled and semi-skilled, low-paying jobs.

Now let us move on to the turn of the century in our examination of the working life of women. The 1890s saw the first stage of the agrarian revolt in Canada. In 1880, less than 25 per cent of the population was urban, and in 1900 the figure was about 37.5 per cent. As the sons and daughters of farm people in central Canada headed for the cities, they faced a kind of exploitation that had not changed significantly since the 1880s, described earlier.

Accompanying this was the last great agrarian boom, the rapid development of the Western wheat economy in the first decade of this century. There was massive immigration to the west, as young men and families, many from other lands, went west to establish roots in this expanding economic area. During that decade occurred the last of the major appeals for the import of women to mate with native men.

The *Saturday Night* publication in Toronto described one of these women-hunting expeditions in 1905:

> Benjamin Pipe, an Assiniboia farmer, is on the way to England to induce 50 healthy, experienced, good-looking girls to accompany him back to the prairies. The girls will begin as servants at about fifteen dollars a month, but it will be understood that the fault will lie in them if they do not soon become mistresses of 50 households. Wives, not servants, are what the west needs. They tell us that female domestics are almost impossible to get for love or money. The west will give both love and money.[16]

Meanwhile, in Toronto, large numbers of women were working, most of them out of financial need. The entry of women into industry continued, but so did their exploitation. In 1915, there were 57,000 women working at 14,887 factories, with only 4,097 of them earning over $12 a week. There were 8,411 children working, with only 115 earning over $12 a week.[17]

The labour movement of this period was weak, but the Canadian Manufacturing Association was growing and gaining strength with moving appeals to its membership, such as the following:

> If you have ever endeavoured to fight a bill single-handed, you will appreciate what a tremendous task it is to produce results. As an individual manufacturer you have neither the time nor the money to devote to work of this kind. . . . The Association needs your assistance. A successful campaign against the 8-hour bill (8-hour day) alone has saved the price of your membership fee a hundred times over. This is but one of a long list of items which go to make a splendid record of parliamentary achievements.[18]

On this optimistic note, we move into the First World War period, during which labour lost many of the tiny footholds it had gained. Factory hours were lengthened and conditions worsened. Women worked 72 hours a week and more in munitions plants. Here's one description of a Toronto munitions plant in 1917:

> . . . the management increased hours from 13 to 14 a day. At least 7 women refused to work the extra hour. Of these, 2 had husbands at the front, one had lost a brother overseas, one had a brother on active service, and one had been

awarded the munitions workers good service medal. The 7 went to the office of the Toronto Daily Star. "Look at our hands!" cried one, and she thrust out hands blackened with oil from which the skin had peeled in big patches. A member of the delegation said: "One of the girls was too sick to come with us. Oil in her system is killing her. Two have died!" Another said: "They are killing us off as fast as they are killing the men in the trenches!"[19]

Out of such human tragedies, profits were made and millionaires were given their knighthoods.

But do not despair, protective legislation was passed during this period. Following on the heels of Ontario, Manitoba and Saskatchewan, British Columbia also passed racist legislation prohibiting white women from working or living in places kept or managed by any Chinese persons.

I want to draw a parallel here between the two world wars of this century as times of great deception by governments of working women. During both wars, women were used as a reserve labour force to replace men who had gone into the services and to meet the increased demands of wartime industry. During both wars, the federal government officially recognized the principle of "equal pay for equal work." Between the two world wars and after the second, the noble statements disappeared immediately into the never-never land of government archives. During the second world war, the government somehow found the financial energy to set up a program of day-care centres for those much-needed women workers, a program which was dropped after the war. Not only was this program dropped, but married women were once again deprived of jobs by the reincarnation of pre-war civil service regulations stipulating that upon marriage, a woman was deemed to have resigned, except in some special circumstances. This policy was continued until 1955. To conclude, the war periods illustrated clearly the strength of government in the service of industry's needs, and the weakness of government in the service of any abstract moral values such as justice for women workers.

World War II was a time of tremendous expansion in the strength of unions, and after the war, naturally enough, these stronger unions demanded seniority for returned men ... casting their eyes upon industries such as airplane factories, where women made up half of the work force. Many women were ready to go back into the work of the household, but many others were not, and needed or wanted to work outside the home. Once again, as after World War I, they were faced with their low status in the light of a labour surplus.

World War II was also a time of major industrial development, accompanied by renewed and innovative attempts at labour exploitation. Just as an illustration: after the war, the Dominion Textile Company, inheritors of a long tradition of interesting labour practices, increased the workload for employees by 25 per cent without any increase in pay.[20] And then, of course, there was the classic manoeuvre which has caused so much tragedy among women and men workers both, and hatred between them, the transfer of women to do what had come to be called men's jobs at what were called women's wages.[21]

Before I leave the subject of the wars, let me draw attention to the special exploitation and suffering of the people who are not only workers, not only women, but also part of a minority group, be it racial, ethnic, or religious. Nowhere has this struck me more deeply than in a quote reproduced in a speech by Sylva Gelber regarding the Japanese-Canadians whose belongings and small properties were confiscated during the Second World War and who were relocated, often in internment camps. Here are the thoughts of a Canadian-born Japanese woman, Shizuye Takashima, who was still a child at the time: Vancouver, March 1942

> Japan is at war with the United States, Great Britain and all the Allied Countries, including Canada, the country of my birth. My parents are Japanese, born in Japan, but they have been Canadian citizens for many, many years, and have become part of this young country. Now, overnight, our rights as Canadians are taken away. Mass evacuation for the Japanese!
>
> "All the Japanese," it is carefully explained to me, "whether we were born in Tokyo or in Vancouver are to be moved to distant places. Away from the west coast of British Columbia – for security reasons."
>
> We must all leave, my sister Yuki, my older brother David, my parents, our relatives – all.
>
> The older men are the first to go. The government feels that my father, or his friends, might sabotage the police and

their buildings. Imagine! I couldn't believe such stories, but there is my father packing just his clothes in a small suitcase.

Men crowd at the windows. Father is still on the steps, he seems to be searching the crowd, finally sees us, waves. Mother does not move. Yuki and I wave. Most remain still. The dark brown faces of the men become small. Some are still shouting. Yuki moves closer to mother. The long, narrow, old train quickly picks up speed as it coils away along the tracks, away from all of us who are left at the station. Mother is silent. I look at her. I see tears are slowly falling. They remain on her cheeks. I turn away, look around. The women and the children stare at one another. Some women cry right out loud. A bent old woman breaks out into a Buddhist prayer, moves her orange beads in her wrinkled hands, prays out aloud to her God. Mother and the other women bow their heads. The Silent God seems so far away.[22]

As you may have read in a Canadian Magazine article not too long ago, some of these people "went to sugar beet fields in Alberta and Manitoba; a few went to Ontario as household maids or farm workers; 42 chose to go to Japan; and 11,600 were sent to the B.C. interior" to internment camps.[23]

These things I have been writing about are not aberrations, strange inexplicable occurrences. They are part and parcel of the history and values of capitalist development in this country.

Let us continue the saga of Canadian working women. From the latter part of the nineteenth century on, there were shifts in the nature of the labour force and development of the economy that were of great importance to working women. One was the transformation of lower level clerical and teaching jobs from men's work to women's work. Let us look at teaching, for example. In 1877, male teachers in Ontario public schools numbered 3,020, and female teachers numbered 3,448. By 1889, male teachers numbered only 2,774 and females had risen to 5,193.[24] An academic of the time reports that as more women came in at lower salaries – for the same work, of course – men abandoned the profession or used it as a stepping stone to better things.[25] In Toronto in 1892, 460 of the city's 500 teachers were women.[26] In the clerical field, the major transformation came with the invention of the typewriter, opening up a field for low-paid female secretaries.

Nursing continued as it had always been, a proper profession for females, calling them to service and to sacrifice with few labour protections and traditionally poor wages. The most fundamental development in the economy affecting the futures of working women was the shift that occurred in industrial demands with the development of new technologies. It was a shift away from the need for massive numbers of cheap bodies, towards the need for relatively fewer but more skilled and educated workers to manage and repair machines and to populate higher levels of the growing public sector of the economy, which was needed to service industry and the urban concentrations resulting from industrialization.

What did this mean? The economic pressure for women to produce huge families for the labour force was relieved. To meet the demand for more skilled workers, public education was extended to include masses of children and young people who would otherwise have been in the unskilled labour force. Women had more years of life free from child-bearing and child-raising, years that could be spent in the workplace to improve the living standards of the family as a whole. And the gap in the labour force created by the education of children either disappeared or was taken up by women.

Let us take a quick look now at the major 20th century changes that have occurred in the lives of women. Later, we will examine the basic things which have not changed.

To relieve you of the painful experience of reading statistics upon statistics, I will generalize from the figures to give you the flavour of the transformations. First, the rate of participation of women in the labour force has more than doubled since 1901.[27] The greatest explosion has taken place since World War II in the ranks of married women, whose entry into the labour force is expected to continue to expand through the 1970s. Women are living much longer, bearing fewer children, and taking advantage of increasingly sophisticated means of birth control to exercise more exact control over the size of their families . . . control they have always had to some extent, but never before so efficient. Also, with medical advances, fewer infants die, which means that fewer babies have to be conceived to achieve a chosen family size. Women are freer to leave the bondage of marriages that are intolerable. Before 1900, there wasn't a single year when there were more than 20 divorces in Canada. In 1968, there were 54.7

divorces for every 100,000 persons in Canada. In 1970, with the impact of the 1968 liberalized divorce legislation, the rate had reached 139.8 per 100,000.[28] The mass education of female children, as well as males, has expanded enormously at the public and secondary levels. With regard to legal rights over children, the weight of discrimination has swung from women to men. The influence of religion over women's lives is waning. There are more mechanical, disposable, drip-dry and ready-mix goods in the home to lighten the burden of household labour. And, most significantly, new job opportunities have been created with the rapid expansion of the white collar and service sectors of the economy.

On the legislative scene, we have witnessed a tidal wave of laws in various provinces and on the federal level . . . regarding minimum wages, hours of work, social benefits, holidays, sexual discrimination in employment, equal pay, and maternity protections. There are still many gaps remaining, of course, in the federal and provincial legislative records, and many laws on the books that have yet to be effectively enforced, but one would have every reason to be optimistic from the perspective of the early suffragists . . . so much seems to have changed for the better.

But has it really? Let us examine the situation of working women today, with their historical experience in mind. Is the labour force basically divided into men's and women's jobs? Yes. Are women still earning much less than men for the same or similar work? Yes. Are women still used as a source of cheap labour? Yes. Do we still see a contrast between the propagandistic platitudes about 'womanhood' and the living experience of most working women? Yes. Have the corporate and political leaders of this country become suddenly more sensitive to the plight of working women? No.

Let us review the postwar experience of Canadian working women to find the factual basis for these "yesses" and "nos."

The 1950's is what I call the GRP period of Canadian history – the Great Rip-Off Period. Some might call it lack of foresight, others might see it as fitting right into the free enterprise ethic of getting more for less, but during the 1950s and 60s, Canada imported huge numbers of skilled and professional people to meet the increasingly sophisticated demands of higher phases of industrialization. Where did the rip-off come in? John Porter points it out well, as do subsequent studies.[29] In taking advantage of other countries' investments in higher education, Canada was able to neglect for a time the higher training of its own indigenous population, men and women. Don't forget that in 1951, more than half of the men in the labour force had only elementary school education or less.[30] Porter estimates that "about one-third of all the new professional occupations that came with the industrial expansion between 1951 and 1961 were filled from immigration and about one-half of all the new skilled and technical manual occupations were also filled from immigration."[31] Meanwhile, as he notes, university education was more costly for Canadian students than in any other comparable industrial society, even in the sixties, when we saw great expansion in higher education relative to the country's earlier records. At that time, 26 per cent of university operating costs were being passed on to Canadian students through tuition fees, compared to 9.9 per cent in the U.K., and student awards were painfully inadequate.[32] The 1970-71 Canada Year Book notes with regard to the country's intensified recruiting of immigrants abroad in the early sixties: "The achievements of 1964 were accomplished despite strong competition in Europe for skilled and educated workers and new postwar levels of prosperity."[33] There was a heavy cost involved in this policy, however, and the cost was the relief of pressures which might otherwise have forced the training of some of the native Canadians who were lower on the social scale and who, be they men or women, have remained low.

This was a phenomenon affecting both men and women, but let us now look at the specific situation of women in the postwar period and up to the present day. With the fantastic growth of the white collar sector of the labour force, we have seen the concentration of more than one-third of working women in clerical jobs, many of these less-skilled and low-paying.[34] The clerical field has replaced the assembly line in offering vast opportunities for routine, repetitive, monotonous and alienating labour, and the large majority of jobs in this expanding field have been taken up by women.[35] The new sweatshops are huge offices with dozens or hundreds of women crammed together with their fingers dancing endlessly and frantically on clicking keyboards. That is not to say that the old sweatshops, the laundries, textile plants, etcetera, are not still around. They are, of course.

Statistics for the late 1960s indicated that women as a group in the labour force had better educational backgrounds (in terms of their levels of education) than men as a group.[36] In spite of this, there was a tremendous disparity in the average earnings of male and female full-year workers, in all major occupational groups.[37] Women were channelled into lower-paying occupations, their conditions of work were manipulated to justify lower wages, their pay rates for jobs similar to those performed by men were less, and their opportunities for promotion were much more limited.[38] Even in traditionally female occupations such as teaching and nursing, the men as a group have done better than women in pay and promotion. But then, that is not surprising, for that has always been the case.

The basic reality of two almost separate labour forces, male and female, with men's jobs and women's jobs, still dominates the present and future prospects of working women. It is reinforced by tradition, prejudice, discriminatory education and vocational counselling, and discriminatory hiring. As recently as 1970, the Canada Career Directory had 3,268 listings of jobs open to men with 1,244 open to women, and Canadian employers recruiting through services, even on campuses, were refusing to interview female graduates for those men's jobs.[39]

Despite legislation on the books, we see innumerable examples of illegal discrimination to which government and industry turn a conveniently blind eye. Take, for example, the totally sex-based wage differences in hospitals funded by the government.[40] The average monthly salary of male lab technicians in Canada, for example, is 5.2 per cent higher than that of female lab technicians. The salary of male lab assistants is 6.5 per cent higher, and with Xray technicians the difference is 7.8 per cent. Not too long ago we saw a court suit in Ontario regarding the pay differentials between male orderlies and female nurses' aides.[41] The case was finally settled in favour of the nurses' aides, but for all the difference it made in the paying practices of Canadian hospitals, the case might never have taken place.

Despite legislation on the books, we see some strange rulings in the courts. In 1968 a justice of the Ontario high courts ruled that, although a woman was a police constable in the same sense as men were,

She is not being discriminated against by the fact that she

receives a different wage, different from male constables, for the fact of difference is in accord with every rule of economics, civilization, family life and common sense.[42]

This ruling was overruled by a higher court subsequently – but imagine the time and human energy consumed by every such effort, and the human will needed to motivate it.

Then there are the kinds of decisions *permitted* by the law, one of which reflects on a subject I want to touch on briefly . . . the control of women's lives in the name of morality. Consider, for example, the court judgment that a woman whose three-year-old son fell to his death from a faulty balcony could not claim damages from the landlord because her child was illegitimate.[43]

Similar moral injunctions have been laid upon female welfare recipients living alone. Penalties for sleeping with men, for example. And families have been left to fend with no money because of "immoral" behaviour.

This brings me to the question, "What is the real social status of women in the home?" We know their economic status: they are not paid for their work, their labour is not counted in the GNP and they get none of the social benefits or pensions accorded other workers. But what of the noble statements of the importance of woman's home-work which are used to keep them vacillating between household work and workplace labour according to the fluctuating demands of industry. The real attitudes of our industrial and political barons towards the woman at home, I think, are best measured by their attitudes towards the woman at home, alone, with no husband. Let us use the welfare recipients as an example. According to a 1970 survey, nearly two-thirds of all welfare recipients in Canada were women.[44] Of this group, 69.2 per cent were widowed, separated or divorced and 54.2 per cent were women with children under 21. Many of these women cannot afford to work because of the low wages available to women in the labour market. This is borne out in a study by Dr. Roslyn Kunin of the University of British Columbia.[45] With Vancouver daycare costing $65 a month, and the average female job paying $100 a week, a woman with three children would be better off getting the $246.50 a month available to her through social assistance.

Let us now examine the attitudes towards women in this situation

... housewives without husbands to depend upon. One indicator was the passage of a resolution by the Union of Manitoba Municipalities in 1970, calling for the removal from the voters' list of any persons receiving welfare assistance, most of whom are, of course, women.[46] This reflects a very poor attitude towards jobless men as well. But the social myth is that *women* working in the home are respected. What is clearly apparent, as it has always been, is that the small respect that housewives do get for their work is derived from having husbands, and from the status of those husbands.

The myth that household work is respected as socially important work is one of many establishment views nourishing male workers' prejudices against female workers, views that help keep the entire workforce weak and vulnerable to the profit-making manoeuvres of large corporations. The fact is that most working women are forced to work by economic necessity. Does anyone really think that it is the social pleasures of a night cleaning job in an empty office building that keep a woman in the labour force? Or the stimulating company of an endlessly chattering typewriter? An increasing number of women are supporting themselves, or their own children, and others are trying to bring the family income up to a subsistence level or a level of moderate comfort in the light of rising costs, prices, and company profits. Of course, there are some who are in the workforce because the climate of their lives at home, whatever the factors involved, has become mentally and emotionally intolerable, or at least undesirable. Are these people really the villains responsible for unemployment among men? Are these the scapegoats to be driven back to their homes? Is this the price women must pay for labour's collective blindness and proud ignorance of the nature of its own exploitation? Women have always been the scapegoats for male workers' fears of the arbitrary powers of corporations to seek profit at any cost. And when women replace men in jobs, it is the women who are attacked, and not the economic system that allows workers to be replaced or laid off arbitrarily, that allows the exploitation of people for profit, that allows underemployment and overwork. The economic system is taken for granted, and the weakest members of our society, the second-class employees ... be they women, or immigrants, or Indians or blacks ... become victims of the ignorance of the trade union aristocracy, which is too wrapped up in the contract negotiations of the underwater boiler room to see the icebergs approaching the vessel. What are these icebergs? I'll describe them as I see them in a moment. But first I must establish the basis for my reluctant, but unavoidable criticism of what I think are the prevailing prejudices in the trade union movement and among working class men generally.

Why am I now picking on working class men? Because they are the class allies of working women. Because their interests in the long run are the same: to fight for a freer and more fulfilling life for all human beings, without the human torture imposed by an economic system in which the lust for profits prevails. In the short run, of course, their interests are to keep their own jobs, their means of survival. But does this justify a collective agreement which, in June 1968, allows for the dismissal of a married woman because she becomes pregnant?[47] The Ontario Labour Relations Board found, in this case, that had this woman not been covered by the collective agreement, she would not have suffered this injustice, because restrictions of this kind were not placed on non-union employees in the same firm. Even if we were to totally ignore the question of the small numbers of women in the leadership of the union locals where women predominate, we would still have a multitude of problems to deal with: pension plans which provide for the earlier retirement of women employees or lesser benefits for the survivors of women employees; collective agreements with separate salary schedules for men and women; life insurance plans agreed to by union locals with lesser benefits for women workers; collective agreements which allow the firing of women once they marry; collective agreements which allow married women to be laid off first in the event of labour cutbacks; collective agreements which prevent married women from achieving permanent status in their jobs; agreements which allow women to be re-employed in a lesser capacity after pregnancy leave; agreements which give the boss the right to decide when maternity leave should begin. For some of these examples I owe thanks to an honest, self-critical and promising document produced by the Canadian Union of Public Employees.[48]

For a moment I wish to dwell on what is certainly one of the most crucial areas of women's exploitation today. Not only are they destined to work, by and large, in low-paying jobs with fewer protections – but they are also destined to spend many hours, days, weeks, and years of their lives worrying about the social care of their children. The vacuum created by the federal government's withdrawal from its commitment to daycare during the Second World War has never been adequately filled since then. And in our sympathy for the financial problems of today's government, let's not forget that less than a century ago, children who were five years old were only three or four years away from a government-sanctioned, brutal, and lifelong exploitation in the workforce. That gives us the perspective to be somewhat skeptical of the elites in our economy, who are now arguing that the hard-pressed working women of the day are guilty of child neglect in their efforts to find socially-respectable, safe and emotionally responsive child-care arrangements for their offspring. One of the dangers on this front is that the serious lack of public community daycare will open the way to new sources of profit for private industry with diminishing public control. This is already happening on a significant scale in the United States, where firms like Singer, Gerber baby foods, and Hasbro toys are getting into the daycare racket, and to a lesser, but still significant extent in Canada, starting with the Winnipeg Mini-Schools which were inspired by the philosophy that nurseries can be money-makers.[49]

Another threat to the public interest is that the sanctioning and development of workplace daycare under the control of employers will open up opportunities for new kinds of exploitation, as women are tied even more closely to their present jobs, with the risk of even greater losses if they rebel.

Finally, what are the prospects for the future . . . the icebergs on the horizon . . . and our possibilities of dealing with these dangers and overcoming them?

First, our continuing acceptance of the separate labour forces, men's and women's jobs, with different salaries and status, is fundamental to the exploitation of women workers as second-class employees.

The continuing acceptance of the principle of equal work for less pay is fundamental to the use of women workers to replace men whenever possible.

The extension of part-time work without any labour protection or fringe benefits (as is the case with department store employees classified as non-regular, who are growing in numbers) represents a renewed attempt on the part of employers to escape those protective laws that exist, in order to exploit cheap womanpower in labour-intensive industries.

The areas in which women now predominate, the lower-paid and lesser-skilled clerical and service jobs, are increasingly vulnerable to automation and relative decline as the more skilled professional and and technical jobs, where men predominate, expand in their relative share of the labour force of the future.

Most important in terms of the immediate future is the fact that the service sector of the Canadian economy, where women are employed in large numbers along with men, is overextended with respect to the country's population and industrial base. As we see the weakening of that largely foreign-owned industrial base with new protective measures in the United States, we must also expect to see employment problems, not only in the service sector, but also in other areas of the labour force.

Where is the hope for the future? The hope is in the development of an understanding in the women's movement of the present needs and the potential collective power of women in the workplace. It is in the labour movement's renewed attempts to organize women in all those jobs which have thus far resisted organization or have been given up as hopeless. The hope is in the recognition that part-time workers must be included under labour protection. It lies in the possibility that men and women workers both will recognize the need for experiments with integration of their separate work forces, and the need to encourage young women to enter "men's" jobs. The hope is in the rising expectations of women workers, with their increased education, and in their developing consciousness of the history and nature of their exploitation by private entrepreneurs and by politicians who service big business. It lies in a kind of solidarity which Canadian male and female workers have had only rarely, but which I think is a not unlikely possibility, as more women are organized and the impact of their numbers and militance is felt in the Canadian labour movement of the future. And, in my opinion, the hope lies ultimately in the building of a movement dedicated to the creation of an independent, socialist Canada, organized around the needs and hopes of all Canadian working people, be they men or women.

Notes

[1] For much of the historical content of this sketch, I am indebted to *An Historical Almanac of Canada*, edited by Lena Newman. (Toronto: McClelland and Stewart Limited, 1967).

[2] Lipton, Charles, *The Trade Union Movement of Canada 1827-1959*. (Montreal: Canadian Social Publications Limited, Second Edition, 1968), p. 43.

[3] *Ibid.* [4] *Ibid.*, pp. 58-64.

[5] *Royal Commission on the Relations of Capital and Labour, 1889*, as quoted in Charles Lipton's *The Trade Union Movement of Canada 1827-1959, op. cit.*, p. 61.

[6] *Ibid.*, p. 60.

[7] Amot, Guillaume, 1894. As quoted in *The Lace Ghetto*. Maxine Nunes and Deanna White. (Toronto: New Press, 1972) New Woman Series: 3, edited by Adrienne Clarkson, p. 14.

[8] E. G. P. Littleton, Military Secretary to Lord Lorne, Governor General, Montreal, 1878, as quoted in *An Historical Almanac of Canada.*

[9] Scott, Jean Thomson, "The Conditions of Female Labour in Ontario." Toronto University Studies in Political Science, First Series, No. III. W. J. Ashley, Editor. (Toronto: Warwick & Sons, 1892), p. 14.

[10] *The Ontario Workman*, Toronto, May 2, 1872, as quoted in *A History of the Rise of Women's Consciousness in Canada & Quebec Including Various Tracts on the Ideology of Women in the Working Class, The Movement for Female Emancipation & its Links with the Temperance Struggle & with some Conclusions Drawn Concerning the Struggle of Canadian Women Today*, by Maureen Hynes. (Toronto: Hogtown Press, Publication #30).

[11] Robin, Martin, *Radical Politics and Canadian Labour – 1880-1930*. (Kingston: Industrial Relations Centre, Queen's University, 1968), p. 27, footnote 39.

[12] *Ibid.*

[13] *Toronto Globe*, August 15, 1877, as quoted in Martin Robin's *Radical Politics and Canadian Labour*, p. 14, footnote 34.

[14] Russell, L. Case, *Toronto Globe*, September 28, 1912, as quoted in *The Lace Ghetto*.

[15] Mahood, Sally, "The Women's Suffrage Movement in Canada and Saskatchewan," in *Women Unite!* (Toronto: Canadian Women's Educational Press, 1972), pp. 25-28.

[16] From *Saturday Night*, Toronto, 1905, as quoted in *An Historical Almanac of Canada.*

[17] Lipton, Charles, *The Trade Union Movement of Canada 1827-1959*, p. 99. He quotes the figures from George Kleiner, *Capital ... Canada*, p. 117.

[18] From *Voice*, July 1, 1907, as quoted in Charles Lipton's *The Trade Union Movement of Canada 1827-1959*, p. 117.

[19] From Canada, House of Commons Debates, August 2, 1917, as quoted in Charles Lipton's *The Trade Union Movement of Canada 1827-1959*, pp. 167-168.

[20] Lipton, Charles. *The Trade Union Movement of Canada 1827-1959*, p. 303.

[21] *Ibid.*

[22] Takashima, Shizuye, *A Child in a Prison Camp.* (Montreal: Tundra Books, 1971), as quoted by Sylva M. Gelber in an address to the Status of Women Council of B.C., Vancouver, October 25, 1972.

[23] *The Canadian Magazine*, November 27, 1971, also quoted in Sylva Gelber's address, above.

[24] Scott, Jean Thomson, "The Conditions of Female Labour in Ontario,"

Toronto University Studies in Political Science, First Series, No. III, W. J. Ashley, Editor (Toronto: Warwick & Sons, 1892), p. 24.

25 *Ibid.*

26 *Topical Quarterly*. (November, 1970), p. 23.

27 *Report of the Royal Commission on the Status of Women in Canada*. (Ottawa: Information Canada, 1970), p. 54.

28 Statistics Canada, *Vital Statistics Preliminary Annual Report 1971*. (Catalogue No. 84-201 Annual).

29 Porter, John, "The Human Community," in *The Canadians 1867-1967*, edited by J. M. S. Careless and R. Craig Brown (Toronto: Macmillan of Canada, 1967), pp. 385-409. For further documentation, see *Canada's Highly Qualified Manpower Resources*. A. G. Atkinson, K. J. Barnes and Ellen Richardson, Research Branch, Program Development Service, Department of Manpower and Immigration. (Ottawa: Information Canada, 1970).

30 Porter, John. "The Human Community," in *The Canadians 1867-1967*, pp. 404-405.

31 *Ibid.*, p. 407.

32 *Ibid.*, p. 408. These figures are for 1962-63.

33 *1970-71 Canada Year Book*. Dominion Bureau of Statistics (Ottawa: Information Canada, 1971), p. 266.

34 Dominion Bureau of Statistics, Labour Force Special Tables, 12-month averages, Table 3c. (Ottawa: DBS Special Surveys Division, 1969).

35 Canada Department of Labour. *Women's Bureau '71*. (Ottawa: Information Canada, 1972), p. 9.

36 Dominion Bureau of Statistics, *Labour Force Survey*. (Ottawa: DBS Special Surveys Division, unpublished, March 1969).

37 Dominion Bureau of Statistics. *Income Distributions by Size in Canada 1965* (Ottawa: Queen's Printer, 1968), p. 44. In four out of six occupational groups, men's average earnings were double, or slightly less than double, those of women. The figures include women whose daily hours of work were less than those of men. This accounts for some of the disparity. However, it should also be kept in mind that employers will shorten the work hours of women slightly, to justify lower wages.

38 *Report of the Royal Commission on the Status of Women in Canada*. (Ottawa: Information Canada, 1970), pp. 52-97.

39 Canada Department of Labour. *Women's Bureau '69*. (Ottawa: Queen's Printer, 1970), p. 27.

40 Gelber, Sylva M., address to the Annual Meeting of the Ontario Public Health Association, Toronto, October 19, 1972.

41 Regina v. Howard *et al.*, Ex Parte Municipality of Metropolitan Toronto. (Ontario Court of Appeal), Ontario Reports, Vol. 3, 1970, p. 555.

42 Beckett *v.* City of Sault Ste. Marie Police Commissioners *et al.*, Vol. 67, Dominion Law Reports (2d), p. 294 (Ontario High Court, Ferguson, J., 1968).

43 *Montreal Gazette*, November 28, 1969.

44 The Social Survey Research Centre Limited. *The World of the Welfare Recipient, January 1971*. Submitted to the Federal-Provincial Study Group on Alienation. (Toronto: Canadian Facts Co. Ltd., 1971).

45 *Chatelaine*, November, 1972, p. 18.

46 *Globe and Mail*, November 26, 1970.

47 Mrs. Mary Anne Wortley and Hiram Walker and Sons Limited.

48 *The Status of Women in CUPE*. A special report approved by the CUPE national convention, September 1971.

49 Nankivell, Joan. "Day Care: If Government Won't, Private Chains Will." *Chatelaine*, September, 1972, p. 52.

Resources and Underdevelopment
Mel Watkins

In January, 1973, a Town Hall meeting was held in Toronto on the pros and cons of the Mackenzie Valley Pipeline. Five hundred people jammed the auditorium – and perhaps as many wanted to get in, but didn't – to listen to a panel of William Wilder, Eric Kierans, Douglas Pimlott, and Donald Macdonald.

The event was highly revealing of the politics of this country. Consider the panelists. Mr. Wilder is Chairman of the Board of Canadian Arctic Gas Study, the consortium that wants to build the gas pipeline. Consisting of the giant international oil companies, Trans Canada Pipelines, the CPR, the CNR, and the Canada Development Corporation, it makes even the syndicate that built the CPR look like small potatoes – while, unlike the CPR, it is not intended to bind Canada together but rather to move Alaska gas and Canadian Arctic gas to the U.S. Jim Laxer calls it "the most powerful array of corporate and state power ever gathered on behalf of any project in this country's history."[1]

Wilder himself is the former head of the financial house of Wood Gundy. He is the personification of Tom Naylor's thesis about the Canadian capitalist – competent as a merchant/finance capitalist, unable to make the transition to being an independent industrial capitalist, but, unfortunately, only too able to become a resource capitalist fronting for an international consortium, with final decision-making power lying outside of the country and the object of the exercise being to export. When Mr. Wilder says, as he did at the Town Hall meeting, "I took on this job on the basis that it was in the national interest," we need not question his sincerity, but we should point to the underdeveloped national consciousness of Canadian capitalists.

Mr. Kierans is certainly not open to that charge, but that

simply makes him a rare bird. Each decade we are allowed to have one genuine bourgeois nationalist folk-hero, but only one – Walter Gordon in the sixties and now Kierans. Mr. Kierans came to his present position as a result of the decision of the Johnson Administration in 1965 to use the multi-national corporations as a vehicle to help the U.S. balance of payments. But now he goes much further. In his 1973 *Report on Natural Resource Policy in Manitoba,* he writes of "neo-colonialism" and says, "It is not wildly imaginative to suggest that the day may not be far distant when Canada's resources will be controlled, not by the ten provinces, but by fewer than ten giant resource corporations."[2]

Indeed, both Kierans, in that report, and Gordon in a speech in February, 1973, are now advocates of public ownership – the former advocating that crown corporations in Manitoba should undertake all exploration, development and mining to the primary metal stage, the latter that a crown corporation control all oil and gas production in the Canadian Arctic. The contradictions for a dependent capitalist country that arise from foreign private ownership of its resource industries, and particularly of the energy resource industries, have become such that public ownership can be advocated by default. So it is, too, that the Science Council of Canada in its 1973 report, *Natural Resource Policy Issues in Canada*, concludes by suggesting that increased revenues from resources can be obtained not only by increasing royalty rates and by an export tax, but also by "public ownership of specific and carefully selected Canadian resources."[3]

Dr. Pimlott of the University of Toronto's Department of Zoology is an academic drawn into an increasingly public role through his concern for the environment and original people of the north, the founder and ex-Chairman of Canadian Arctic Resources Committee (CARC). A former civil servant, he set out to lobby the government to make its decision objectively and democratically but has, by his own admission, learned something about the nature of decision-making in Canada today. He has learned that "public participation was not welcome" and that "government at the political and bureaucratic levels is doing everything possible to stifle the debate" about the Mackenzie Valley pipeline.[4]

In a speech in May, 1972,[5] he presented in an extremely revealing way the response of Canadian Ministers to the possibility, first raised in February 1971, that the Trans Alaska Pipeline (TAPS) might be indefinitely delayed by the court actions of American conservationists. Virtually within hours, the then Minister of Energy, Mines and Resources, Joe Greene, speaking in Vancouver, offered the Mackenzie Valley route as an alternative to TAPS, and on March 2nd repeated the offer to highranking officials of the Nixon Administration in Washington. In March, Jean Chrétien, Minister of Indian Affairs and Northern Development, told a Dallas, Texas audience: "We in Canada would welcome the building of such a gas pipeline through our country and would do everything reasonable to facilitate this particular development . . . An oil pipeline would also be acceptable. In other words, if it is felt desirable to build an oil pipeline from Prudhoe Bay direct to the mid-continent market, then a right-of-way through Canada, I am sure, can, and will, be made available."

Shortly thereafter, Jack Davis, Minister of the Environment, stated in Vancouver that he was 90 per cent sure that the building of the Mackenzie Corridor could begin by 1973. Pimlott concludes from this that "the Mackenzie Valley would probably have had a hurry-up pipeline if the international petroleum executives had opted to put one there."

Finally, we come to the present Minister of Energy, Mines and Resources, Donald Macdonald, his predecessor having been incapacitated for politics but not for a directorship with Petrofina of Canada. This is the man who in May 1972 wrote to U.S. Interior Secretary Rogers Morton, with respect of an oil pipeline:

> There would be many advantages arising from the use of a Canadian pipeline route. We believe it would enhance the energy security of your country by providing an overland route for your Alaska oil production . . . Canada has an interest in the energy security of your country, and this land route for Alaska crude oil would enhance that security of supply . . . [6]

Macdonald, as befits his portfolio, does not so much represent, as over-represent, the multi-national energy companies. He is really an advance man for their circus. As well, he perfectly portrays the mentality of the happy hinterlander. At a time when there were 655,000 unemployed that we knew about, he was non-plussed at the Town Hall meeting by Wilder's statement that 400 jobs would be provided directly by the pipeline and simply went on to insist that no other activity was so worthwhile for Canada in the 1970s.

While it is hard to out-do a federal cabinet minister in inanity, justice requires us to point out that provincial premiers are not above trying to run a close second. Hence, the spectacle of Premier Barrett of B.C. – the most radical premier in Canada, though it is admitedly not a hard race to win – dashing down to Washington to offer his province as a right-of-way to link Alaska to the other 48 states. Nothing plays more into the hands of the big companies and Washington than turning the future of the Canadian north and ultimately of southern Canada as well, into a second-order debate about routes and preferred modes of transportation.

Harold Innis, the greatest political economist and historian that this country has produced, once said that the risk of being a social scientist in Canada was that one might die laughing. But the serious moral is that it is of the essence of the political economy of Canada as a resource hinterland that the major issues in our politics are imposed on us from the outside, from the United States. The recent Deutsch Report for the Ontario Government[7] speaks of the "spillover" of the U.S. energy crisis into Canada, and the phenomenon is pervasive. It is the hallmark of a hinterland that it not only cannot generate its own solutions – so long, that is, as it operates within the capitalist framework – but it cannot even generate its own problems.

The $5 billion Mackenzie Valley gas pipeline is just one of a number of major resource projects planned for the seventies. There is an oil pipeline for the Mackenzie Valley of comparable dollar magnitude. There is the $6 billion James Bay project which involves flooding an area in Northern Quebec twice the size of England and destroying the economy of 6,000 natives – all for the benefit of Con Ed in New York. There is the Northern Manitoba water diversion plan, the "largest single diversion ever undertaken by man on this continent" according to its promoters, which will destroy the Churchill River and flood Southern Indian Lake. The water level is now to be raised only 12 feet rather than the originally planned 30 feet, the difference presumably being a measure of the benefits of social democracy. The plan will export the surplus power not needed by Manitoba till 1990 to the U.S. There is the high Arctic oil and gas play, with the possibility of a pipeline from the eastern Arctic down either the western or eastern side of James Bay. There is exploration offshore the Atlantic Provinces. Add these extraordinary developments to the ordinary developments, and the sum to be spent on the development of energy resources is variously estimated as $50 billion to $100 billion for this decade.

A Socialist Perspective

It is this spectre that underlies the gathering debate in this country that is increasingly bringing together disparate groups in opposition to resource ripoffs. Within that opposition, there is an urgent need for socialist analysis, as a basis for political action and a socialist program.

Socialists, beginning with Marx, have understood that capitalist development was uneven development. Not only was there an uneven distribution of benefits among classes – with capitalists benefiting much while workers benefited much less or lost – but globally the same was true for countries; that is, the phenomenon of imperialism and underdevelopment, and within countries for regions, with some prospering while others stagnated.

Of contemporary Marxist writers, this analysis has been articulated best by Andre Gunder Frank.[8] Capitalist economic development is a dialectical process simultaneously creating development and underdevelopment. Economic underdevelopment is generated by the same forces which generate economic development, and to search in each case for special reasons for the former is to miss the point.

The capitalist world is structured in terms of the interrelationship of metropolis and hinterland, and is characterized by hierarchical links in long imperial chains. The metropolis is the seat of manufacturing, importing staples – raw materials, food – from the hinterland and exporting manufactured goods. The role of the hinterland, to export staples and import manufactured goods which embody their own staples, is pre-determined. The metropolis, then, develops – or over-develops – while the hinterland is locked into a pattern of underdevelopment. As Bruce Archibald observes: "In contemporary terms, the overdevelopment of the highly industrialized polluted areas is the other side of the coin of underdeveloped rural farming and fishing communities and regional centres which cannot sustain their own population."[9]

Now, under capitalism a surplus is everywhere created by the exploitation of wage-labour, but this is particularly so in the case of resource development. Indeed, even orthodox economics, with

111

its notorious limitations, recognizes that the scarcity of resources yields an "economic rent" which is then appropriated by the owner of the resource for merely owing the resource. In 1848 John Stuart Mill in his *Principles of Political Economy* said of the owners of such resources: "They grow richer, as it were in their sleep, without working, risking or economizing."

The issue then is: who owns the resources? In Canada, except for the North West Territories, the answer is the provinces. But in fact, they have alienated rights to explore and develop into private hands through lease arrangements, and typically for a price which is a fraction of the rents – this being demonstrably the case, given the profitability of resource companies *after* such payments. Typically, the private owner is a foreign corporation, two-thirds of all activity in the resource sector being controlled by non-residents. So the surplus, in the form of dividends, goes outside Canada. Any initial capital brought in tends to be repaid in a few years, and the remaining investment, while under foreign control, is made by capital formed within Canada. It follows that the so-called returns to capital are unambiguously "rents" or "super-profits."

In principle, the government of the hinterland – federal and provincial in the case of Canada – can tax corporate profits, thereby appropriating a portion of the surplus. Notoriously, Canadian governments do not do this, a fact widely known after the 1972 federal election campaign, that being the only fact established in that campaign.

The extent of the surplus appropriated, or of the overall rip-off by the corporations, has been documented by Kierans for the metal-mining industry in his Manitoba report. In 1969, wages and salaries, which accrued mostly to Canadians, constituted 11 per cent of the value of resources, or the selling price of the output. Rents, or surplus – after deduction of all costs – constituted 30 per cent, a substantial portion thereof accruing to foreigners.

Profits in the metal mining industry, before taxes, were $3,165 million for 1965-70. Only $519 million were subject to corporate income taxes, that is, more than $2.5 billion escaped corporate taxes. For 1965-69, according to Kierans, the distribution of mining industry profits came down to this: "The return to the owners of the natural resources, the people, amounted to 14.7 per cent of net profit. The operators of the leases received the remaining 85.3 per cent of profits."

For the three major metal-producing firms in Manitoba – Inco, Sherritt Gordon and Hudson Bay Mining and Smelting, which together account for more than 95 per cent of production in Manitoba – the value of production in 1968-70 was $676.1 million, yielding book profits of $192 million or 28.4¢ for every dollar of sales. The Government of Manitoba received in taxes $15.6 million, or 2.3¢ per dollar of sales, and the Government of Canada received $15 million, or 2.2¢; this left 24¢ for the corporations, little of which remains in Manitoba and much of which does not remain in Canada.

The resources involved are, of course, non-renewable. Kierans warns: "If . . . surpluses are not retained, then the people become progressively poorer as their resources are depleted and the sometime assets are not replaced." (p. 5) The failure to retain the surplus is crippling in the long-run:

> Resource rich nations that continually yield up the value of their wealth in return for the labour employed in its exploitation will never be more than resource nations. They lose the opportunity to form their own capital, capital which will enable them to break out of that very reliance on their resource base and reduce their dependence on foreign investment. When a nation or province can generate capital out of its own resources and retain it, it will be less dependent on others. (p. 37)

It is by this line of reasoning that Kierans arrives at the case for public ownership. He himself insists: "It is not a question of capitalism or socialism. It is simply searching for the better way." But we are entitled to point out that it is no accident that socialism is the better way.

Another aspect of the relationship between resource exploitation and development or underdevelopment is that resources are, by their nature, inputs into goods-producing industries. A critical question, then, is where the further processing – down to full-blown manufacturing – takes place. Now the metropolis/hinterland relationship will clearly tend to work in such a way that the hinterland will export the staple in the most unprocessed form feasible, given transport costs. At the same time, so obvious is the move to further processing that hinterland governments tend to make some effort in that direction, though typically by bribing the resource exploiter, and in an exorbitant fashion. Hence, Inco,

Sherrit Gordon, and Hudson Bay Mining and Smelting have received two 21-year extensions of their original leases from the Manitoba Government in return for more smelting and refining activity.

But, without exception, conventional governments lack the vision to see the possibility of a quantum leap from a resource base to an industrial complex. The extent of Canada's failure is evident from the following statement by Pierre L. Bourgault in his study for the Science Council of Canada:

> We are the world's largest producer of nickel, but we are net importers of stainless steel and manufactured nickel products . . . ; we are the world's second largest producer of aluminum, but we import it in its more sophisticated forms such as . . . precision aluminum parts for use in aircraft; we are the world's largest exporter of pulp and paper, but we import much of our fine paper and virtually all of the highly sophisticated paper, such as backing for photographic film; we are one of the world's principal sources of platinum, but it is all exported for refining and processing and reimported in finished forms; we are large exporters of natural gas and petroleum, but we are net importers of petrochemicals; and although we are the world's foremost exporter of raw asbestos fibres, we are net importers of manufactured asbestos products.[10]

Orthodox economics speaks of "linkages" between activities, by which one thing leads to another. It is clear that the reality is "blockages" by which one thing leads to more of the same. We began more than three centuries ago as "hewers of wood and drawers of water. . . ." A decade ago, economic historians agreed that the pace and pattern of Canada's development was still fundamentally determined by foreign demand for its resource exports.[11] And in the very recent past, which may be the harbinger of things to come, we are becoming increasingly reliant on staple exports, with employment in manufacturing stable or falling; that is, we are being subjected to a process of de-industrialization from an already weak base. In the long run, as Bourgault warns us, if we keep on this path, "before the children of today could reach middle age most of the resources would be gone, leaving Canada with a resource-based economy and no resources." (p. 126)

At the root of our problem lies foreign ownership. In the resource industries, it means the export of staples in unprocessed form and the outward drain of surplus. In the manufacturing industries, it means a truncated, branch-plant structure with a high propensity to import parts and a demonstrated incapacity to export finished products, or even to hold the Canadian market without tariff protection. The combination is deadly. The government speaks one day of a "resources policy," the next day of an "industrial strategy." The proper antidote is a new national policy that combines both, and that would mean, particularly in the resource sector, a much smaller role for the multi-national corporation, down to its complete elimination, and a much expanded role for the public ownership and operation of resource firms.

The Historical Experience

It is no exaggeration to say that throughout our history foreign domination of resource industries have been the key to our dependency – and it is for that reason, as Jim Laxer has put it, that they are also the key to our liberation.[12] It has been our lot over the centuries, as we have moved from the French to the British to the American Empire, to serve as a resource supplier to more advanced and industrialized metropolitan areas.

Canadian history has been written in these terms by our best historians, and particularly by Innis:

> The economic history of Canada has been dominated by the discrepancy between the centre and the margin of western civilization. Energy has been directed toward the exploitation of staple products and the tendency has been cumulative. The raw materials supplied to the mother country stimulated manufacture of the finished product and also of the products which were in demand in the colony.... Energy in the colony was drawn into the production of the staple commodity both directly and indirectly. Population was involved directly in the production of the staple and indirectly in the production of facilities promoting production. Agriculture, industry, transportation, trade, finance, and governmental activities tend to become subordinate to the production of the staple for a more highly specialized manufacturing community.[13]

And again:

Concentration on the production of staples for export to more highly industrialized areas in Europe and later in the United States had broad implications for the Canadian economic, political and social structure. Each staple in its turn left its stamp, and the shift to new staples invariably produced periods of crises in which adjustments in the old structure were painfully made and a new pattern created in relation to a new staple.[14]

The history of Canada, then, is the history of its great staple trades: the fur trade, the cod fisheries, square timber and lumber, wheat, and the new staples of this century – pulp and paper, minerals, oil and gas. Let us try to draw some lessons from that historical experience.

The pattern of development and underdevelopment, of metropolis and hinterland, are evident in the early staples of fur and cod. The attraction of the New World for the Old World was its resources. Initial interest was in precious metals, and the plundering and looting of colonial people, particularly in Central and South America, was an important source of primitive accumulation for Europe. Promoters – also called explorers – were driven as well by the search for a passage to the Orient. Permanent settlement tended to be discouraged and even inhibited, taking place only if necessary to resource exploitation and then to be contained to that necessary for resource exploitation. Hence, in both the fisheries and the fur trade, settlement was actively discouraged. In the fisheries, English West Country fishermen discouraged settlement in Newfoundland, and Newfoundland was long denied responsible government in the hope of making it a less hospitable place to live year-round.

In the fur trade, the word "trade" is critical. The traders made contracts with the Indian who did the trapping, collecting and transporting; the white man penetrated the interior over time only by necessity, as the beaver was destroyed in the closer area, and under the exigencies of competition between English and French traders, and later between the Hudson's Bay Company and the Northwest Company. The fur trade companies consistently refused to establish viable settlements for fear of competition in the trade from interlopers, and New France was to receive a sufficient infusion of settlers to guarantee survival only because of the intervention of the French state in the 1660s.

The Hudson's Bay Company was a predecessor to the giant multi-national resource corporations of today. Its charter of 1670 gave the company "the sole trade and commerce of all these seas, straits, bays, rivers, lakes, creeks and sounds ... that lie within the entrance of the straits, commonly called Hudson Straits," and the Company's powers were further defined as "true and absolute lords and proprietors of the entire territory." Profits, or surpluses, were enormous. Fifty years after incorporation, the original investor of £100 would have received 343 per cent in dividends plus stock bonuses of £800. Kierans, after citing these facts in his Manitoba report, continues: "Despite the improvement in the fortunes of the shareholders, the existence of the inhabitants and trappers of the region remained marginal, precarious and at a subsistence level." (p. 4)

When the importance of the fur trade to empire declined, and the attractions of the Canadian West to outside capitalists shifted to opening it up to settlers, wheat growing and railways, the Bay Company's sovereignty was removed, that is, transferred at a handsome price to the new Government of Canada. The intent of the federal government was, in effect, to take over the mandate of the Company and to administer the West as a territory of the Dominion. The Métis under Riel were able to obtain provincial status for Manitoba, but, unlike the other provinces, Manitobans were not given control over their resources. This practice was extended with the granting of provincial status to Saskatchewan and Alberta in 1905, and the three western provinces were not given their proper rights until 1930. Under the guise of managing resources "for the purposes of the Dominion," the federal government alienated vast sections of land into the hands of the CPR, and gave the latter a monopoly which was broken only under intense pressure from the western farmer and with compensation paid to the CPR. It also worked out a "national policy" which drained surplus from western Canadian farmers to eastern capitalists, who in turn channelled much of it to British bondholders and American corporations. The late Vernon Fowke of the University of Saskatchewan, a student of Innis and the West's most important economic historian, was right to see the wheat grower as the successor to the Indian as "native" producer of the staple product, and as a hinterlander to be exploited.[15]

The legacy of the cod-fisheries for the Atlantic Provinces is their underdevelopment. Per capita incomes are 30 per cent below the average for Canada, unemployment runs about 50 per cent higher, and there is proportionately less manufacturing than in Canada as a whole. The obverse of the latter is that the Atlantic Provinces have a greater proportion of workers in primary industries; that is, resource industries are proportionately more important for the country as a whole, that being a characteristic feature of underdevelopment. Mining accounts for 13.4 per cent of net commodity production and forestry for 4.2 per cent. Nova Scotia produces almost 80 per cent of Canada's gypsum, but the bulk of this is shipped to the U.S. for processing into wall board and other items which are then sold back to Canadians. A study by Roy E. George, *A Leader and a Laggard: Manufacturing Industry in Nova Scotia, Quebec and Ontario* (1970) shows that transport costs are a problem, but not a primary cause of underemployment. It also shows that the absence or high cost of materials and fuels and inadequate supplies of hydro-electric power are not sufficiently significant to explain the lack of manufacturing development relative to central Canada.[16]

Vested interests in the metropolis notwithstanding, the fisheries led over time to permanent settlements, and to the development of shipbuilding and the carrying trade. Unlike New England, whose economy was similarly based, the Atlantic Provinces remained in the British Empire. In the short run, this meant the benefit of imperial trade preferences, notably for square timber from New Brunswick, and the general expansion of shipbuilding and the carrying trade. But as Britain moved to free trade and the removal of special status for its colonies, the Maritime Provinces discovered that, rather than being able to create their own industrial base, they simply became a hinterland of Central Canada within the new Confederation.

Tom Naylor has shown how Central Canadian banks took over the banking system of the Maritime Provinces – hence the anomaly of the head office of the Bank of Nova Scotia being in Toronto – and that local banking which tended to aid industrial development was replaced by external control and the draining of surplus out of the region. The tariff attracted American branch plants to Canada, but mostly to central Canada where it was easier to form capital. The tendency of capitalists' development to be uneven has been accentuated by the tendency of foreign-controlled capital in Canada to be even more mal-distributed regionally than Canadian-controlled capital. The geographer Michael Ray estimates that 45 per cent of American-controlled manufacturing employment is within 100 miles of Toronto, 64 per cent within 300 miles, and 83 per cent within 400 miles, and calculates that if American-controlled manufacturing employment had the same distribution as Canadian-controlled employment, there would be an approximately 20 per cent increase in employment for the Atlantic Provinces.[17]

The moral of the story is that the failure to establish indigenous control over resources, and to escape from the metropolis/hinterland bind, is crippling in the long run. The solution, as Archibald argues – much of the above is drawn from him – is regional public ownership in the context of national planning. As he says:

> Public ownership of the resource industries in the Atlantic provinces would not only ensure that a more reasonable price could be obtained for these raw materials which were to be exported, but also the retention of the economic surplus being produced by the workers in the region. This could then be put to use in developing the manufacturing industries . . .

Imperial preference created the basis for a square timber trade not only for New Brunswick but also for Quebec City, spreading ultimately up the Ottawa River. Over time, the British market for square timber was replaced by the American market for sawn lumber – the latter representing the first example of what has now become common, namely, America's depletion of its own resources, in spite of the abundance of its original endowment, and the search for supplies from the rest of the world, and particularly from Canada, given our proximity and our eagerness to be assaulted. The title of A. R. M. Lower's book, *The North American Assault on the Canadian Forest,* could be used to describe a wide range of cases, merely by substituting other words for "forest." The continentalism inherent in the lumber trade is evident in the impetus it gave to the Reciprocity Treaty of 1854, which first formally defined for Canada a special status within the American Empire, and in the tendency for American businessmen to migrate northward and establish themselves in the Canadian industry; by the late 19th century and thereafter, the migration has been by the multi-national corporation and the control has become perpetual.

Another striking feature of more general relevance was the

tendency of the industry to mine rather than to conserve. Hence, the great pine stands of Simcoe, Muskoka and Parry Sound are no more, and a once-prosperous area has regressed to subsistence farming and to tourism. In the Ottawa Valley, lumbering encouraged some local development in agriculture and commerce, but once the resource was depleted the population was stranded. This is to suggest that present talk about, for example, the jobs that will be created in the service sector around oil and gas development in the Arctic, should be taken with a large grain of salt; such activity has no viability independent of the resource base, and in that particular case the resource is clearly non-renewable.

There is a moral here of profound importance: that conservation matters, that once resources are mindlessly depleted all that is left are impoverished people and ghost towns. What will be left of Sudbury after its nickel is depleted, or of Calgary with its 400,-000-plus inhabitants after Alberta oil and gas is gone?

Meanwhile, back on the farm, the new menace is agribusiness. Much of the urban wealth of this country, that of Winnipeg in particular, was created by surpluses ripped-off the western wheat farmer. Yet, as Roy Atkinson of the National Farmers Union has observed, the farmers are now a dying tribe, with their quaint institutions, like the family farm, deserving of study by anthropologists. The consequences are profound. The farmer, though long exploited by the banks and the moneylenders, the railways, the grain speculators, the elevator companies and the eastern industrialists, was an independent owner; now he is being reduced to something like a mini sub-contractor of the multi-national corporation. It is not because he hasn't tried; in terms of productivity gains, agriculture has consistently outperformed manufacturing – where the corporation rules supreme. The spread of agribusiness – which, like our industry in general, will be predominantly under foreign control – promises to reduce our agriculture to the second-rate status of our manufacturing sector.

Nor is that all. Whatever the corporation touches, tends to deteriorate. The many cheese factories of Ontario once produced world-famous cheeses; now Kraft pushes them to the wall by colluding with the Ontario Milk Board to deny them milk, and itself produces a genuinely new product called "corporate cheese." As the corporation spreads its tentacles, it is becoming increasingly unsafe to eat food – which is no small matter – so perhaps it's all for the best that it's becoming too expensive to buy.

As for the western grain farmer, capable of growing surpluses to feed the hungry at home and in the Third World, his new role is to produce meat for the affluent of North America. There could be no more striking evidence that continentalism is indeed not internationalism.

The new staples of this century have a number of characteristic features:

> The export market is overwhelmingly in the U.S., which has meant increasing integration of the Canadian economy into a continental structure.
>
> The instrumentatility of resource exploitation is the multi-national corporation, and it is a highly efficient instrument for appropriating not only the resource, but also the economic surplus for the benefit of the metropolis, with benefits for Canadians being coincidental and haphazard.
>
> The production of the staple increasingly uses large amounts of capital, or machinery, and relatively little labour – and much of the machinery is imported. As a result, the effect on jobs of staple production has declined, with oil and gas, for example, having a decidedly lower labour-component than wheat and it is that component, and little else that constitutes the economic benefit for Canadians.

In effect, the new staples reinforce and accentuate tendencies inherent in staple production. Rather than the Canadian economy becoming more mature and diversified, we find instead that we are increasingly dependent on the U.S.; increasingly dominated by a handful of giant multi-national corporations; and increasingly saddled with an underdeveloped industrial structure.

Our historic role as a resource-exporter has clearly left us ill-prepared for the heightened competition that is characteristic of the new era of inter-imperialist rivalry into which the capitalist world has moved. Indeed, the possibility, that is increasingly becoming a reality, is that further resource exploitation for exports will bring into play mechanisms of de-industrialization that will reverse previous industrial gains painfully made.

De-Industrialization

That benefits for Canadians are small, or even negative, can be established by looking again at present and planned development

121

in the Mackenzie Valley Corridor and the Arctic. In our investigation we will identify four mechanisms of de-industrialization.

Exploring for oil and gas and bringing it to well-head creates few jobs directly. Building pipelines creates some jobs, but on a one-shot basis. If direct employment is small in general, it is even less for the native people and mainly in low-paying manual jobs. For instance, during the construction of the Pointed Mountain Pipeline, only 30 native people were employed for a maximum of three months, while 320 workers were brought in from the South. In 1970, after the federal government had invested $9 million in Panarctic, it had employed only 6 natives at $1.75 an hour.

The results of this are profound. While the majority of the population in the North West Territories is still native people, the pattern is quickly changing, particularly in the Mackenzie Delta where the biggest oil and gas play is taking place. Ten years ago, the town of Inuvik had 1,000 native inhabitants; today, there is a population of 3,000 and the majority is white. Furthermore, the whites live in modern, subsidized housing, the natives in slum conditions. What begins as an employment effect ends up creating a segregated town and racial discrimination. The losers just happen to be the original people, those who are, in lawyer Peter Cumming's moving phrase, "truly of the very land that they occupy." The multi-national corporation and the Canadian state have become invaders, creating a pattern of oppression that we like to imagine is found only in Third World colonies.

Tax revenues, which might potentially be used to encourage industrialization, will be slight. Oil and gas companies don't pay corporate income taxes, except in theory, and royalties have been set particularly low in the North West Territories – at between 5 per cent and 10 per cent, compared to 16.7 per cent in Alberta and 20-22 per cent in Alaska – to encourage exploration for high cost gas and oil.

The first potential de-industrialization effect arises with respect to the financing of the pipeline. The proposed gas pipeline will partly be financed inside Canada, and to that extent will attract capital away from manufacturing and limit potential jobs in that sector. It will partly be financed by importing capital, and to that extent, will drive up the value of the Canadian dollar on the foreign exchanges. That, in turn, increases the cost of exports, decreases the cost of imports, and by both routes destroys jobs.

To offset this latter effect, capital imports would have to be fully offset by importing pipe, etcetera. The pipeline consortium now appreciates this point and argues that this is what will be done. Of course, to the extent goods are imported, the favourable effects on employment while building the pipeline, which the consortium constantly cites, are reduced.

Now the ultimate *raison d'être* for all this development is the voracious U.S. appetite for oil and gas. The Mackenzie Valley gas pipeline is primarily intended to carry Prudhoe Bay gas, but Mackenzie Delta gas can be piggybacked. At least 95 per cent of the throughput will initially go to the U.S. This alienation of Canadian resources for the U.S. market cannot have any other long-run effect than to raise energy costs in Canada. The American industrial base is strengthened, while Canada's industrial potential is eroded. This is a second, and potent, de-industrialization effect; even the Davis Government in Ontario is worried, and they don't worry easily.

It is this harmful effect on Canadian industry, rising energy costs, that also underlies Ontario's concern about Alberta's intention to force up oil and gas prices. The point may seem obvious, but in fact it is a complicated problem that is indicative of the bind that hinterland countries get put in. The Social Credit government of Alberta did not exactly bargain with the oil companies with the shrewdness of an Arab sheik, and it may seem laudable for the new Conservative government to increase royalties. But the fact of the matter is that Alberta has signed, and remains bound to, royalty agreements that entitle its government to one-sixth of gross revenues. To get the additional $70 million revenue that the government now wants will therefore require price increases of $420 million in gross revenues. The remaining five-sixths of $350 million goes to the handful of giant companies which control the licenses for oil and gas in Alberta. Since Ontario imports significantly from Alberta, its oil and gas costs will go up significantly more than $70 million. That is, in order to re-distribute income from Ontario to Alberta – if that is thought desirable – a payoff has to be made to the oil companies. It is this latter effect, of course, that explains why the oil companies are not objecting to what Lougheed is doing. Nor is that even the end of the story, for Ontario's energy costs will rise significantly more than costs in the U.S. as a result of Alberta's move. While the U.S. will also pay more for Alberta gas, high-cost Alberta sources are rela-

123

tively less important to them; and the effect on the average cost of gas is therefore less.

The same phenomenon, with adverse effects on Canadian manufacturing, will tend to operate with respect to Mackenzie Delta gas once it goes on-stream. It is estimated that Delta gas, coming out of a pipeline in Chicago, will have cost $1.25 M.C.F. but that Chicago consumers will pay only 45¢ M.C.F. This may seem absurd, but in the crazy world of oil and gas economics almost anything is possible. This particular number works because small quantities of Delta gas will be mixed with large quantities of much cheaper gas, the whole mixture averaging out to less than 45¢ M.C.F. But just as Ontario is much more reliant on Alberta gas than the U.S., so it will be compelled to become much more reliant on Delta gas, precisely because so much Alberta gas has been alienated to the U.S. market. The Deutsch Report for the Ontario government comes down on the side that the Mackenzie Valley gas pipeline should be built, because Ontario will need the gas; it implies that increasing supply will moderate price increases in Ontario. But the actual effect will be precisely the opposite.

It is worth pointing out that the absurdity involved runs even deeper and it is not simply an Ontario problem. That gas which costs $1.25 M.C.F. should sell for 45¢ can be explained, but not justified. If consumers were made to pay the marginal cost rather than the average cost – a rule which appeals to economists and would make sense to a socialist planner – then not only would Delta gas remain in the ground for some time, but gas prices would rise in the U.S. This would encourage increases in domestic supply and decreases in demand through less wasteful use, and the world would be better off.

There is another de-industrialization effect that grows out of the export of Canadian oil and gas to the U.S. The oil and gas embodies little Canadian labour, but its importation by the United States encourages Americans, given their serious trade problems, to insist that Canada buy back manufactured goods which embody relatively more labour. The result is the destruction of jobs in Canada. This third de-industrialization mechanism may be very much in evidence in Canada in the balance of this decade.

Finally, as the first Innis quote implies, resource development in this country tends to become a mania, absorbing energies in a cumulative fashion and reducing our capacity to consider alternatives. In the contemporary context, that means never getting around to working out an industrial strategy. It also means not achieving our potential for industrial growth, for more jobs and more diversified employment opportunities. Instead we have the Donald Macdonalds who think that the only way to create jobs is to give free rein to the multi-national corporations – indeed, to bribe them, the better to rape us. This fourth de-industrialization effect, this imposition of blinders, is ultimately the most powerful of all.

The essence of the relationship between resource exploitation and the combined forces of development and underdeveloped can perhaps be put most starkly by considering the case of Sudbury and nickel. Nickel is a classic example of the new staple – mostly exported to the U.S., and capital-intensive from the outset and increasingly so over time.

Over the past ninety years, the wealth of minerals taken out of Sudbury is unquestionably enormous, but little has remained in Sudbury. Now surpluses drained from Sudbury enable Inco to develop new and distant mines that will be to Sudbury's disadvantage.

It is true that the employees in the mines and mills are the highest paid of any in North America – a tribute not to Inco and Falconbridge, but to the historic militancy of the unions – but labour turnover is high, and living conditions for migrant workers oppressive.

Nevertheless, if we count that as development, then take note that with a population of 100,000 there are at the most 1,000 jobs in manufacturing in Sudbury – and count that as underdevelopment. Sudbury is located on the trans-continental rail line – the nickel was discovered while building the CPR – and is now on the Trans Canada gas pipeline, and it has good access to water and to hydro-electric power. Yet even the refining of nickel is in Port Colbourne, not Sudbury. Incidentally, it was only moved there from New Jersey by fiat of the Canadian Government during World War I to block Inco selling to the Germans.

It is unnecessary to dwell on the environment of Sudbury, although it is perhaps not widely known that U.S. astronauts have been trained on this company-created moonscape. After the nickel runs out, will anything be left but the monumental scarring?

. The political implications of this analysis, for political action and for a political program, should be evident by this point. The case for public ownership of the resource industries, and particularly of the energy resource industries, is overwhelming. It is important, however, that what results is socialism and not expanded state capitalism: that ownership be regional, planning national, and decision-making communal.

With respect to the array of big resource developments in oil and gas and hydro-electric power, the case is similarly overwhelming for moratoria – until, in each case, there is adequate environmental protection, a full respecting of the legal and moral claims of the native peoples, and a demonstrable need for the resources within Canada.

Notes

[1] James Laxer, "The Energy Crisis: Turning up for the Sell-out," *Last Post,* March 1973, p. 19.

[2] Eric Kierans, *Report on Natural Resources Policy in Manitoba,* Government of Manitoba, February 1973, pp. 11, 17.

[3] Science Council of Canada, *Natural Resource Policy Issues in Canada,* January 1973, p. 46.

[4] Douglass H. Pimlott, Speech at a symposium in St. Catharines, Ontario, March 17, 1973, sponsored by the St. Catharines and District Labour Council.

[5] Douglas H. Pimlott, "People and the North: Motivations, Objectives and Approach of the Canadian Arctic Resources Committee" in Douglas H. Pimlott, Kitson M. Vincent and Christine E. McKnight, *Arctic Alternatives* (Ottawa, 1973).

[6] Cited in James Laxer, "The Energy Crisis: Tuning up for the Sell-out," p. 20.

[7] John J. Deutsch, *Advisory Committee On Energy,* (Toronto, 1972).

[8] Andre Gunder Frank, *Capitalism and Underdevelopment in Latin America* (New York, 1969).

[9] Bruce Archibald, "Atlantic Regional Under-development and Socialism" in Laurier La Pierre *et al.,* eds., *Essays on the Left* (Toronto, 1971).

[10] Pierre L. Bourgault, *Innovation and the Structure of Canadian Industry,* Science Council of Canada, Special Study No. 23, October 1972, p. 51.

[11] Melville H. Watkins, "A Staple Theory of Economic Growth," *Canadian Journal of Economics and Political Science,* May 1963.

[12] James Laxer, "Canada's resources: the piecemeal surrender," *Last Post,* October 1971, p. 13.

H. A. Innis, *The Fur Trade in Canada* (Toronto, 1962), p. 385.

[14] H. A. Innis, *Empire and Communications* (London, 1950), pp. 4-5.

[15] Vernon C. Fowke, *The National Policy and the Wheat Economy* (Toronto, 1957). p. 93.

[16] Roy E. George, *A Leader and a Laggard: Manufacturing Industry in Nova Scotis, Quebec and Ontario* (Toronto, 1970).

[17] D. Michael Ray, "The Spatial Structure of Regional Development and Cultural Differences: A Factorial Ecology of Canada, 1961," Paper presented at the Annual Regional Sciences Association Meeting, November 8, 1968.

Canadian Manufacturing and U.S. Trade Policy
Jim Laxer

Instead of developing its own domestic manufacturing, Canadian capitalism has invited foreign corporations, particularly American, to enter Canada to establish branch plant firms. This phenomenon has been developing since the time of the National Policy in the late 19th century. Branch plant corporations now dominate manufacturing in most of the key sectors, ·such as transportation equipment, electrical products, machinery, chemicals, rubber and plastics and petroleum products.

Since World War II foreign corporations in resource extraction and in manufacturing have become so dominant in Canada that they have replaced Canada's native trading and banking bourgeoisie as the predominant force in the Canadian state. Foreign corporations manage the Canadian economy and state in their interest, and distort and confine Canadian development within a framework that is most profitable to them.

Branch plant manufacturing in Canada developed behind the wall of the Canadian tariff. It was established to exploit the Candian domestic market. Prior to World War II, it was a means by which American corporations could get behind the tariff wall of the British empire. Canadian capitalists, specialists in profiting through enlarging the volume of trade rather than through producing themselves, were the architects of this sub-imperial strategy, which featured Canada as the place in the British empire where the Americans did their manufacturing.

As long as the British empire remained a significant economic entity in the world, the sub-imperial strategy had meaning. But the growing disparity in power between the United States and Britain between the World Wars, and then finally in the post-1945 period, spelled the end of this strategy. During the 1920s and 30s

127

Canadian trade shifted significantly away from the classical east-west axis of the wheat economy and the national policy. As British and European markets for Canadian foodstuffs declined, American markets opened up for Canadian mineral resources. American direct investment entered Canada on the heels of retreating British portfolio investment. Following 1920, Canada was becoming an increasingly important source of raw materials for the United States, at the same time as American firms were expanding their Canadian operations in the production of industrial goods, in the new growth industries such as automobiles, electrical products and chemicals.

This rise of American branch-plant manufacturing in Canada has established the key institutional form within which the bulk of commodity production takes place in Canada. Since World War II, Canadian manufacturing has lost its role in supplying American goods to Commonwealth countries. Instead, Canadian manufacturing is now locked into an overwhelmingly American orbit; its primary purpose is simply to hold the Canadian domestic market for American goods. The branch-plant manufacturing sector has not been designed since World War II to enter export markets. The decline of the earlier sub-imperial strategy of Canadian capitalists is reflected in the almost exclusive reliance of Canada on trade links with the U.S. since World War II. At the same time as the United States has been declining relative to other capitalist countries over the past two decades, Canadian trade has been centred even more on the United States. Between 1950 and 1970 the proportion of Canadian exports destined for the American market has increased from 60 per cent to 68 per cent, while during the same period the proportion of Canadian imports from the United States has increased from 67 per cent to 71 per cent.[1]

The twin features of Canadian government policy after World War II were encouragement of resource development in Canada and an open door for the continued build-up of branch plants of U.S. corporations in Canada.

As Canada has moved more completely into the American economic orbit, the nature of the American impact on the manufacturing sector of the economy has altered. Since World War II Canada's manufacturing industries can increasingly be characterized as warehouse assembly operations which rely on imports of technology, machinery and parts and components. Moreover, as

U.S. investment in Canada has more and more derived from the reinvestment of profits made in Canada and from loans on the Canadian money market, the net flow of interest and dividends out of Canada has surpassed the inflow of new foreign investment.

Approximately half of Canada's manufacturing is located in Ontario, including the bulk of heavy manufacturing, one-third is located in Quebec and the rest in the west and the Maritimes.[2]

A striking feature of Canadian manufacturing is the relatively small percentage of the country's work force it employs. In 1965, only 24.5 per cent of the paid non-agricultural work force in Canada was employed in manufacturing. By 1971, the percentage had dropped to 21.3 per cent.[3]

Among western countries, only Greece and Ireland have a lower percentage of their work force employed in manufacturing. For the United States the comparable figures are these: in 1965, 29.7 per cent of the paid non-agricultural work force was employed in manufacturing; in 1971 the figure was 26.3 per cent.[4] The disparity in proportions of the work force employed in manufacturing in Canada and the United States is not, of course, accounted for through greater Canadian productivity. In 1970 while Canadian manufacturing activity accounted for 20 billion dollars in value added, U.S. manufacturing activity accounted for 300 billion dollars in value added – a ratio of 3 to 2 in terms of the size of the two economies.[5]

The qualitative make-up of the manufacturing sectors in the two countries differ as fundamentally as these broad quantitative differences. While durable goods production involves the employment of less than half the manufacturing workers in Canada, it involves the employment of 60 per cent of manufacturing workers in the U.S.[6] It is revealing to examine manufacturing sector by sector in comparing Canada with the U.S. Canada has relatively greater manufacturing employment than the U.S. in only three categories: food and beverages, tobacco products and wood products. In all other categories there is relatively greater U.S. employment. This is particularly the case in high technology industries such as machinery, electrical products, chemicals and scientific and professional equipment. Extremely significant in understanding the nature of American dominance of Canada in manufacturing is the production of machinery. Production in this sphere, of course, makes possible industrial production in all other categories. In

1971, there were 72,800 workers employed in this field in Canada and the value added in the industry was just over 700 million dollars. In the U.S. there were 1,791,000 workers employed in this category and value added totalled over 31.5 billion dollars. In other words, while U.S. relative employment in this field was two-and-a-half to one compared to Canada, the value of U.S. relative output was four-and-a-half to one compared to Canada.[7] In 1970, Canada imported 1,783,268,000 dollars worth of machinery, more than the total value of machinery produced in Canada, and of this amount 1,421,809,000 was imported from the United States.[8]

In 1970 in the field of production of electrical products, while the ratio of American relative employment was about one-and-a-half to one compared to Canada the relative ratio of value of output was over two to one. In the production of chemicals the ratios were about the same. In the production of scientific and professional equipment, the relative ratio of Americans to Canadians employed is three to one.[9]

In general, United States manufacturing is markedly superior to Canadian manufacturing in quantitative and, more significantly, in qualitative terms. Canadian manufacturing tends to be characterized by a relatively high level of capital investment and by a relatively low level of proportional employment. That the shape of Canadian manufacturing is a direct result of its branch-plant character is further amplified by examining both the nature of Canadian trade and the effect on Canadian industry of reliance on the importation of foreign technology.

Canada has been a net importer of most types of manufactured goods and has been paying for these with net exports in pulp and paper, minerals, primary metals, lumber, wheat and whiskey.[10] In 1970, Canada imported over eight-and-a-half billion dollars worth of manufactured goods from abroad and exported six billion dollars worth of manufactured goods.[11]

Canadians are by far the world's leading importers of manufactured goods, amounting to $463 per capita per year in 1969 compared with $239 per capita per year in the European common market, $116 per capita per year in the United States and $31 per capita per year in Japan.[12] While imports of manufactured goods in 1970 amounted to nearly 20 per cent of the final value of the manufactured goods produced in Canada, in the United States imports of manufactured goods amounted to only 4 per cent of the final value of the manufactured goods produced in the United States. It is significant that the four per cent figure was regarded in the United States as so high that it merited measures to protect American manufacturing. Many Canadians were still wondering whether any problem existed in the field of manufacturing with nearly five times the invasion of the domestic market with foreign-manufactured goods.

In major high-technology industries that have been growing rapidly in the industrialized countries over the past ten years, Canada has been left behind, and has been running up increasing trade deficits. This is true of the plastics industry, pharmaceutical products, scientific instruments and electronic computers. It is highly significant that in science-intensive manufacturing, based on minerals in which Canada is a world leader at the level of raw extraction, the country is often a net importer of the finished product. Canada is the world's largest producer of nickel, but a net importer of stainless steel and manufactured nickel products; as the world's second largest producer of aluminum, Canada nonetheless imports it in its more sophisticated forms. As the world's largest exporter of pulp and paper, the country imports much of its fine paper. Canadians are net importers of petrochemicals in spite of their large exports of natural gas and oil. Canada is a net importer of manufactured asbestos products.[13]

It is ironic to note the way government agencies attempt to explain the continued reliance of Canada on resource exports. In the chapter on Mines and Minerals of the *Canada Year Book, 1972,* the Mineral Resources Branch of the Department of Energy, Mines and Resources proudly reports that while the manufacturing sector of the economy has been in serious trouble in recent years, Canadian mineral production was experiencing an 11 per cent annual growth rate. The report notes that in spite of the enormous increase in Canadian exports of end products due to the Canada-U.S. auto pact, exports of raw materials have maintained their high percentage of total Canadian exports over the past decade. The chapter states:

The great size of Canada's mineral industry is based largely upon export sales. Apparent domestic minerals consumption is equivalent to proportions of mineral output ranging from 6 per cent for potash and nickel to about 20 per cent for iron ore and about 43 per cent for copper. The value of minerals and fabricated minerals exported in 1970 was 90 per cent of mineral production value.

Exports of minerals and fabricated mineral products have led several great and sustained booms in the Canadian economy in the past and they have been a major factor in the surge in recent Canadian export trade.[14]

In spite of statements by people like Donald Macdonald, Canada's minister of energy, mines and resources, that the country's future depends on further resource development, it is becoming apparent that resource development as an alternative to manufacturing is a strategy involving seriously diminishing returns. A recent background study for the Science Council of Canada included the following statement on the growing problem of expanding mineral output in Canada:

> While mineral reserves . . . have noticeably increased in recent years as a result of accelerated exploration activities, the growth in reserves has not been proportionate to increases in production. Indeed the relationship of reserves to annual production in 1967 was less for several minerals than it was in the mid-1950s. . . . Exploration expenditures of up to $1 billion a year by 1985 (in '68 dollars) will be necessary to sustain a 4.5 per cent growth in this industry.[15]

The study points to potential reserve problems in nickel, copper and natural gas. It concludes that the life index for many of Canada's minerals is not as favourable as are those of certain other countries. It warns that exploitation at a too-rapid rate would move Canada up the cost curve ahead of other countries, and would make Canada a high material cost country.[16]

The Science Council study points to the link between branch plant manufacturing in Canada and the low level of technological innovation in the Canadian economy. In spite of spending relatively high amounts per capita on education, Canada is near the bottom among developed countries in technological innovation. One reason for this is the fact that where end-product manufacturers are foreign-owned, they normally import technology wholly conceived from the parent company. This means that parts and components for end product manufacturers are usually designed according to specifications also developed by the parent company. Companies engaged in end-product manufacturing and companies which produce parts and components often establish interconnected research communities which operate in the field of product innovation. This process cannot develop in a branch plant economy where would-be local suppliers have to compete with foreign firms with several years lead time in producing parts and components for new end-products.[17]

In the 1960s, the federal government attempted to promote research and development in Canadian industry through generous tax incentives. Many corporations established research and development components, which they promptly shut down at the end of the Sixties when the government ended the tax incentives.[18] The government theory that the companies would get into the habit of innovating once they set up R and D units was disproven by experience.

The stagnation of innovative activity in high technology industries in Canada is revealed by the fact that between 1969 and 1971, of the 25,000 scientists and engineers graduated in Canada, only 2,000 got jobs in manufacturing. In the early sixties, half the graduates in these fields were hired by manufacturing firms.[19]

The tendency for foreign-owned manufacturing to become warehouse-assembly operations is increasing Canada's dependency on foreign technology and also on foreign manufacturing for many of the stages that go into the production of goods finished in Canada. This phenomenon shows up drastically in certain industries. For example, the production of office and store machinery, is a Canadian industry in which only 25 per cent of the employees are involved in production. Of $297 million value added in the industry in 1969, only $84 million came from manufacturing activities. The rest came from sales and service.[20] Obviously these branch plant operations do little more than finish American manufacturing in Canada. It is not surprising that the industry then lobbies the federal government to reduce tariffs in this field so that parts and components can be imported more cheaply. Far from advocating protection from foreign competition as independent manufacturers in developed countries often do, these so-called manufacturers behave like importers who are working to open up the country to further manufacturing imports.

A further effect of the branch-plant nature of Canadian manu-facturing is to be found in the existence in Canada of a large number of competing foreign firms in many lines of production in Canada. The fact that many large U.S. companies locate in Canada means that each of them tends to be inefficient in not having a large enough market to achieve maximal efficiency. Thus the Canadian market, already small in comparison to that of the U.S., is fragmented by foreign ownership.

It is often thought that because Canada's market is slightly less than 10 per cent of the U.S. market, that Canada is doomed to inefficiency in manufacturing and poor performance in high technology industries. But it makes much more sense to compare Canada's performance with that of the second tier of capitalist countries. The U.S. market is five times as big as that of the second largest capitalist market, West Germany. The West German market is two-and-a-half times as big as Canada's. In the range between West Germany and Canada fall the following countries: Japan, France, Britain and Italy. For the European countries mentioned which are in the European Common Market, their own domestic markets rather than the markets of all Europe remain overwhelmingly important for the sale of high-technology manufactured goods.[21]

Canada's performance in most high-technology manufacturing in comparision to these second-tier capitalist countries is poor indeed. The only conclusion one can draw is that this stems not from the size of the Canadian market but from the dependent character of Canadian capitalism.

The uniquely high level of Canadian per capita manufacturing imports, of course, cuts down the manufacturing sector of the Canadian economy and the number of jobs in it. If Canada reduced its level of imports of manufactured goods to the U.S. per capita level, a new domestic manufacturing market of over 7 billion dollars a year would be created. Supplying that market with domestically-produced goods would substantially reduce Canadian unemployment.

Having looked at the general characteristics of Canada's branch plant manufacturing sector, let us now examine the specific case of the automobile industry in Canada and this country's experience with the Canada-U.S. auto pact.

In 1965 the Canada-U.S. Auto Pact was started as a means of

rationalizing the North American automobile industry. It sought ultimate free trade in assembled autos and in auto parts. One continental auto market, serviced by giant American producers, was the vision. It meant that Canadian auto plants would not be geared to producing for the Canadian market. Instead they would produce for segments of the entire North American market. The pact was rightly condemned by many Canadians as a step toward a fully-integrated economy.

Had the Auto Pact not emerged, Canada would have been forced to take protective steps to guarantee the reservation of Canada's market for the sale of cars produced in this country. Considering that Canada's auto industry is almost entirely foreign-owned, there would have been long term pressure in favor of producing a Canadian car, either with government assistance or public ownership. The Auto Pact had the effect of preventing pressure to follow the Swedes and other Europeans, who have produced their own cars.

The condition of the Canadian auto industry in 1964 is striking proof, for those who need it, that foreign ownership does not bring efficiency and competitiveness. After all, the Canadian auto industry was 100 per cent foreign owned, and yet it was so uncompetitive that it couldn't maintain control of its own domestic market, let alone export its products.

The Auto Pact contained the following safeguards for Canadian auto production:

(1) The provision of a base level of production in Canada below which Canadian production could not go. This level was calculated in terms of 1964 as the base year. It provided that production could not fall below the dollar value of autos and auto parts produced in Canada in 1964. Nor could it fall below the ratio of production in the auto industry to the sale of North American cars sold in Canada in 1964. In that year Canada's share of North American automotive production and sales was roughly 5.3 per cent and 9.1 per cent, respectively. Whichever figure was higher from these two methods of determining the Canadian production floor would be the one to apply.

(2) An undertaking that, as the sales of North American cars in Canada increased, so too would auto production in Canada. Increases in sales of cars were to be matched by at least an

amount of production equivalent to 60 per cent of that increase. For commercial vehicles the increase was to be at least 50 per cent.

(3) A third safeguard came in the form of an agreement not between the two governments but between Canada and the four U.S. auto corporations. The U.S. auto firms, in letters of commitment, agreed to increase Canadian production over and above the pact's safeguards by the following additional amounts by the end of 1968: General Motors $121 million, Ford $74.2 million, Chrysler $33 million and American Motors $11.2 million. The commitment of the auto producers was achieved by the end of 1968, after which it expired.[22]

Many with short memories might imagine that the growth of the Canadian auto industry since the signing of the auto pact has been the most dramatic chapter in the history of the industry in this country. But far from being a recent industry just getting off the ground here, Canada has been firmly established in the auto industry from the first decade in this century.

The auto industry is perhaps the best example of an industry where Canadian businessmen who were in at the start failed to maintain control of their firms. Canada's best known auto magnate was R. S. McLaughlin of Oshawa, Ontario. In 1907 he signed a contract with the Buick Motor Company of Flint, Michigan for the importation of Buick engines to his Oshawa plant, where they were installed in McLaughlin's assembled cars. In 1915, McLaughlin organized the Chevrolet Motor Company of Canada to produce Chevrolets under agreement with American Chevrolet.

During these years McLaughlin owned these two firms in Canada and made use of U.S. technology by contracts with U.S. firms. His weakness as an independent capitalist was his dependence on the higher level of U.S. technology and mass production techniques in the production of engines. In 1918 the McLaughlin enterprises met a familiar fate. The two companies were sold to General Motors and were reorganized as General Motors of Canada.[23]

The Canadian auto industry had now moved into phase two of its history. The American industry now owned the Canadian firms. The Canadian tariff forced them to manufacture in Canada if they wanted this country's market. They were further enticed to do so because their plants in Canada were located not only behind the Canadian tariff wall but also that of the British empire. Autos produced here could be sold directly in other British empire countries.

The decade of the 1920s was one of rapid growth in auto production in Canada. By 1929 the industry produced 263,000 vehicles of which 102,000 were exported.[24] A nation of under ten million people outproduced all the great nations of Europe including the United Kingdom, France and Germany. In world terms, 1929 was the high point of the Canadian car industry.

During the depression of the 1930s and the war years, Canadian auto production was cut back sharply (although Canada's production of war vehicles was mammoth during the Second World War). By the time the industry found itself in a situation of "normalcy" again in the late 1940s, it faced competition from the exporting nations of western Europe. Auto production in Canada slowly grew to a high of 481,000 vehicles in 1953 and then slumped by 1960 to 396,000 vehicles. In that same year Canada imported 180,000 cars, mainly from the u.k. and Europe, while its exports were a mere 20,000.[25]

In a period of three decades the Canadian auto industry had plummeted in world terms, compared to countries like Germany which produced 2 million cars in 1960. Furthermore, since 1929 the Canadian industry had experienced a clear decline in the number of jobs it provided relative to the growth of the work force.

By the beginning of the 1960s, it was clear to all that the Canadian auto industry was in grave trouble. In response to this situation, the federal government established the Royal Commission on the Automotive Industry under economist Vincent Bladen to investigate.

Looked at from the perspective of the early sixties, the issue was whether Canada's auto industry would be integrated into the American industry or whether it would be rationalized to produce for the Canadian market. While the Bladen Commission came down in favor of an approach never implemented, which attempted to avoid this choice, some of the briefs to the Commission did advocate one or the other alternative. Some of these briefs are of interest today.

Naturally, the U.S. auto manufacturers favoured increased integration of the Canadian with the American auto industry. And, not surprisingly, the Canadian parts producers, generally small firms, many of them Canadian-owned, opposed integration and advocated greater protection for themselves.

The United Auto Workers were clearly split internally on the issue. The Canadian district of the U.A.W. with its brief endorsed by the Canadian Labor Congress, favored integration. The U.A.W. brief stated:

> In essence, we suggest that the Commission examine the feasibility of an international agreement which would permit free trade in the products of any motor vehicle manufacturing company provided that the company produced in Canada or had produced for it in Canada, a quantity of motor vehicles and parts, sufficient to assure maintenance of current levels of employment at current production volume and future increases in employment parallel with the growth of the company's Canadian market.[26]

This approach was precisely the kind adopted by the Auto Pact a few years later, a fact which led the U.A.W. to claim credit for the pact once it had been achieved.

Local 444 of the U.A.W. (Chrysler, Windsor) and the General Motors council of the U.A.W., however, did not agree with the national office or the CLC. They struck out against a continentalist approach, advocating instead an immediate increase in Canadian content in cars produced in Canada as a "step in the direction of an All-Canadian car."[27]

The condition of the auto industry in the early 1960s was so desperate that the choice between a continental or a Canadian auto industry had to be made quickly. Canadians in those years were watching the growth of a vast balance of payments deficit with the U.S. in auto trade. In 1965 the United States enjoyed a $768 million surplus in its auto trade with Canada.[28]

In 1965 the Pearson government opted for continental integration with the United States in the car industry when it signed the Auto Pact.

Under the Auto Pact the Canadian industry was rationalized to produce fewer lines of cars for the entire North American market. With this rationalization, there has been a marked increase in productivity in the Canadian industry and transfer of management functions from Canada to the United States. Since the commencement of the pact, Canada has increased its share of North American auto production. In 1970 and 1971, for the first time, Canada had a small surplus in its auto trade with the U.S., although even in these two years there was a Canadian deficit counting the sending of profits to the U.S. from their subsidiaries in this country.[29]

Growth in the industry in Canada tended to be concentrated in the first years of the agreement. By the end of 1968 vehicle-producers in Canada had over-fulfilled their commitments by $396 million.[30]

The present extent of integration can be learned from the following figures: by 1968 imports of autos from the U.S. supplied more than 40 per cent of the Canadian market compared with three per cent in 1964; about 60 per cent of vehicles produced in Canada in 1968 were exported compared with seven per cent in 1964. One-third of all trade between Canada and the U.S. now takes place in the field of assembled autos and auto parts.[31]

The early benefits of the Auto Pact for Canada appeared to confound the critics. The industry had grown and had become more productive. It was a shining success story for the Liberal Party.

But what was not immediately clear was that the pact meant long-term Canadian vulnerability in its auto industry and an increasing incapacity of the Canadian government to affect the growth rates of the Canadian industry.

By the end of 1968 the special agreement between Canada and the auto producers for heightened growth targets had lapsed. One safeguard was already out of the way. Since then pressure has been mounting steadily for the removal of the formal safeguards in the pact.

In the fall of 1970, the Ways and Means Committee of the House of Representatives recommended that President Nixon terminate the auto pact unless progress was made toward eliminating the protective clauses for Canada. In a report to Congress on the subject in the fall of 1970, Nixon heightened the pressure for removal of the protective clauses. He said:

> The continued existence of the transitional measures . . . represents an unnecessary burden on the automotive industry

and is an obstacle to full realization of the agreement objectives.[32]

Canada's External Affairs Minister, Mitchell Sharp, helpfully admitted at the same time that "eventually" cars produced in Canada and the United States would have completely unrestricted access to the entire North American market. He showed how well he could fit into the American agenda when he suggested that if the U.S. opened up the oil market for Canada in the United States, we would consider scrapping the protective clauses in the Auto Pact.

The removal of the safeguards would allow American auto producers completely free access to the Canadian market, no matter what the level of their production here. It means they could shift production out of this country, and even more important, locate future growth in the industry on the American side of the border. Without the safeguards there is no guaranteed future for the industry in Canada.

Convinced free traders will, of course, reply "So what? Now that our auto industry has become more productive, why shouldn't the auto producers locate future growth here, as much as in the U.S.?"

Even the continentalist Liberal government knows the answer to that question. In the fall of 1970, in talks with the U.S. the Canadian government insisted that it must obtain a new five-year production level commitment from the auto industry. Its reason was simple: "free market" forces simply do not exist in the auto industry. A monopoly American-owned industry, closely integrated with the American government, will be influenced by many factors that have nothing to do with whether a Canadian plant could theoretically produce as efficiently as an American plant.

The removal of the safeguards means the placing of a ceiling on the growth of the Canadian auto industry. It means total U.S. access to our market and control of our production, with future growth concentrated in the U.S. Such a development will contribute to Canadian unemployment and to a return to a steep deficit in our auto trade with the U.S.

Even without the removal of the safeguards a dramatic shift in Canada – U.S. auto trade has begun to occur. In 1972 Canada returned to a deficit in its auto trade with the U.S.; when the deficit involved in the importation of automobiles from overseas, is added, the Canadian deficit was approximately $500 million, now two-thirds as high as the deficit in 1964. It was the latter figure which convinced the Canadian government that the auto pact was necessary.[33]

Nixon's economic policies since August 1971 have already begun to affect Canada's position in the auto industry, the key industry in southern Ontario. The Nixon administration's current assault on Canada's share of North American auto production must be understood in the broader context of the U.S. agenda for the Canadian economy. Of critical importance is the fact that the historic "special relationship" between Canada and the U.S. which allowed Canada to be a relatively industrialized hinterland between 1945 and 1971 came to an end with Nixon's new economic policies launched on August 15, 1971.

On August 15, the Nixon administration formally responded to what had been apparent for some time: the end of U.S. domination of the world capitalist economy. Japanese and western European invasion of U.S. markets and the weakness of the American dollar forced Nixon to move away from the system of an "internationalism" within the capitalist world dominated by the U.S. and toward a system of threatened protectionism and regional division of the capitalist world into economic blocs. Since August 15 we have been living through the heightening monetary crisis, with its two U.S. dollar devaluations. We have seen the end of the gold standard in the United States and the temporary 10 per cent surcharge on imports into the United States. In addition to these measures, Nixon has been attempting to improve the relative position of U.S. business by increasing the exploitation of American working people through wage control policies. In order to strengthen the position of U.S. manufacturing in world competition, the U.S. has enacted the seven per cent investment tax credit, involving tax cuts for U.S. businesses that increase capital investment, and the Domestic International Sales Corporation or DISC, which allows U.S. companies exporting goods to write-off 50 per cent of the taxes on their foreign sales. DISC has been designed to encourage multi-national corporations to shift their production from branch plants abroad back to the United States.

During the current crisis, the position the Nixon government has taken has been that the problem stems from what he calls the unfair trading practices of other nations. This is a euphemism for

141

saying that America's competitive position has worsened. American industry has been losing its lead in productivity in a whole range of industries due to too-low a rate of capital investment. In part, the U.S. has allowed its industry to deteriorate relative to that of other countries because of the flow of American investment abroad. In addition to these factors, the high cost the U.S. has assumed as gendarme of world capitalism has placed enormous burdens on the U.S. economy through defence spending that is proportionately much higher than that in other developed capitalist countries.

Although Nixon claims to prefer a move toward free trade among all countries, he has made it clear that if the supposed unfair trading practices of other nations do not end, he will move even more toward protectionism. Early in 1973 he placed a bill before the U.S. Congress which would allow him wide discretion to raise and lower U.S. tariff schedules in negotiations with other countries as a means of giving him extra muscle at the bargaining table.

Within the United States three clearly discernible blocs can be distinguished in the debate on how far protectionism should go. Clearly the U.S. financial community on Wall Street wants to maintain an open door policy among capitalist nations so that the increasingly high flow of profits back to the U.S. from foreign operations will not be threatened. At the other end of the spectrum is the leadership of the American labour movement. The AFL-CIO leadership has been pushing the Burke-Hartke bill in the U.S. Congress which would replace tariffs with quotas to limit the amount of industrial imports into the U.S.

The Nixon administration has been pursuing a policy that can be described as one of moderate protectionism, involving both a determination to end America's trade deficit and an emphasis on the importance of the operations of U.S. multi-national corporations abroad to the health of the American economy.

In response to the charge from the AFL-CIO that the creation of branch plants abroad by U.S. companies has meant job losses for U.S. workers, the Nixon administration has produced studies which show how the operation of U.S. firms abroad acts to de-industrialize countries like Canada and to maximize production for American industry at home. One study showed that there are between 250,000 and 500,000 high paying jobs in the U.S.

involved in servicing the foreign activities of U.S. corporations. These jobs would not exist if the corporations had not moved abroad. An example from one study reported in Fortune magazine showed how the operations of a U.S. firm abroad actually reduced the number of jobs abroad rather than increasing it. The article states:

> When Kimberly-Clark built a $23 million paper mill in Huntsville, Ontario, to serve the Canadian market, it purchased enough equipment in the U.S. to supply 51 man years of employment. Had Kimberly-Clark not built the mill, a Canadian competitor would have captured the market and bought less equipment in the U.S. (resulting in only 16 man-years of employment). As for the balance of payments, the investment resulted in no net outflow of capital, and as soon as Kimberly-Clark pays off a Canadian bank loan, the subsidiary expects to pay $2.8 million a year in dividends to the parent company in the U.S.[34]

An article in the Wall Street Journal which draws on the thought of former U.S. Secretary of the Treasury, John Connally, summarizes the mood of the Nixon administration:

> "There will have to be less competition among American businesses so that there can be more competition against foreign businesses; Washington must become less of an antagonist for U.S. industry and much more of a cooperative partner."

> To achieve these ends, might require many profound and politically explosive changes. These changes include:

> Turning anti-trust policy inside out so that in many cases the government would encourage mergers instead of discourage them. More long-range government planning for the economy. Much more federal assistance to key industries – along with much more influence over them. Diverting many young people away from the universities and into vocational training. Convincing – or compelling – unions to abandon lengthy strikes.

> Impelling the administration to contemplate such initiatives is the same nightmarish fear that led it to devalue the dollar – the fear that the U.S. has lost its competitive edge to nations, such as Japan and Germany. Unless the U.S. recoups rap-

idly, the consequences will be inability to meet military and diplomatic obligations abroad and a deteriorating standard of living at home that ultimately could lead to outright revolution in this country, Mr. Connally says.

"The U.S. sends its business executives out like Don Quixote, to do battle but we don't give them much of a lance to do battle with," Mr. Connally contends. He declares, "this has got to change." Others say the changes could involve greatly increasing tax incentives or starting direct federal subsidies to some businesses engaged in foreign trade.

"Unlike the U.S., other countries own their raw materials," Mr. Connally says. "So any time a private U.S. company goes overseas to acquire timber, copper or other resources, they deal with governments." Those governments may change policies drastically enough to result in the expropriation of the U.S. interests, he notes.

But if a U.S. company goes overseas with any sort of federal insurance coverage and enters into any agreement with a host government, the U.S. might well say "this agreement cannot be altered, amended or terminated in any form or fashion without the prior written approval of the U.S. government." "And that, "he says," might make the other governments think twice before acting against U.S. companies."[35]

The American agenda for the Canadian economy has been abundantly clear since August 15, 1971. It involves the quest for greater U.S. access on a permanent basis to Canadian resources, especially energy resources, and the sale, in return, of more manufactured goods from the U.S. to Canada. Early in 1973 President Nixon singled out Canada for criticism in a message to Congress because the U.S. has been buying more resources from Canada without Canada purchasing back sufficient U.S. manufactured goods. As U.S. pressure for a continental energy deal mounts, so too will the tendency toward de-industrialization increase.

Resource export agreements will mean higher costs in energy and other resources for Canadian industry and therefore, a worsening of the competitive position of Canadian manufacturing. Furthermore, the huge inflow of U.S. dollars into Canada to proceed with projects like the Mackenzie Valley Pipeline and the James Bay Hydro development will drive up the value of the

Canadian dollar, perhaps by five to ten per cent relative to the American dollar.

A California economist, concerned about the U.S. balance of payments crisis, has worked out the following estimate for the trade effects of an upward revaluation of the Canadian dollar: a five per cent increase would result in a $715 million negative trade shift for Canada with the U.S.; a 10 per cent increase would result in a $1.6 billion negative trade shift.[36]

The result of Nixonomics has been to move Canada's economy from one phase of development to another. Before Nixonomics, Canada had a truncated manufacturing sector which was quantitatively and particular qualititively stunted because of U.S. control. Now Nixonomics means de-industrialization, even in terms of this already truncated manufacturing sector.

A recent report of the U.S. tariff commission revealed that the process of de-industrialization due to the American impact on Canada pre-dates Nixonomics. The report showed that U.S. corporations began shifting their capital investment out of Canadian manufacturing and into western Europe in 1966. Furthermore, there has been a shift of U.S. investment within Canada away from manufacturing to resource extraction.

Because resource extraction involves many fewer jobs for the value of production, in comparison to manufacturing, de-industrialization means permanent high level unemployment.

Using statistics from a Waffle study of Ontario manufacturing, let us look at manufacturing employment in the city of Hamilton between 1966 and 1972. Of the 72 firms employing 100 or more workers in manufacturing in 1966, 12 had shut down by 1972 while four new ones opened in their place. The total number of manufacturing jobs in Hamilton in 1966 was about 65,000. In spite of the fact that the size of the labour force in Hamilton by 1972 had increased by almost 20 per cent, the number of manufacturing jobs declined by about 2,300. Two thousand of these job losses were in American owned firms and almost all of the rest were in British and European-owned companies.[37]

As de-industrialization proceeds, Canada's economy is becoming more dependent on the resource industries and on the service industries. It is essential to realize that the entire Canadian population lives off the wealth of productive labour in the economy. As manufacturing shrinks relatively, the economy is burdened with an ever-larger proportion of its work force in service industries. About two-thirds of the work force is now in service industries, the highest proportion of any country in the world.

This places an increasing squeeze on the salaries of workers in the service industries, both in the private sector and among government employees. It is no accident that white-collar workers, teachers, and civil servants are becoming increasingly militant as their livelihood and economic security are threatened by the effects of Canada's stagnant manufacturing sector.

De-industrialization of course, threatens the sections of the work force that have enjoyed the greatest relative prosperity and security in Canada, the workers in the large capital-intensive manufacturing firms.

De-industrialization is the price workers pay for Canada's dependent status in the American empire. As the American empire enters a period of decline, the costs of its decline are passed in disproportionately high amounts to workers in dependent countries like Canada and to minorities like the blacks within the United States.

For Canadians, de-industrialization grows out of the nature of Canadian capitalism and its relation to American capitalism. Only an anti-imperialist struggle bringing together workers in manufacturing and in the service sector along with workers in resource-extractive regions where no industrial infrastructure has been established can reverse the present stagnation in Canadian industry, with its attendant costs for the Canadian people.

Notes

[1] Statistics Canada, *Canada Year Book 1972*, (Ottawa, 1972), pp. 1094, 1095.
[2] *Ibid.*, pp. 758, 759.
[3] This figure was arrived at by comparing figures in the *Canadian Statistical Review* for 1965 and 1971. *The Canadian Statistical Review* is published by Statistics Canada.
[4] U.S. Bureau of the Census, *Statistical Abstract of the United States 1972*, (93rd. edition), (Washington, D.C., 1972), p. 219.
[5] Statistics Canada, *Canada Year Book 1972*, (Ottawa, 1972), p. 776. U.S. Bureau of the Census, *op. cit.*, p. 697.
[6] Statistics Canada, *Employment earnings and hours August 1972*, (Ottawa, 1972), p. 12.
[7] Statistics Canada, *Employment earnings and hours April 1972*, (Ottawa, 1972), p. 16.
[8] Statistics Canada, *Canada Year Book 1972*, (Ottawa, 1972), p. 1090.
[9] Statistics Canada, *Employment earnings and hours April 1972*, (Ottawa, 1972),

p. 16. Statistics Canada, *Canada Year Book 1972*, (Ottawa, 1972), p. 751. U.S. Bureau of the Census, *op. cit.*, pp. 710, 711, 712.

[10] Pierre L. Bourgault, *Innovation and the Structure of Canadian Industry*, Background Study for the Science Council of Canada, October, 1972, Special Study No. 23, (Ottawa, 1972), p. 30.

[11] Statistics Canada, *Canada Year Book 1972*, (Ottawa, 1972), pp. 1086, 1090.

[12] Pierre L. Bourgault, *op. cit.*, p. 83.

[13] *Ibid.*, p. 51.

[14] Statistics Canada, *op. cit.*, p. 589.

[15] Pierre L. Bourgault, *op. cit.*, p. 32.

[16] *Ibid.*, p. 32.

[17] *Ibid.*, p. 105.

[18] *Ibid.*, pp. 55-59.

[19] Science Council of Canada, *Innovation in a Cold Climate*, October, 1971, Report No. 15, (Ottawa, 1971), p. 19.

[20] Pierre L. Bourgault, *op. cit.*, p. 89.

[21] *Ibid.*, p. 80.

[22] Statistics Canada, *op. cit.*, p. 1064.

[23] James Laxer, "Lament for an Industry," *Last Post*, Dec. 1971.

[24] *Ibid.*

[25] *Ibid.*

[26] *Ibid.*

[27] *Ibid.*

[28] *Ibid.*

[29] *Ibid.*

[30] *Ibid.*

[31] *Ibid.*

[32] *Ibid.*

[33] The Globe and Mail, Feb. 12, 1973.

[34] *Fortune Magazine*, April, 1972.

[35] *The Wall Street Journal*, April 24, 1972.

[36] Fortune Magazine, March, 1972.

[37] The study cited here is a research project being carried out by Toronto Wafflers. It is a study of the behaviour of U.S. and Canadian-owned manufacturing firms in Ontario between 1966 and 1972. For an account of this study, see "Appendix."

The De-Industrialization of Ontario
Jim Laxer and Doris Jantzi

The preceding essay on manufacturing presents the general problem of de-industrialization in Canada. What follows in this statistical essay is an examination of trends in manufacturing employment, industry by industry and region by region, in Ontario. The figures are drawn from a research project begun in the fall of 1972 by a group of Wafflers in Toronto.[1]

The study examines the behaviour of large American and Canadian manufacturing firms in Ontario for the period 1966-1972.

For the period studied there was a small absolute decline in manufacturing employment in Ontario. In June 1966 there were

776,831 workers employed in manufacturing in Ontario; by June 1972 the number was 772,200. During this period the work force in Ontario grew by approximately 27 per cent. Thus the shift from manufacturing to service industries in Ontario is evident from the complete stagnation in manufacturing employment in the province. Ontario's manufacturing employment situation is similar to the national pattern for these years. In August 1966 there were 1,549,628 workers employed in manufacturing in Canada; in August 1972 the number was 1,536,600.

During this period considerable consolidation of manufacturing took place into larger firms with small firms driven out of business. The growth which occurred in manufacturing during this period centred in the large firms.

The tables which follow reveal the changes in employment in the large firms. These tables present a sample of large firms for which employment figures could be obtained for both 1966 and 1972 and firms which shut down after 1966 or opened prior to 1972. The sample includes only firms for which ownership could be ascertained as either American or Canadian. It contains no firms owned in foreign countries other than the U.S. The sample includes only plants which employed 100 or more workers and includes approximately 45 per cent of all manufacturing employment in Ontario.

In the sample studied there was a marked difference in the behaviour of U.S.-owned and Canadian-owned firms.

The U.S.-owned sample had the following results: there were 511 establishments studied for both 1966 and 1972; 85 establishments shut down between 1966 and 1972 and 122 new ones opened up. Over all employment in this sample of U.S. owned firms grew from 221,137 to 238,961, an increase of 8.1 per cent. The average size of establishment in the sample increased from 371 employees to 377 employees.

The Canadian-owned sample had the following results: there were 296 establishments studied for both 1966 and 1972; 35 establishments shut down between 1966 and 1972 and 75 new ones opened up. Overall employment in this sample of Canadian owned firms grew from 106,900 to 129,513, an increase of 21.1 per cent. The average size of establishment in the sample increased from 323 employees to 349 employees.

It can thus be seen that there was a striking difference in the creation of new employment in the large Canadian-owned as compared to the large American-owned plants. It is evident from the above statistics on overall employment in manufacturing in Ontario, that growth was centred in the large establishments and decline was evident in the small establishments. Canadian and American firms studied in the sample were not much different in average size.

It is evident that while large firms grew in employment whether they were Canadian- or American-owned, there was almost three times as much employment growth in the Canadian-owned firms.

In light of the analysis presented in the previous chapter on manufacturing, it appears that as the economy moved out of recession and into a boom phase in 1971-72, American firms passed on most of the new jobs created by their increased activity in Canada to the parent firms in the U.S. or other foreign countries. This factor would explain the enormous difference in the behaviour of large American and large Canadian firms. The difference is clearly not explained by a U.S. withdrawal from the Ontario economy, as the significantly higher figure for U.S. plant openings over shutdowns attests. Therefore, it is necessary to conclude that American firms maintained their share of the market while importing more parts and components for final manufacture from their parent firms in the U.S. This resulted in a qualitative undermining of manufacturing in Ontario, since most of the new jobs were exported abroad.

The Canadian sample reveals what happened to firms that operated almost entirely in Canada. It can be regarded as representing the "natural" growth rate for large manufacturing establishments in Ontario for this period.

The samples presented roughly represent the relative relation of U.S.-owned manufacturing in Ontario to Canadian-owned. It is therefore, clear how serious are the implications of American ownership of the bulk of manufacturing in Ontario during a period when the American government is pressuring American firms to shift employment from branch plants abroad back to the United States.

Table One (p. 151) shows the behaviour of the American and Canadian-owned firms in the sample by industrial category. It reveals the American control of most of the vital sectors of Ontario manufacturing: chemicals, rubber and plastics, fabricated metals, machinery, electrical products and transportation equipment. It reveals stagnation in employment in the large American firms in: machinery, electrical products and transportation equipment.

Table Two (p. 152) shows the behaviour of American and Canadian-owned firms in the sample region by region in Ontario. It reveals that the pattern of greater employment growth in Canadian-owned compared to American owned firms is general for most parts of Ontario. It reveals that key areas of Ontario that have been industrial centres for a very long time have experienced complete stagnation during the years studied. This is especially noteworthy for the Niagara region, which includes Hamilton, Brantford, and the Niagara peninsula. This region has experienced an absolute decline in employment in the large American firms.

It is evident as well that some large firms have migrated from old industrial regions to newer ones, particularly the Georgian Bay region where a marked employment increase is shown. This reflects the desire of large corporations to move from high wage unionized areas to low wage areas.

The strikingly uneven development of manufacturing in the province is shown by the fact that well over half the sample is drawn from the first three regions examined in the table, regions which make up the "Golden Horsehoe" from Oshawa around the end of Lake Ontario to Niagara Falls.

The study demonstrates the fact that during the present period of inter-imperialist rivalry among the great capitalist nations, American ownership of Canadian manufacturing leads to de-industrialization for Canada – the quantitative and qualitative undermining of this country's manufacturing sector.

Thus the term "de-industrialization" refers not to the general phenomenon of the reduction of the percentage of the work force employed in manufacturing (evident in most countries), but to the special distorting effects of U.S. ownership of Canadian manufacturing, in particular, U.S. attempts to enhance American employment at home at the expense of Canada.

Notes

[1] Figures from: Statistics Canada, *Employment, earnings and hours,* (Ottawa, 1966 and 1972); *Scott's Ontario Industrial Directory,* (Oakville, 1966 and 1972); and Statistics Canada, *Inter-Corporate Ownership 1969,* (Ottawa, 1971).

In addition to the authors of this essay, the following people have worked on this study: Bonnie Benedik, Paul Craven, Ann Forrest, Corileen North.

Tables

TABLE ONE: Ontario Sample: Manufacturing Employment In
Plants Employing 100 Or More
Industry By Industry

Standard Industrial Classifications	U.S.-Owned Plants		Canadian-Owned Plants	
	1966	1972	1966	1972
20. Food and Allied Products	17,505	17,103	9,260	10,846
21. Tobacco Products	826	643	146	231
22. Textiles	2,680	5,147	8,479	8,377
23. Clothing	3,466	3,844	3,265	3,007
24. Lumber and Wood Products	1,994	1,379	2,928	4,543
25. Furniture	3,369	4,112	2,986	4,874
26. Paper and Allied Products	5,536	7,085	10,053	11,553
27. Printing and Publishing	1,275	2,087	14,496	15,540
28. Chemicals and Allied Products	14,800	18,505	5,796	5,433
29. Petroleum Refining Products	640	665	259	116
30. Rubber and Plastics	14,290	15,795	2,598	3,089
31. Leather Products	3,634	2,116	3,305	4,077
32. Stone, Glass and Clay Products	6,118	7,153	1,874	3,518
33. Primary Metals	7,054	7,400	12,341	14,891
34. Fabricated Metals	13,900	20,323	8,016	10,284
35. Machinery except Electrical	29,701	32,098	5,426	10,688
36. Electrical Products	29,329	30,883	8,867	11,192
37. Transportation Equipment	58,547	55,483	4,561	4,932
38. Scientific and Professional Equipment	2,942	2,358	400	539
39. Miscellaneous	3,531	4,782	1,844	1,783
TOTALS	221,137	238,961	106,900	129,513
	increase 8.1%		increase 21.1%	

TABLE TWO: Ontario Sample: Manufacturing Employment Region by Region

Regions (by County)	U.S.-Owned Plants		Canadian-Owned Plants	
	1966	1972	1966	1972
1. Metropolitan Toronto	47,765	52,662	36,069	43,681
2. Metropolitan Region Without Toronto (Halton, Peel, York, Ontario)	42,855	45,562	6,955	11,596
3. Niagara Region (Brant, Wentworth, Haldimand, Lincoln, Welland)	49,961	48,399	21,972	25,172
4. Lake Erie Region (Middlesex, Oxford, Elgin, Norfolk)	13,547	14,775	5,254	5,452
5. Lake St. Clair Region (Essex, Kent, Lambton)	20,325	21,687	5,561	6,236
6. Upper Grand River Region (Huron, Perth, Waterloo, Wellington)	20,258	22,110	10,528	12,120
7. Georgian Bay Region (Bruce, Grey, Dufferin, Simcoe Counties; Muskoka, Parry Sound)	7,045	11,668	2,361	3,665
8. Lakehead Nor-West. Ontario (Kenora, Thunder Bay, Rainy River Counties; Patricia Portion)	1,990	1,752	3,191	4,460
9. Nor-East. Ontario (Cochrane, Algoma, Sudbury, Nipissing, Timiskaming)	278	590	3,743	3,698
10. Lake Ontario Region (Durham, Victoria, Haldimand, Peterborough, Northumberland, Hastings, Lennox & Addington, Prince Edward)	6,047	7,015	1,490	1,913
11. Eastern Ontario Region (Frontenac, Renfrew, Leeds, Lanark, Carleton, Granville, Dundas, Russell, Stormont, Prescott, Glengarry)	11,066	12,741	9,776	11,520
TOTALS	221,137	238,961	106,900	129,513

The Capitalist State in Canada
John Hutcheson

Many people in Canada are ready to believe that politicians are self-serving even to the point of corruption. But it is more difficult for them to see that governments serve specific class interests and thus systematically act against the interests of the overwhelming majority of the population. In an earlier chapter of this book, it has been demonstrated that Canada's energy policy is clearly in the interest of U.S. corporations. In spite of rising public indignation, the government continues to pursue a policy which results in non-renewable resources, along with the profits from these ventures, flowing out of Canada at an increasing rate. In return for this few jobs are created and energy costs for Canadians are driven up; moreover, these resource exports set in motion de-industrializing effects which undermine the manufacturing sector of the economy.

Why does the Canadian government pursue a policy so clearly in violation of the interests of Canadians? In order to answer this question it is necessary to look at the nature of political power in this country.

There is a widely-held view of political power which suggests that the government is merely a focal point for pressures from all parts of the society, and that the government, as a neutral force, merely reflects, adjudicates and resolves the competing pressures. Those who hold this view may also believe that some interest groups are better organized and more articulate and thus get their way more often than others. But in the long run, the argument goes, all the competing interests have to be taken into account. This can be called the "pluralist" view of politics. Pluralism starts from an assumption that society is an aggregate of individuals who come together in many different kinds of groupings to pursue their individual interests.

There is a variety of this view that can be called "radical pluralism." Radical pluralists believe that the disadvantaged and the poor in our society have no say in our society and they thus call for "participatory democracy," that is, for a real voice for the poor. While such a concept complains that not all the interests in society receive equal treatment, it holds that there is a harmony of interests which will be realized if all groups of people are able to have a say in decision-making.

There are also some people who believe that, while capitalism may have been marked by gross injustices in the past, the growth of the government has offset the unequal distribution of power which results from ownership of property. These people are encouraged in this view by unrealistic conservatives who mutter about "creeping socialism," and who complain that Canadians are being mollycoddled by the welfare system. Also many Canadians no doubt believe that the capitalist economy has been replaced by a modern, "mixed economy."

It is of course true that from World War I, though more obviously from the second half of the 1930's, the direct economic role of the government has increased markedly. It is equally true, however, that any close analysis of this development will show that the nature of the mix in the mixed economy is of a very particular kind. In fact, what the Canadian government is doing is continuing a policy of creating the conditions for the maintenance of capitalism, but under changing conditions in the forces of production and the social relations of production. As has been argued in Chapter 3, the achievement of a high rate of profit is the driving force of capitalism. What has happened in the twentieth century is that the direct use of the government has become necessary for the maintenance of a high rate of profit.

Much of the ideological justification of the "new" economic role for capitalist governments was provided by the economist John Maynard Keynes. In concluding his analysis of twentieth century capitalism, Keynes wrote:

> I conceive, therefore, that a somewhat comprehensive soci-alisation of investment will prove the only means of securing an approximation to full employment; though this need not exclude all manner of compromises and of devices by which public authority will co-operate with private initiative. But

beyond this no obvious case is made out for a system of State Socialism which would embrace most of the economic life of the community. It is not the ownership of the instruments of production which it is important for the State to assume. If the State is able to determine the aggregate amount of resources devoted to augmenting the instruments and the basic rate of reward to those who own them, it will have accomplished all that is necessary. Moreover, the necessary measures of socialisation can be introduced gradually and without a break in the general traditions of society.[1]

Another ideologue of the "welfare state", William Beveridge, spoke of the desirability of the "socialization of demand without the socialization of production."

In Canada the Department of Regional Economc Expansion has eagerly taken up the role of "augmenting the instruments [of production] and the basic rate of reward to those who own them." A recent study[2] shows how much public finance is used to support such social enterprises as I.B.M., I.T.T., Westinghouse, and Proctor and Gamble. And DREE is not the only agency for this type of activity. Recently the Canadian Export Development Corporation loaned "Brazil" $26.5 million for the purpose of buying electrical equipment. That this is not altogether charitable aid to a struggling bastion of democracy can be seen from a closer analysis of the terms.[3] The money, rather than being loaned to the people of Brazil, who are represented neither by those who rule in Brazil nor by the companies concerned, was loaned to a "private Brazilian utility company," (Light-serviços) which is 83 per cent owned by Brascan, one of Canada's very own multi-national corporations. Also the equipment was to be purchased from a specified group of corporations operating branch plants in Canada.

The situation is well summarized in the Quebec Federation of Labour's Manifesto, "The State is Our Exploiter":

> ... under the liberal state, public financing injected into the economy is given outright to private capital, or supports it so as to raise profit ratios. This strengthens the private sector at the expense of the public sector.[4]

The government in Canada has always been essential to the

development strategy of capitalism and it continues to act in the interests of a capitalist class.

The Marxist analysis of political power in fact recognizes that the government is merely one aspect of a wider political framework which can be called the "state." Ralph Miliband, in his study of the contemporary capitalist state, defines the state as "a number of particular institutions which, together, constitute its reality, and which interact as parts of what may be called the state system."[5] Thus, apart from governments at various levels, there is the administrative element of the state, which is not just the government bureaucracy but also public corporations, central banks, regulatory commissions, etc. There are also the military and police forces, the coercive apparatus of the state. There is also the judiciary which in constitutional theory is independent of the government. In practice, the legislature, too, is distinct from the government, and thus parliamentary assemblies form part of the wider sphere of the state.

There is a further aspect of power in capitalist societies which cannot be neglected. This is the power that results from what the Italian Marxist Antonio Gramsci called the "hegemony" of the dominant class, that is, its ideological predominance over subordinate classes. This hegemony is exercised through a variety of institutions; political, cultural and social. These institutions include political parties, churches, radio, television, newspapers, cinema, theatre, schools and universities, and the family. (I do not mean to imply that the existence of these institutions *inevitably* serves the capitalist state, but at present most manifestations of them do reinforce the capitalist state.) Not all of these institutions are normally reckoned to be part of the state, but it is important to see how they are used to buttress the capitalist state.

In Chapter 3 of this book there is a discussion of class in Canada and of the class conflict that is inevitably part of the capitalist mode of production. The nature of the state grows out of this fundamental aspect of capitalist society. As Miliband puts it:

> The economic and political life of capitalist societies is *primarily* determined by the relationship, born of the capitalist mode of production, between . . . two classes – the class which on the one hand owns and controls, and the working class on

the other. Here are still the social forces whose confrontation most powerfully shapes the social climate and the political system of advanced capitalism. In fact, the political process in these societies is mainly *about* the confrontation of those forces, and is intended to sanction the terms of the relationship between them.[6]

That is to say, the power of the capitalist class does not arise simply from its control of the state. One can identify *three levels* at which the power of the capitalists is exercised: through control of the means of production, through control of the dominant ideological institutions of society, and through control of the state. Within each of these three levels there is a spectrum of control from leadership (or "hegemony" in Gramsci's terminology) to overt domination. Obviously control within any one of these three levels reinforces control within the others. For example, when control is effective within the first two, there is little need to resort to overt domination in the third. But should a serious challenge arise at any one level, power is quickly mobilized at the other levels. Workers in a factory know that they are "under control" once they have passed the steel fence that typically surrounds factories, but should they challenge that everyday control, the forces of the state in the form of the police and the courts are soon brought into action. It is in fact through the state that the power at the other levels is guaranteed and co-ordinated, though it is the control of the means of production that makes possible control at the other two levels. (This type of analysis, incidentally, suggests that it is dangerous to make too sharp a distinction between "base" and "superstructure" when analysing capitalist society.)

The importance of an analysis of power which takes into account all three levels is shown by the history of attempts to transform capitalist societies. Challenges to the capitalists' control which have not been effective throughout the three levels have always met with defeat.

Sometimes even where the government has fallen into the hands of "outsiders," capitalist states have managed to survive. It is a question of the nature of the "outsiders," specifically of their willingness and ability to permanently change capitalist social relations of production. For example, as Miliband argues, the fascists of the 1930s advanced a "rhetoric of total transformation and renewal" with "anti-bourgeois resonances,"[7] but neither Mussolini nor Hitler dislodged big business, because neither sought to transform capitalist social relations. As Miliband says:

> The most telling fact of all about the real nature of the Fascist systems is surely that, when they came to an end, twenty years after Mussolini's "March on Rome" and twelve years after Hitler's assumption of the chancellorship, the economic and social structures of both countries had not been significantly changed.[8]

Perhaps more surprising to many have been the results in countries where social democratic and labour parties have formed governments on programmes which expressed an intention to transcend the capitalist system by means of the use of state power in the service of reform. They have not done so. This is not to say that the presence of such parties has not contributed to important reforms, or to say that it makes no difference which party is in power. The point is that social democratic parties have been unable to control the power of the capitalists and to change capitalist social relations. They have not faced up to the realities of the class conflict which grows out of the capitalist mode of production and which produces the class nature of the bourgeois state.

In the 1890s Rosa Luxemburg clearly indicated the limitations of what are now called social democratic parties. In her essay, *Social Reform or Revolution* she outlines the petty-bourgeois basis of the tendency which refused to acknowledge the real nature of the development of capitalist society:

> The theory of the gradual introduction of socialism proposes a progressive reform of capitalist property and the capitalist state in the direction of socialism. However, in consequence of the objective facts of existing society, one and the other develop in a precisely opposed direction. The process of production will be increasingly socialized and state intervention, the control of the state over the process of production will be extended. But at the same time, private property will take on more and more the form of open capitalist exploita-

tion of the labour of others, and state control will be more and more penetrated with the exclusive interests of the ruling class. Inasmuch as the state, that is the *political* organization of capitalism, and property relations, that is, the *juridical* organization of capitalism, become more *capitalist* as they develop, and not more socialist, they oppose to the theory of the progressive introduction of socialism two insurmountable difficulties.[9]

The development of capitalist property and the capitalist state is not leading in the direction of socialism.

For anyone concerned about the future of this country, it is extremely important to arrive at a clear understanding of this point. Many Canadians believe that there is an inherently progressive tendency at work that is increasing the well-being of the people of this country by substantial modifications of the capitalist system. Many Canadians, for example, support the NDP because they believe that a series of such modifications can remove the undesirable features of capitalism. In that way many hope that capitalism can be controlled without a fundamental challenge to the power of capitalists which results from their control of the means of production. But that is to hope that the capitalists will not use all the power at their disposal to maintain their domination. One weapon that the capitalists have at their disposal is control of the state.

We have already seen some examples of the way in which capitalists are using their control of the state to maintain capitalism. But there are other examples of this which show clearly the economic role of the government. And it is important to realize that these policies affect the lives of all of us and our prospects for the future.

Since the 1950s capitalist governments have attempted to avoid crises by supporting profit rates through control of wage levels, deflationary politites and direct controls. In Canada only the first of these has been used on a comprehensive scale. In the late 1960s, for example, the government decided that it could run the risk of creating high levels of unemployment. Of course this was not explained in terms of income redistribution. Rather, the policy was justified by reference to a creature of some economists' imaginations, the Phillips curve. Essentially the argument was that "society" had to choose between unemployment and inflation. The importance of being able to find such technical arguments to justify unpopular actions was well appreciated by Keynes. In 1925 Keynes had written the following advice to a government:

> We ought to warn you . . . that it will not be safe politically that you are intensifying unemployment deliberately in order to reduce wages. Thus you will have to ascribe what is happening to every conceivable cause except the true one.[10]

It is possible that the grain of truth in the Phillips curve argument lies in a connection between inflation and "unproductive" labour. The concept of "unproductive" labour, that is labour which does not directly produce surplus-value, is discussed in Chapter 3 of this book. What may be happening is that the growing size of the unproductive labour force, which is necessary for the maintenance of profit rates, is also creating a level of inflation which threatens the stability of the system. It has certainly been the experience of several countries, however, that inflation was not reduced by creating general unemployment. The resort to income policies suggests that, in some countries at least, high levels of unemployment have not proved to be satisfactory to the capitalists with respect to income distribution, though the costs of the policy have been very high for the hundreds of thousands of unemployed.

It is worth discussing, briefly, the use of incomes policies since, although they have not been used here, they have been used elsewhere and some have thought that they might be useful in Canada. The first point to notice is that an incomes policy is in reality a wage freeze. The policy is made to appear to demand equality of sacrifice since the reality must not appear to be too seriously at variance with the ruling ideology of pluralism in which the state is the arbiter of competing pressures. But the point of the policy is to reduce wages in order to maintain the rate of surplus-value.

The policy has been introduced in some countries when it was found that deflationary policies did not reduce inflation, thus leaving problems for foreign trade, but did create problems for productivity growth as a result of demand fluctuations. The disadvantages of the incomes policy, from the capitalists' point of view, is that the class nature of income distribution is made clear to all, except presumably to some economists who remain lost in the fogs of their own creation.[11] The class nature of the incomes policy becoming clear, the chances of the policy actually redistributing income are obviously dependent on the balance of political forces.

What we now have to consider is the question of the stability of the capitalist economy under the "new" economic policies. The capitalists have expanded the direct economic role of the government in order to achieve a higher rate of profit and to maintain their domination. But they cannot do this without causing important structural changes in the economy. Many economists have argued that these structural changes promote stability. But many capitalist governments are now finding that they are facing a growing "fiscal crisis."

In Canada the government is now responsible for about 18 per cent of all investment and the proportion of investment coming from the public sector has increased by about 21 per cent from 1950 to 1970. Correspondingly the rate of business investment has been decreasing. Government expenditure, without including transfer payments, is about 20 per cent of GNP. The government directly employs about 12 per cent of the labour force, this figure increasing to about 18 per cent if you include hospitals, education and other indirect government employment.[12] The fiscal crisis is a consequence of the tendency to a declining rate of profit. It is the tendency for the profit rate to decline, which necessitates the high level of government expenditure and creates problems for the financing of that expenditure.

The problem of financing this level of government expenditure is becoming acute and yet it is politically necessary. Government expenditure must be supported out of either surplus-value or out of wages. An important debate is developing on the correct analysis of this expenditure. One side tends to argue that unproductive expenditure, particularly military budgets, maintain rates of profit through providing markets for capitalist production. The other side stresses the problem of the production of surplus-value and argues that unproductive government and private expenditure must be paid for out of increased productivity in some parts of the private sector. Obviously the argument turns on an adequate delineation of productive and unproductive labour, and also on the extent to which taxes redistribute income from wages to surplus-value.

To the extent that government expenditure is supported out of surplus-value and does not contribute to increasing total surplus-value, the output of productive workers must increase correspondingly to maintain rates of profit. This means job speed-up and deteriorating conditions of work. Of course much government expenditure is supported by taxes on wages and in fact the fiscal policy of the government is increasingly redistributing income to the benefit of corporations. The ability to do this, however, is limited by the resistance of the working class to decreased standards of living, and the limits of the process have been indicated by increased militancy of large sections of the working class in recent years.

In Canada, as in other capitalist countries, the contradictions of capitalist growth are becoming increasingly impossible to hide. In Canada, however, these contradictions are heightened by the dependency of the country. As the U.S. attempts to resolve some of its own structural problems, the development of Canada is likely to be further jeopardized.

This latter point is a reminder that one cannot discuss the capitalist state in Canada without taking into account the specific aspects of the state which arise from the dependency of Canadian capitalism. There are features of the Canadian state, some of which have been discussed, which are similar to those in other capitalist states. But the present state in Canada is also the result of a specific historical development of the forces of production and the social relations of production. We must consider that history if we are to understand the way in which the state has both been used to create a dependent capitalist economy and has also been the result of a dependent capitalist development. That history will also help us to understand why the Canadian bourgeoisie has increasingly lost control of the state.

In Canada we live in a society that can be described as "liberal-democratic." There is political competition amongst several parties, there is the right of opposition, there are regular elections, representative assemblies, civic guarantees and various restrictions on the use of state power. But we should recognize, as Professor C. B. Macpherson reminded us,[13] that the democratic aspect of our society was added on to a solidly-established liberal capitalist society and, as we have already seen, this particular kind of democratic government exists to uphold and enforce capitalist society. That is, the democratic element was granted by the ruling class in order to contain popular pressures, but it has been granted in such a way as to maintain the capitalist economy.

It is easy to see that this country was not founded on democratic principles when one considers how recently the franchise was granted to all adults. It was well into the twentieth century before that limited form of democracy was achieved. And it is easy to see how little it was a matter of principle for the ruling class in this country, by considering the two bills introduced by Arthur Meighen and passed by Parliament in 1917.[14] One of the bills denied the vote to conscientious objectors, to those of enemy alien birth, and to those of European birth speaking an enemy alien language and naturalized since 1902. The second, to show that some principles were a fine thing, gave the franchise to all on active service and to wives, widows and other female relatives of servicemen overseas. Thus were women first admitted to this democratic society.

It is necessary to note here that, although liberal-democracy has been associated with capitalism, it does not follow that capitalism requires liberal-democratic politics. As Marx noted:

> Confronted by the working class, the still ruling class – whatever the specific form in which it appropriates the labour of the masses – has but one and the same economic interest: to maintain the enslavement of labour and to appropriate the fruit.[15]

Perhaps because the overtly oppressive state tends to be unstable, there is a tendency towards the apparently "classless" state. For those who believe in the security of liberal democracy, however, it is worth considering the frightening ease with which the War Measures Act was brought into action in 1970.

In order to understand the present liberal-democratic state we have to look at the history of liberal society in Canada and the specific nature of that liberal society. First it is necessary to understand how a liberal capitalist society was created, since it is not a common feature of dependent societies.

The emergence of liberal society in Europe was the result of a long struggle between two social systems – capitalism and seigneurialism. (The latter term is better than the more commonly-used "feudalism," since feudalism designates a particular political system within seigneurialism.) It is impossible to summarize the history of this struggle which was carried on for many centuries and with varying intensity at different times in different countries. It is important, however, to note several points:

1) The triumph of liberal society was achieved after long years of class conflict between bourgeoisie and nobility, and in each country the new liberal society was marked by the particular national form of this class conflict. This is particularly true of the "superstructural" aspects of each society.

2) The method of transforming agrarian society was at the centre of the conflict.

3) The history of the modern working class (or proletariat) begins with the triumph of liberal society.[16]

The first two of these points are not of major importance in Canada. There was no entrenched seigneurial society of lords and peasants (see further comments on this below) and the only significant non-bourgeois rural population, the sparsely-settled Indians, was evicted and to a considerable extent destroyed. There were of course conflicts over land policy once the Indians had been evicted, but these were conflicts within the framework of an emerging capitalist society. The third point is of major importance, and the emergence of a working class defined by capitalist production is a major feature of Canada's development.

In addition to this, in discussing the development of liberal society in Canda, we have to take into account the factor of its dependent status. That is we need to see the link between the development of the metropolis and the hinterland, and the way in which the development of both social relations of production and forces of production in the metropolis have influenced the development of both social relations of production and forces of production in the hinterland.[17]

The basic relationship between metropolis and hinterland is elementary and was stated clearly as long ago as the eighteenth century by a contributor to the great document of the Enlightenment, the *Encyclopedia:*

> These colonies being established solely for the utility of the metropolis, it follows that . . . the colonies would be of no

more use, if they were able to do without the metropolis; thus it is a very law of nature that the arts and cultivation in a colony must be confined to such and such objects, according to the convenience of the country of domination.[18]

The prospects for development, *under capitalism*, of countries placed in such colonial relationships have not been very good. This problem has been discussed by, among others, Paul Baran.[19] As Baran points out, European expansion has been responsible for the destruction of self-sufficient rural societies and, by the seizure of land for production of export crops and by the exposure of rural handicrafts to the competition of industrial exports, has in most places created only vast pools of pauperized labour. Only one Asian country, for example, has escaped its neighbours' fate and developed under capitalism, and that is Japan. As Baran noted, it is perhaps not coincidental that Japan was never part of the capitalist colonial world.

There are, however, a few areas of the world where European expansion has resulted in the development of prosperous capitalist economies. One area is North America. For the U.S. the only obstacle to accumulation and capitalist expansion was foreign domination. The bourgeoisie in that country was strong enough to overthrow that domination and to create a political framework conducive to the growth of capitalism. In fact, as William Appleman Williams has shown,[20] the achievement of capitalist development in the U.S. was not merely the result of independence, but (as with Japan and the major European powers) entailed the creation of a new empire, starting from the date of independence. And the development of the U.S. empire has had profound implications for the other parts of the Americas.

Obviously, then, we have to look at the specific nature of any colonial relationship. The role of the metropolis-hinterland relationship in the distortion of the structure of the hinterland has recently been emphasized by André Gunder Frank.[21] Frank's argument, which has been formulated for Latin America but has been generalized to other situations (in fact "Latin America" is already a generalization), can be summarized as follows: first, Latin America has had a market economy from the beginning of colonialism; secondly, it has been capitalist from the beginning;

and, thirdly, the dependent nature of its insertion into the capitalist world market is the cause of its under-development.

Gunder Frank is right to insist that from the beginning of their colonial period American societies, and this holds for Canada, have been tied to a capitalist world market; but, as several of his critics have observed,[22] it does not follow that the American colonies of Europe developed capitalist relations of production from the beginning of their colonial history. As Marx showed:

> Capital can spring into life only when the owner of the means of production and subsistence meets in the market with the free labourer selling his labour-power. And this one historical condition comprises a world's history.[23]

In fact, in a comparative analysis of dependent societies it is of particular importance to investigate the extent to which capitalist integration has been achieved. That is the extent to which the population is involved in the capitalist mode of production in each dependent country. The degree of capitalist integration is undoubtedly *one* factor in the prosperity of the dependent society. The peculiarly destructive consequences of a non-capitalist society being drawn into an international market dominated by the capitalist mode of production are summarized by Marx's comment: "The civilized horrors of over-work are grafted on to the barbaric horrors of slavery, serfdom, etc."[24]

In Canada an almost fully-integrated capitalist social structure *did* grow out of a colonial society which was already integrated into a capitalist empire. Though the key factor in Canada's development has been the extraction of a series of staple products by a series of imperial powers, Canada has never been *merely* a resource colony. Canada is unlike other colonies in which capitalism promoted plantation production, using slavery or indentured labour, or perpetuated various forms of non-capitalist production based on peasant labour. Canada has become a fully integrated capitalist society, that is a society with capitalist property relations, and a society in which the overwhelming proportion of the population is engaged in capitalist production. It is perhaps for this reason that Canada, despite its colonial aspects, has developed into a rich country. This development is now threatened, as many chapters in this book show. The succession of capitalist development by under-development has been a common fate for many regions of capitalist countries, as the history of the Maritimes testifies. In fact, as the example of Argentina may show, this is a fate that can be visited upon whole countries.

As I have argued above, capitalist social relations in Canada did not arise, as in Europe, out of a prolonged conflict between capitalist society and seigneurial society. The fur trade was long the dominant economic activity in Canada and, after fishing, was the means by which Canada was joined to the European economy. The fur trade, however, was based neither on capitalist nor on seigneurial relations of production, but on mercantile exploitation of Indian production. It is true that in New France a form of seigneurial society had been established, though it is important to see that this was not a simple reproduction of European society and it had little of its tenacity.[25]

That there were some barriers to capitalist development, however, can be seen from an article that appeared in *Le Canadien* about 1810. The article defended bourgeois society, contrasting the U.S.A. with Lower Canada. It is interesting as an example of more than one kind of chauvinism:

> First we have an overwhelming aversion towards feudal tenure ... Since our revolution all our actions are geared towards commerce ... all our institutions tend to favour its operations. For example, suppose you wish to speculate and you do not have enough money. You can go to a banker who knows something of the value of your property and you will soon have the sum you need, for a small discount ... But if your property is held under feudal law its value cannot be so easily determined and it may be subject to [obligations]. But there is a more important consideration in favour of [freehold]. In our country the husband is the sole controller of all goods, we do not have laws which protect wives and children; so that the husband can use as security all his property without his wife being able to prevent him. ... Thus a respectable man can always find credit, while with your Canadian laws a man who appears to have property will find difficulty in raising loans because his wife always retains some rights [over other creditors;]and it is precisely that which we do not like. These laws are all very well for a rural population, but they are insupportable for a people who devote themselves entirely to commerce.[26]

The survival of seigneurial property combined with the dominance of the new colonial merchants and government led to the unstable political situation of the 1830s.[27] Though the struggle was led by pre-industrial social classes, as were many of the democratic struggles in Europe between the 1790s and the 1840s, it was essentially a struggle for a democratic control of the capitalist society that was emerging rather than a struggle against capitalist society. The defeat of the 1837 rebellions meant that in Canada, as in Europe, democracy would be granted later as an appendage to liberal society. But in Canada the particular nature of the bourgeoisie and its colonial situation had the additional result that the defeat of the national and democratic struggles of the 1830s doomed the possibility of the development of an *independent* capitalism. There is an essay by Tom Naylor[28] which is of fundamental importance since it shows the mechanism by which Canada could emerge as a capitalist and yet dependent state. The commercial bourgeoisie in Canada used their position of dominance to bring about precisely this situation. Following the suppression of the rebellion the Canadian mercantile bourgeoisie could settle down to creating a dependent society with capitalist social relations of production.

A main role of the state in Canada has always been the maintenance of "peace, order, and good government," which means ensuring an expanding market economy, allowing for capital accumulation and maintaining the necessary labour supply. Control of the state by the bourgeoisie has been crucial in carrying out this form of development.

First let us look at the provision of the necessary labour supply, that is the creation of a modern working class. As Pentland puts it:

> The capitalistic labour market . . . is the one so well supplied with labour that employers feel free to hire workers as desired, on a short term basis without assuming any responsibility for their overhead costs. There is not much sign of such a market in Canada before 1830. In the next two decades there is evidence of transition towards it. . . . The essential structure of a capitalistic market existed in the 1850's, and the market had attained some sophistication by the 1870's.[29]

In bringing about this situation the role of the government was crucial, both in controlling land policy and in maintaining an appropriate immigration policy, and in controlling the conditions of work of those immigrants when they had arrived. Of course this type of government activity is not particular to any one period in Canadian history. The way in which the government has always controlled conditions of work can be seen from a reading of Charles Lipton's *The Trade Union Movement of Canada, 1827-1959.*[30]

It was not until 1872, and then as the result of considerable demonstrations, that a Trade Union Act was introduced to legislate that the mere fact of combining to increase wages or to reduce hours of work was not a conspiracy and did not violate the common law. Even then, along with the Trade Union Act, the government passed the Criminal Law Amendment Act. This Act, by providing penalties for violence or intimidation during organizing campaigns and strikes, left plenty of room for anti-union interpretation and convictions of conspiracy by anti-union courts.[31] In 1947, following the textile strike at Lachute, at a mill where one woman could work 108 hours for $11.17, two union organizers (Madeleine Parent and Azélus Beaucage) were convicted of seditious conspiracy.

The state has also, from early times, been able to rely on the use of court injunctions to prohibit organization and to end strikes. In Quebec recently the government has gone from the use of injunctions to jail striking workers to the introduction of legislation (Bill 89) to eliminate the right to strike in the public sector and in transport and communications.[32] This is only an echo of the Industrial Disputes Act of 1907 dealing with strikes in public utilities, mining and railroads. And the Federal Government has also used direct legislation to end specific strikes. Consider the National Railway Strike of August, 1950. This strike led the Ottawa correspondent of the Montreal *Gazette* to remind the government of its powers under the War Measures Act (a useful item as we have recently seen). A special session of Parliament was summoned and the Prime Minister stated that the strike was harming the United States, a country which depended on "effective co-operation from Canada." Having heard that, Parliament passed an Act to require workers to return to work within 48 hours.[33] In 1954 a strike vote by 90 per cent of the membership of the unions of non-operating railway employees was met by a federal government announcement that if the strike took place, another parliamentary act would be brought in to ban the strike.[34]

Let us turn now to the particular form of the state in Canada. We have seen that by the mid-nineteenth century Canada had emerged as a liberal capitalist society with a clearly defined dominant commercial bourgeoisie and a growing working class. We have seen that the state performed the classical functions of any capitalist state in suppressing any opposition to this development and the human costs of this type of society. But we have to consider the particular nature of the Canadian state as an instrument of both the ruling class of the imperial country and the ruling class of Canada. The Canadian state has been a critical link between the domestic and foreign ruling classes.

In the days of the British Empire the Canadian state served as a guarantor of the loans of British investors and banking houses and at the same time served their partners, the Canadian bourgeoisie. Both the Act of Union of 1840 and Confederation were identified by Harold Innis[35] as instruments to secure low interest rates for the transportation system. Donald Creighton went even further. In discussing the British government's decision to support the proposals made at Quebec for confederation, he said:

> This British assistance might be interpreted as an effort to assist in the creation of a great holding company in which could be amalgamated all those divided and vulnerable North American interests whose protection was a burden to the British state and whose financial weakness was a grievance of British capital.[36]

And in the same study Creighton explains the true meaning of Canada for the capitalist class:

> Railways were not mere adjuncts to Confederation, they were of its essence; and the *moral bases* of a transcontinental union were the two solemn engagements to provide railway communications from the St. Lawrence valley to the oceans. . . . Political union would at once provide a basis upon which [past obligations resulting from the construction of a transportation system] could be more easily borne, and a fund of resources out of which the transport system could be completed and the existing investments made more profitable.[37]

In fact the constitution of 1867, which was designed for one particular economic strategy, has been a problem ever since as the result of the emergence of an economic reality unlike that imagined by the Fathers of Confederation.[38] The economic goal of Confederation was the creation of a continent-wide trading system. The 1867 Act assumes growth based on the development of the new Western agricultural regions, the emergence of a national industry, large-scale immigration, and a continuation of the commercial system of the British Empire. The powers necessary to guide such development were conferred upon the Ottawa government. Macdonald's National Policy of 1879 showed how the state was to be used in the interests of the Canadian bourgeoisie. The National Policy provided government backing for the building of the railway; it established a tariff which would provide business for the CPR, shipping manufactured goods from the east to the prairies and wheat east towards Montreal and thence to Europe. The government in Ottawa showed that it was determined to bring the west under the control of Canada. In 1885 troops were sent to put down the second Riel rebellion, showing that Métis and Indians would not be allowed to interfere with the "sub-imperial" interests of Canada's merchant capitalists.

As things turned out, however, the major bases for development in much of Canada in the years after Confederation were mining, newsprint and hydro-electric power, and later urbanization and road transportation. This has meant that the provincial governments, which were given control over the public domain have emerged as critical institutions within the Canadian state. In addition, the U.S. branch plants began to appear in Canada in large numbers. And the fact that much of this post-Confederation industrial development has been directed from the U.S. has added a further and profoundly important facet to the role of the state in Canada. Harold Innis pointed to this when he noted that the achievement of "independence" in Canada was connected with the decline of Canada's economic role in the British Empire:

> The end of the period of expansion based on the St. Lawrence and trade with Great Britain coincided roughly with the achievement of Dominion status which followed the Great War and which was marked by the Statute of Westminster. . . . The extension of the American empire, the decline of its natural resources, and the emergence of metropolitan areas, supported capitalist expansion in Canada and reinforced the trend of regionalism. The pull to the north and south has tended to become stronger in contrast with the pull

of east and west. The British North America Act and later decisions of the Privy Council have strengthened the control of the provinces over natural resources such as minerals, hydro-electric power, and pulpwood on Crown lands, resources which have provided the basis for trade with the U.S. and for investment of American capital.[39]

The changing pattern of dominion provincial relations has thus echoed the transition from formal colonial status within the British Empire to informal dependent status within the U.S. empire. Informal empire has a long history of which the variety known as neo-colonialism is only one type. It was in 1824 that the British foreign-secretary, Canning, said "Spanish-America is free and, if we do not mismanage our affairs sadly, she is English."[40] U.S. capitalists had long understood the meaning of this statement, although they had not waited for some Spanish colonies to liberate themselves. It was during the period following World War I that Canada was subjected to the decisive shifts towards the economic structure which we now know. The flow of resources to the south was increased and U.S. branch plants established complete domination in the automotive, electrical and chemical industries in Canada.

It should not be thought that the transition from one empire to another has occasioned much conflict within the capitalist class. The majority of the Canadian bourgeoisie was quick to discover the benefits of continentalism. For them it has paid. For the rest of the country the long-run price has been high, as Harold Innis observed in the concluding pages of *The Fur Trade in Canada*:

> The economic history of Canada has been dominated by the discrepancy between the centre and margin of western civilization. Energy has been directed toward the exploitation of staple products and the tendency has been cumulative.... Agriculture, industry, transportation, trade, finance, and governmental activities tend to become subordinate to the production of the staple for a more highly specialized manufacturing community.[41]

In fact, even a few members of the Canadian bourgeoisie have worried that too high a price would eventually be paid for development within the U.S. empire. Until the 1940's the Canadian bourgeoisie, through their control of a state within the British

Empire, were a valuable asset to the U.S. capitalists. The "North Atlantic Triangle" was then a reality, though the interests of the U.S. capitalists extended well beyond the North Atlantic portion of the British Empire. From the early twentieth century to the 1940s the Canadian bourgeoisie was in a relatively favourable situation as it balanced on the base created by the other two corners of the triangle. With the decline of the British Empire the base for this balance was destroyed though, like a sleepwalker, the Canadian bourgeoisie appeared not to notice. Some voices tried to waken them gently. It was no accident that this gentle alarm was sounded by figures both associated with the financial bourgeoisie and with an active role in the Canadian state. James Coyne and Walter Gordon both realized that, with the rapid take-over of Canadian resources and productive facilities, the Canadian bourgeoisie would be left with an increasingly insignificant role in the U.S. empire. Even the role of the state would pass from that of an intermediary between the U.S. and Canadian bourgeoisie to becoming increasingly a direct creature of the U.S. imperialists.

The loss of sovereignty by the Canadian government can be seen in many ways. In fact the term "special status" is only a euphemism for the sale of sovereignty. As has been shown in the introduction to this book, the process began in earnest in 1940 with the creation of the Permanent Joint Board of Defence. The process was carried further by Canada's participation in NATO and NORAD. The events of the "Cuban missile crisis" of 1962 revealed that the Canadian government had virtually lost ultimate authority over its own military forces. Pressure to mobilize the Canadian forces from NORAD and the U.S. government was stronger than the misgivings of the Prime Minister and the unwillingness of the Minister for External Affairs. It was in vain that the latter pleaded "if we go along with the Americans now we'll be their vassals forever."[42] The delay in jumping to the bidding of the U.S. by Diefenbaker and Howard Green split the Conservative government. Since the Liberal party has been the agency of "special status," it is doubtful that a Liberal government would have even noticed that a fundamental issue of Canada's sovereignty was in the balance.

The defence of U.S. "security" was also an issue in the death of a high-ranking Canadian diplomat in 1957. Herbert Norman, Canadian Ambassador to Egypt, was hounded to his death by accusations from the U.S. Senate Internal Security Subcommittee. This witch-hunting was abetted by the supply of confidential information from the Canadian government.[43] (In May, 1973, in response to an allegation that the Nixon administration had planned to break into the Canadian Embassy in Washington, an external affairs spokesman stated that "all the Americans would have had to do was ask for any information they wished."[44])

In 1965 it became apparent that the Canadian government could not even control its own taxation policy. Walter Gordon's budget proposed to disallow tax deductions for advertising in foreign-owned newspapers and periodicals. Bowing to pressure from the U.S. State Department, the government exempted *Time* and *Reader's Digest* from this legislation. It appeared that the U.S. government used both the quota on oil exports and the auto-pact as levers in the "negotiations."[45] The auto-pact itself is a mechanism by which the Canadian government has ceded control of a critical industry to the U.S. government and foreign corporations.

From resource sell-outs to low taxation for U.S. corporations, from Defence Sharing Agreements to the auto-pact, Canadian governments have surrendered the Canadian economy to U.S. control. The loss of sovereignty has been an inevitable consequence. It is ironic that "special status" has been ended, not by the anger of the Canadian people, but by the measures taken by the U.S. empire to help it digest its other intended victims.

The Canadian state is now in the control of the dominant section of the ruling class in Canada – the U.S. corporations. The Canadian state furthers the interests of U.S. capitalists and by so doing contributes to Canada's further integration into the U.S. empire. This is leading to the disintegration of Canada. But the fact that a Canadian state still exists is of great significance. For the Canadian people to demand the right to control that state would be a profoundly anti-imperialist action. This would not mean the defence of the present state which daily works in opposition to the interests of the people of this country. It would mean the political possibility of creating a Canadian state controlled by the working people which would serve as an instrument of national liberation.

The demand for an independent state would itself be a demand for a state in the hands of the people. The capitalists in Canada are well aware of this danger and for this reason work assiduously to undermine the concept of Canadian sovereignty. That is why it is essential for Canadians to defend Canadian sovereignty and to assert teir right to their own independent state at the same time as they struggle against the policies of the capitalist state in Canada.

Notes

[1] J. M. Keynes, *The General Theory of Employment, Interest, and Money.* Macmillan, London, 1961, p. 378.

[2] R. Chodos, "The Great Canadian DREE machine", reprinted in the Last Post Special, *Corporate Canada.* ed. M. Starowicz and R. Murphy, James Lewis and Samuel, Toronto 1972.

[3] See *The Last Post,* March, 1973.

[4] In D. Drache (ed.) *Quebec — Only the Beginning,* New Press, Toronto, 1972, p. 210.

[5] R. Miliband, *The State in Capitalist Society,* Weidenfeld and Nicholson, London, 1969, p. 49. This is an important study for an understanding of the class nature of the capitalist state. One of the difficulties with Miliband's analysis, however, is that he does not show the way in which the nature of the state is linked to a theory of social change resulting from class conflict. That is, he provides an essentially static analysis, influenced by the fact that he is refuting the pluralist argument, which does not specify the structures by which movements at the different levels of capitalist society are linked together and determined by one another. He emphasizes the cohesion of the capitalist state but not the way in which the state adjusts to make certain of the *reproduction* of the conditions of production under changing conditions of forces of production and social relations of production.

Miliband in fact notes that the Marxist theory of the state has lagged behind other aspects of Marxist analysis. (A summary of its development can be found in Miliband's article "Marx and the State" in *Socialist Register,* 1965.) It could be argued that a Marxist theory of *the* capitalist state is impossible since analysis of elements of the superstructure must take into account the historical specificity of class structures in each capitalist state. Of course a theoretical problematic is necessary and an important contribution to this has been made by Nicos Poulantzas in his *Pouvoir Politique et Classes Sociales,* Maspero, Paris, 1970. An English edition of this book has just been published by New Left Books, London, 1973. There is an interesting exchange between Poulantzas and Miliband which first appeared in *New Left Review,* nos. 58 and 59, and is reprinted in R. Blackburn (ed.) *Ideology in Social Science* (Fontana), London, 1972.

[6] Miliband, *The State in Capitalist Society,* p. 16.

[7] *Ibid.,* p. 88.

[8] *Ibid.,* p. 92.

[9] This passage from *Social Reform and Revolution* can be found on p. 84 of *Selected Political Writings of Rose Luxemburg,* Monthly Review Press, 1971. On the general nature of social democracy see the essay by Lucio Colletti, "Bern-

stein and the Marxism of the Second International" in L. Colletti, *From Rousseau to Lenin,* New Left Books, London, 1972.

[10] J. M. Keynes, *Essays in Persuasion,* Norton, N. Y., 1963, p. 253.

[11] For a discussion of some of the strange inhabitants of the mystical world of the "neo-classical" economists, see E. K. Hunt and Jesse Schwartz, *A Critique of Economic Theory,* Penguin Modern Economics Readings, 1972.

[12] R. Deaton, "The Fiscal Crisis of the State "*Our Generation,* v.8, no. 4 and also available as a reprint. This is an important article with the exception of the last section which is curiously unrelated to what has gone before. The nature of the "fiscal crisis" should be seen as an issue in the debate referred to below.

[13] C. B. Macpherson, *The Real World of Democracy,* CBC Publication, Toronto, 1965.

[14] They are mentioned in A.R.M. Lower, *Colony to Nation,* Longmans, Toronto, 1957, p. 465.

[15] K. Marx, *The Civil War in France.*

[16] There is of course an outline of the conflict between capitalism and seigneurialism by Marx in the *Communist Manifesto.* Some detailed discussion can be found in the important work of E. J. Hobsbawm. See, for example, his essay "The Crisis of the 17th Century", reprinted in T. Aston (ed.), *Crisis in Europe, 1560-1660,* Anchor, Garden City, 1967, and also his book *The Age of Revolution, 1789-1848,* Mentor, N.Y., 1964. The importance of the type of agrarian revolution has been stressed by Barrington Moore in *Social Origins of Dictatorship and Democracy,* Beacon, Boston, 1966. For the history of the early years of the English working class and an example of the kind of history we need, see E. P. Thompson, *The Making of the English Working Class,* Penguin, Harmondsworth, 1969. The continuing importance of all these points was stressed by Antonio Gramsci. See, for example, his essay "The Southern Question" in Gramsci, *The Modern Prince and Other Writings,* International Publishers, N.Y., 1957.

[17] See E. Genovese, *The World the Slaveholders Made,* Vintage Books, N.Y., 1971, Part I.

[18] Article "Colonies" by Véron de Forbonnais in *L'Encyclopédie.* Quoted by S. B. Ryerson in the *Founding of Canada,* Progress Books, Toronto, 1972, p. 178.

[19] P. Baran, *The Political Economy of Growth,* Monthly Review Press, N.Y. 1957, Ch. 5.

[20] W. A. Williams, *The Contours of American History,* Quadrangle Books, Chicago, 1966. For a brief review see his article in *Canadian Dimension,* Vol. IV, 1967.

[21] See, for example, his *Capitalism and Under-development in Latin America,* Monthly Review Press, N.Y., 1969.

[22] For example, Ernesto Laclau, *New Left Review,* 67, 1971 and also the argument in Genovese's book cited in n.19

[23] K. Marx, *Capital,* v. 1, ch.6.

[24] *Ibid.,* ch. 10.

[25] On this see Phillipe Garigue, "Sociological Interpretations of the Social Evolution of French Canada", in M. Rioux and Y. Martin, *French-Canadian Society,* McClelland and Stewart, Toronto, 1964.

[26] Translated from Gilles Bourque, *Classes Sociales et Question Nationale au Québec,* 1760-1840, Parti Pris, Montreal, 1970, p. 196-8.

[27] For an understanding of the events of 1837 and their significance for the emergence of the capitalist state in Canada the studies by S. B. Ryerson, *Unequal Union,* International Publishers, N.Y. 1968, and Gilles Bourque (cited above) are of major importance. For an understanding of the democratic struggles in

Europe from the 1790's to the 1840's, with which the events in Canada should be compared, see the important work of George Rudé. One example is *The Crowd in the French Revolution*, Oxford U.P., 1959.

[28] Tom Naylor, "The Rise and Fall of the 3rd Commercial Empire of the St. Lawrence" in G. Teeple (ed.) *Capitalism and the National Question*, University of Toronto Press, Toronto, 1972. An understanding of the nature of the Canadian bourgeoisie is essential for an understanding of the Canadian state. See also Gustavus Myers, *A History of Canadian Wealth*; Libbie and Frank Park, *Anatomy of Big Business*. The last two are published by James Lewis and Samuel, Toronto, 1972 and 1973. The books by Stanley Ryerson and Gilles Bourque, cited in n.27, are both important for an understanding of the development of the class structure in Canada.

[29] H. C. Pentland, "The Development of a Capitalistic Labour Market in Canada, *Canadian Journal of Economics and Political Science,* v. 25, 1959, p. 455.

[30] C. Lipton, *The Trade Union Movement of Canada,* 1827-1959, Canadian Social Publications Ltd., Montreal, 1968.

[31] *Ibid.*, p. 32.

[32] See *Last Post,* March, 1973.

[33] Lipton, op.cit, p. 285-6.

[34] *Ibid.*, p. 308.

[35] H. A. Innis, *Essays in Canadian Economic History,* Vol. 8, Toronto, 1956, p. 174.

[36] D. Creighton, *British North America at Confederation*, Queen's Printer, Ottawa, 1963, p.10. This was Creighton's submission to the Royal Commission on Dominion Provincial Relations (Rowell-Sirois Commission).

[37] *Ibid.*, p. 59 (My emphasis).

[38] On this see A. Dubuc, "The Decline of Confederation and the New Nationalism" in P. Russell (ed.) *Nationalism in Canada,* McGraw Hill-Ryerson, Toronto, 1966.

[39] H. A. Innis, *Essays in Canadian Economic History,* p. 209.

[40] Quoted in F. Clairmonte, *Economic Liberalism and Under-development,* Asia Publishing House, Bombay, 1960, p. 14.

[41] H. A. Innis, *The Fur Trade in Canada,* University of Toronto Press, Toronto, 1962, p. 385.

[42] Quoted in Peter C. Newman, *Renegade in Power: The Diefenbaker Years,* McClelland and Stewart, Toronto, 1963, p. 337.

[43] W. L. Morton, *The Canadian Identity,* University of Toronto Press, Toronto, 1964, p. 81.

[44] *Toronto Star,* May 30, 1973.

[45] See Peter C. Newman, *The Distemper of Our Times*, McClelland and Stewart, Toronto, 1968, pp. 224-26.

The Trade Union Movement in Canada
Mel Watkins

In a capitalist society, unions are the largest institutions of the working class. To know anything of labour history is to know that they were literally created by the blood, sweat and tears of workers. To know the indigenous songs of workers is to know how many are related to particular strikes and to particular unions. I say this because a socialist analysis of unions is, in many respects, critical of unions as we know them today, and I do not wish to be misunderstood. At a time when unions are under sustained attack from the right, it is necessary to understand that a critique from the left is a very different matter. To criticize is not to undermine, but to help to transform – to make them more powerful and more militant. In short, the socialist position on unions is, in the words of the famous song, "The union makes us strong."

In 1971 there were 2,200,000 trade unionists in Canada, comprising 33.3 per cent of the paid non-agricultural work force. Sixty-two per cent of unionists in 1971 belonged to international, that is to say, to American unions operating in Canada. The Canadian Labour Congress (CLC), the main trade union central, had 74.8 per cent of union members affiliated to it.[1] There are three other centrals: the Confederation of National Trade Unions (CNTU) and the new Confederation of Democratic Unions in Quebec, and the Confederation of Canadian Unions (CCU).

If continentalism is one striking feature of the Canadian trade union movement, a second is fragmentation. The 2.2 million unionists in 1971 were grouped into 10,056 locals with an average membership of about 220.[2]

A third feature – notwithstanding the second – is the tendency for the larger work places to be organized. Conversely, we can ask: which workers are least likely to be organized? The answer is those working for small employers, white-collar workers in the private sector, and women.

Historically, skilled workers tended to be organized first, into *craft unions*, and later all workers of a plant or industry into *industrial unions*. In recent years, major gains have been made in organizing public employees.

In a capitalist society, there are two basic classes – the capitalists and the workers. They are defined in terms of their respective relationship to production, that is, ownership vs. non-ownership of the means of production. To exist, the worker must sell his labour-power to the capitalist, but that labour-power then produces a greater value than it itself costs; that is, it produces surplus value, which is simply unpaid labour, appropriated by the capitalist.

The question then becomes: how is the value which the worker produces divided between capital and labour, that is, what portion will be wages? The role of unions is evident from the answer that Marx gave to that question (in *Value, Price and Profit*):

> Although we can fix the minimum of wages, we cannot fix their maximum. We can only say that, the limits of the working day being given, the maximum of profit corresponds to the physical minimum of wages; and that wages being given, the maximum of profit corresponds to such a prolongation of the working day as is compatible with the physical forces of the labourer. The maximum of profit is therefore limited by the physical minimum of wages and the physical maximum of the working day. It is evident that between the two limits of the maximum rate of profit, an immense scale of variations is possible. The fixation of its actual degree is only settled by the continuous struggle between capital and labour, the capitalist constantly tending to reduce wages to their physical minimum, and to extend the working day to its physical maximum, while the workingman constantly presses in the opposite direction. The question resolves itself into a question of the respective power of the combatants.

Marx then proceeds to make two very important points about strategy. The first has to do with what he calls legislative interference. "As to the *limitations of the working day*, in England, as in all other countries, it has never been settled except by *legislative interference*. Without the workingman's continuous pressure from without, that interference would never have taken place. . . . The result was not to be attained by private settlement between the workingmen and the capitalists. This very necessity of *general political action* affords the proof that in the merely economic action capital is the stronger side."

The second has to do specifically with unions. "Trade unions work well as centres of resistance against the encroachments of capital." It is true that unions struggle within a system in which workers sell their labour power as commodities. But, to merely demand "A fair day's wage for a fair day's work," would be to accept wage slavery under capitalism. In addition to these demands, the workers must also use "their organized forces as a lever for the final emancipation of the working class, that is to say, the ultimate abolition of the wage system."

What should be stressed at this point is that unions can modify the distribution of income between capital and labour in favour of labour.

During the period of rising productivity since World War II, labour has only been able to hold its own in bargaining with capitalists, that is to say, in the economy as a whole, wage gains have not outstripped productivity gains. This suggests that without unions, in the post-war period, the share of production going to labour would actually have fallen.

Thus the fallacy of the view that unions cause inflation. This is an important matter, particularly because many people, including unorganized workers, believe that they do, and harbour anti-union sentiments as a result. This issue, indeed, is very relevant to the divide-and-conquer tactics of the corporations, aided and abetted by the media.

Corporations are clearly powerful and reserve to themselves the unilateral right to set prices. We know that wage settlements are followed by price hikes, but we also know that the big companies use the occasion of wage settlements to hike prices by more than wage costs have risen. Even John Young of the Prices and Income Commission finally admitted – though only after a lot of loose and damaging talk – that unions are not the major culprit.

The root cause of inflation lies not with unions, but rather with the contemporary structure of corporate capitalism. Capitalism is now monopoly capitalism, not *laissez-faire* capitalism. Inflation results, therefore, from corporations administering prices; they avoid competing through price cuts, but compete through sales promotion which drives prices up, and they may raise rather than lower prices when demand slackens, hence contributing to the simultaneous occurrence of unemployment and inflation.

Inflation, of course, erodes the income of working people and reduces the value of wage increases previously won. Unions, in turn, properly endeavour to protect their members by making further wage demands sufficient to compensate for the loss through inflation.

Seen in this light, unions protect their members from an inflation not of their making. It follows that those workers who are not organized – and those outside the labour force, such as the aged – are the real losers. The latter, being only too conscious of this, feel split off from the unionized workers and are often easy prey for the propaganda that unions are themselves the cause of their impoverishment.

The appropriate response for the labour movement, as well as doing educational work, is to adopt a class perspective rather than simply an economist perspective. It must put forth as political demands that old age pensions and minimum wage levels be tied in full to the cost-of-living escalator. They must agitate politically for price controls – but not, of course, for wage controls.

The latter point is particularly relevant, for it is possible – indeed probable, in the new era of inter-imperialist rivalry – that Canada will shortly have wage/price controls. Since price and wage controls are simply a guise for freezing wages so as to keep costs down for Canadian capitalists, unions must refuse to go along with them. But they should be more than ready to call for price controls as a way to protect the working class as a whole from being exploited by the corporations.

Class Consciousness and Business Unionism
In terms of class consciousness, unions represent, in Lenin's distinction, trade union consciousness rather than socialist consciousness. Unions are defensive organizations operating within the system, which is no small matter, but they are not necessarily socialist or anti-capitalist. The class consciousness of the Canadian trade union movement is overwhelmingly trade union consciousness.

Eric Hobsbawm, the British historian, suggests there are four stages, or levels, of the labour movement: 1) individual revolt, crime, and machine-wrecking; 2) trade unionism and strikes; 3) political movements in general; 4) socialist movements in particular. He also observes that the development of labour parties is so common in industrial capitalist societies that it is necessary to explain the infrequent cases where they have not developed, as in the United States.

Class consciousness must be understood as an historical phenomenon, as rooted in the interaction of capitalist relations of production and the specific nature of culture and institutions. The Canadian working class has been powerfully influenced, on the one hand, by British social democracy and, on the other hand, by the Gomperism of American unions. Social democracy is the politics of the British labour movement at the height of British imperialism, and Gomperism or business unionism is the politics of the American labour movement at a critical phase of American imperialism. The result has been to inhibit anti-imperialist consciousness among Canadian workers.

Affecting the consciousness of workers is the fact that between capitalists and workers there stand an array of middle groups belonging to neither of these basic classes. There are declining groups – independent farmers, fishermen and tradesmen – and also new middle groups – industrial and government bureaucrats, salesmen, publicists, and professionals. However, Leo Johnson argues[3] convincingly that the petty bourgeoisie has declined in Canada, largely by being proletarianized. Furthermore, he observes the relative stability of blue-collar workers, and evidence of their increasing alienation; the rapid growth of the white-collar sector, particularly clerical workers, but growing proletarianization and alienation, with white-collar unions now the most rapidly expanding sector of the labour movement. He also notes the growth of professionals with enormous income gains, as in the case of doctors, particularly by the self-employed, but an overall decline in the proportion of professionals in independent practice and an increasing tendency, particularly among teachers, towards an income squeeze, that is, some tendency toward proletarianization, and in Quebec to unionization. From an examination of both the old and the new middle classes, Johnson suggests the Canadian class structure is being simplified and polarized, and this has very important implications for both unionism and socialism.

When we observe actual class structures, it is necessary for us to see the diversity. For as well as diversity, we observe fractionalization of the working class, selective bribing, co-opting, false consciousness. And that too is in the nature of capitalism, for it is in the interest of the capitalists to divide and conquer and to prevent the solidarity of the working class. Hence workers are divided between countries and within countries, between organized and unorganized, and are encouraged to be sexist and racist. The reverse of the coin is that unions, to fight capitalism, have to struggle against sexism, racism, bourgeois nationalism and elitism (*vis-à-vis* the unorganized and those on welfare), and by recreating solidarity, create class consciousness.

Workers' consciousness is powerfully affected by the nature of unionism. Business unionism has reduced the fighting capacity of Canadian workers in their confrontations with the corporations. Because business unionism accepts the view that, given certain specified reforms, capitalism as a system serves the best interests of workers, it blunts the edge of workers' militancy and trade union consciousness, not to mention class consciousness.

It is no accident that business unionism in Canada has managed to eliminate militant traditions in the trade union movement. For example, in 1946 the Canadian Congress of Labour, which brought together all the industrial (CIO) unions in Canada, organized a co-ordinated campaign of several key unions in Canada for negotiations and demands. Even the timing of strikes was co-ordinated, with IWA in British Columbia as the lead-off union. This co-ordination produced the biggest and most successful strike movement in English Canadian history which made the important break-through on the eight-hour day and the 40-hour week as the norm for the country. It led to the victory of the Steelworkers union in Stelco in Hamilton against fierce odds, and the success of seamen, woodworkers, rubber, electrical, chemical and many other workers. It consolidated unions like the USWA, the UAW, and the UE, the IWA (in B.C.) and several more.

But such co-ordination of negotiations, which once confronted the large corporations and the Canadian state with the power of several hundred thousand workers, has vanished. Now, the skill of a few top experienced business negotiators, rather than the power and mobilization of the rank and file, must force the employers to realize that the workers know their power and intend to exercise it.

For the most part union leaders have accepted the philosophy

183

of the cooling off period in negotiations to avoid strikes. They have failed to fight the whole battery of labour legislation whose purpose it is to soften the class struggle, through certification, conciliation, arbitration and the illegalization of strikes between contracts. Although they have raised objections to anti-labour injunctions and the use of strike-breaking agencies they have avoided the powerful weapon of direct workers' actions. Labour legislation objectively has the purpose of tying workers' hands, reducing militancy by confining strike action to specified periods. With this legislation has evolved the tendency to prolong existing contracts. In the 1940s, for example, union contracts were negotiated annually, thus giving the rank and file a chance as an organized force to confront the boss once a year. This kept the union in fighting trim by having at least several months of intensive activity each year. Today, many if not most contracts have been stretched to three years. When one takes into account the period of negotiations beyond an expiry date and a possible strike, as in De Havilland in Toronto, the average contract period can be as high as three and one-half or four years.

No wonder that unions have become less and less active, with attendance at meetings in large locals dropping to a low of one or two per cent of the membership. The local union has less and less meaning in the life of the average worker because the union's activity centres on a rather staged exercise every few years, in which top negotiators meet behind closed doors with the company and keep developments secret. The workers become alienated from their union just as they are alienated from each other and themselves, because of their role in work under capitalism. Little wonder that an increasing number of trade union members become anti-union, and even accept anti-labour, anti-strike attacks by the media and corporate spokesmen. Trade union leaders decry such sentiments among their members, but are unable to cope with them because their advocacy of business unionism is the real source of a drop in trade union militancy and support.

The most dramatic expression of this consequence of business unionism is seen in the U.S., the headquarters of American unions in Canada. The AFL-CIO leadership after some initial hesitation supported Nixon's 1971 wage freeze. Leaders of the Steelworkers in the U.S. have been in the forefront of the movement to curtail strikes. They unveiled this latest policy in 1973 at a meeting of union presidents, called by the Pittsburgh headquarters without prior discussion by the membership. They agreed to accept a no-strike policy for three years – a policy which they hoped would set a new pattern for peace in industry and become a permanent feature of labour-management relations in the U.S.A.

Such a policy of eliminating even "legal" strikes, results in restricting the dimensions of negotiations to existing issues of wages, hours and fringe benefits. Issues such as lay-offs, plant shut-downs, technological changes, control of foremen (and thus defense of the dignity of the worker), elimination or curtailment of boredom and mind-dulling repetition on the job – such issues receive little or no attention. The illegalization of walk-outs between contract periods hampers union activism and militancy – the very issue over which the British trade union movement developed great militancy and a near general strike in the spring of 1973.

Perhaps the most obvious expression of business unionism is to be found in the argument often heard on the issue of organizing the unorganized. "It takes $300.00 to $500.00 to organize a worker and it would take many years to get our union investment back in the form of dues," goes the argument. The conclusion is that workers in small and medium-sized plants are thus not worth organizing.

The effect of the fragmentation of unions, of union locals often going it alone is the smashing of strikes in small and medium-sized enterprises. Such locals have been easy prey for strike-breaking agencies like Canadian Driver Pool and Grange, with the labour movement as a whole either coming in too late to help or not helping at all. An example is that of the Dare Strike in Kitchener, Ontario, where it took the labour movement almost a year to rally to support of the strikers – support which culminated in the demonstration of 5,000 workers in Kitchener in May 1973. This demonstration of support happened largely because of the work of Support Committees in general, and the Waffle group in particular – people who supplied the drive, organizational cohesion and human power in support of the active strikers to help mobilize the labour movement. But by that time it was too late to win the strike on the picket line, and the only prospect open was for a prolonged boycott campaign against Dare Cookies. The prospects were less promising than they would have been two or three months after the strike began.

Allowing smaller locals to be smashed by anti-labour injunctions and strike-breaking agencies has sapped the morale of the trade union movement and weakened the drive to organize the unorganized. If business unionism has become the life-style of the union as seen by the rank and file, for the full-time officialdom it has become truly a business and a prosperous one at that.

There is now a large complement of full-time officials who tend to get cut off from their rank and file. Once in a full-time staff position there is a tendency, as with all bureaucracies where removal or change of staffers is difficult, for officialdom to hold on at all costs. Nothing is considered worse than the possibility that they might have to return to their previous job or type of work. For many staffers holding on to their job has become more important than anything else in the union. Approximately 4,000 full-time staffers constitute the permanent "civil service" of the trade union movement in Canada. The tendency is for them to reach a standard of pay, with special daily and travel allowances and a way of life which is far removed from the members whom they are hired to serve. Top officers in the Steel Workers or Auto-workers in Canada now have salaries and perquisites which are equivalent to about three times that of the highest-paid workers in that industry and five times that of the average worker.

Symbolizing business unionism is the physical location of the Ontario Federation of Labour building in Toronto. Nestled among corporations like the I.B.M. and Texaco, it is in an area far removed from workers in the plants and institutions who make up the membership of the OFL. On the bottom floor, there is a bank.

While dozens of local halls where the rank and file gather are often beehives of activity and expressions of working class militancy and consciousness, the top business leaders of unions tend to separate themselves off in plush offices and into areas which are free from the smell of the factory or mine.

The fact that the headquarters which pay these officials are in the U.S. and that officials are ultimately responsible to Pittsburgh, Chicago, Detroit, New York or Washington, removes them still further from ordinary workers in Canada. Much of the anti-union feeling which exists among union members stems from this phenomenon. The feeling that the union is not really the rank-

and-file, but that it consists of the staffers and that the union serves the staffers first, is largely responsible for the low level of union activism and morale.

The loss of the Kitimat local of the USWA to a Canadian union was presumably due to such loss of contact between staffers and rank and file. The Canadian leaders of the USWA have admitted this condition under pressure to explain the much-publicised loss of the local to a Canadian union.

Probably the most flagrant expression of business unionism and the ready acceptance of capitalism as a desirable system for the workers is the movement of union leaders into company or government jobs. This has happened in the very field of "labour-relations" – where just prior to becoming corporate men, they had presumably been representing the workers. A recent case of a president of a large USWA local in Ontario who went to work for the company on "labour relations" before his term had expired was a logical out-come of business unionism.

Unions and the National Question

The issue of international or American unions in Canada must be put into the broadest possible framework. The lot of workers and the nature of their institutions in one country cannot be discussed except with reference to the political economy of that country as shaped by its place in the imperial chain, in the hierarchy of metropolis/hinterland relations. Canada is a dependent capitalist country now deeply integrated into the American empire. The history of Canadian unions is coincidental with the increasing Americanization of the economy, with the northward spread of the American-based multi-national corporation since the late 19th century, and with "special status" for Canada from 1945 to 1971.

The classic defense of international unions in Canada is to point to the multi-national corporation as a fact of life, to say that it should be fought by multi-national unions, and to imply that that is what international unions really are. The problem with this line of reasoning is that it misidentifies international unions. It pretends they are multi-national unions, while in fact they are continental, or American unions operating in Canada with their head office, in every case, in the United States.

But there is no denying that the name of the game is to do battle with the multi-national corporation. Corporations have gone multi-national, and if workers are to protect their position, they must act multi-nationally as well. But a multi-national labour movement would mean, not American unions operating outside the United States – which smacks of piling one kind of imperialism on top of another – but rather national labour movements closely co-operating with each other. From that perspective, each country needs to have a powerful labour movement, a body able to protect the interest of its workers in the real world of corporate imperialism where whole countries can be exploited, and able to establish fraternal relations with workers in any and all countries.

Nor need the fight against the multi-national corporation be confined to accepting its existence in perpetuity. The socialist alternative to the multi-national corporation is public ownership and national planning. The struggle for that will not be easy and a powerful and national labour movement is a prerequisite to its success.

To put things this way is to see that American unions in Canada necessarily inhibit the development of a Canadian labour movement. They do this by fragmenting the union structure. They do it by causing Canadian workers to relate in a limited economic way with U.S. workers in the same industry, rather than in a political way with Canadian workers in other industries. They do it by dampening national consciousness, since to raise the national question at any level is to risk having it spill over to the area of the labour movement itself.

The issue is not only the fact of American unions in Canada, but the nature of American unions. Of all industrial capitalist countries, the American labour movement is the most committed to business unionism, and is also the most conservative if not the most reactionary. Hence, we are not surprised when John Crispo[4] tells us that international unions have a moderating influence on Canadian labour. He cites that as a benefit – a plus for the internationals – but others are allowed to disagree.

Consider two infamous interventions by the AFL. During World War I a number of Canadian workers either were anti-conscriptionist, or were saying that if labour was to be conscripted, so should wealth. Samuel Gompers, President of the AFL, at the invitation of Prime Minister Borden addressed our House of Commons in favour of conscription. Again, during the Winnipeg General Strike of 1919, Canada's Minister of Labour got the

AFL to use its influence on its Canadian affiliates to stop the strike spreading outside Winnipeg, specifically to Toronto, and did so by citing the threat of the One Big Union (OBU), which stood for industrial unions and militancy, to the AFL, which stood for craft unions and conservatism.

Is it possible, however, that American unions would willingly yield to national unions were they desired by Canadian workers? The historical experience is suggestive. American unionism began to spread into Canada by the 1860s, basically for skilled tradesmen like the printers who wanted to continue to have mobility across the border. By 1873, the first trade union central, the Canadian Labour Union had been established – 13 years before the formation of the AFL in the U.S. In the 1880s, a second trade union central emerged, the Knights of Labour – also imported, but devoted to the unskilled industrial workers rather than the skilled craftsman. In 1886, the craft unions of the CLU and the Knights joined to create the TLC (Trades and Labour Congress), in contrast to the U.S. where the AFL excluded the Knights from its inception. In the 1890's the Knights declined in the U.S. but remained as unions in Canada, and particularly in Quebec; that is, the Knights became in practice a Canadian trade union central. At the same time, AFL influence was growing inside the TLC. At the 1902 Convention, a motion was passed that "no national union be recognized when an international union exists." As Charles Lipton argues,[5] the Knights were automatically excluded, the unity of the Canadian labour movement was split, and the effect was "a counter-revolution" in the Congress. In the first decade of the century, 90 per cent of all unionists in Canada were ensconced in international unions, but it was not a decision freely arrived at.

In the 1920s – 1927 to be precise – a new Canadian trade union central emerged, the All-Canadian Congress of Labour, or ACCL, around the Canadian Brotherhood of Railway Employees. The ACCL was militantly nationalist and committed to industrial unionism. In the 1930's, a period of smashing of trade unions in both Canada and the United States was followed by a great spurt of industrial unionism and the emergence of the CIO in the United States. Simultaneously, industrial unionism grew rapidly in Canada. In the late 1930's, this was particularly marked after the great sit-down strike by the GM workers in Oshawa in 1937, an event which reflected not only spontaneous trade unionism but also the role of the political left, the Communist Party and the CCF. Overwhelmingly, these unions were organized by Canadians, and just as overwhelmingly chartered into American unions. In 1941, a weakened ACCL merged with the CIO unions to create the CCL (Canadian Congress of Labour), and the ACCL had to yield to CIO demands that all locals within the CIO jurisdiction must automatically join the appropriate CIO union. Labour historian Irving Abella argues that the victory of the internationals was finally consolidated at the 1952 CCL convention, when CIO unions achieved full control over CCL affairs and "the last lingering hopes for a purely Canadian national labour organization disappeared."[6]

This discussion is not intended to portray Canadian unions through rose-coloured glasses. In 1937, Aaron Mosher, president of the ACCL, supported General Motors' and Premier Mitch Hepburn's anti-labour movement in their futile attempt to smash the CIO. The point is rather that the short-run benefits of American unionism in Canada are offset in the long run by their entrenched put-down of Canadian unions.

In spite of all the current claims by the large industrial international unions that the Canadian sections have full autonomy, flagrant cases of interference from the American head office point to the centre of real power.

Canadian supporters of American unions argue that for the most part Canadian workers benefit from the U.S. connection, because the U.S. headquarters often finance Canadian workers in strikes. This argument runs in the face of the figures of CALURA, a government agency which reports a substantial financial balance in favour of U.S. union headquarters in terms of union money flowing between the two countries.

Even more important is the claim that U.S. headquarters never interfere with Canadian workers. Well, it happened in 1971 in the Douglas Aircraft strike in Toronto, in a union which makes great claims to "Canadian Autonomy" – the UAW.

Briefly, the American union was anxious for a settlement with the Douglas corporation in the U.S. The strike at the Douglas plant in Canada threatened production in the U.S. plants. The American union leaders tried several manoeuvres, including the appearance of some 25 or 30 international representatives at a meeting in Massey Hall, Toronto, where the strikers turned down the high-pressure attempt to force a settlement. After this failed, the Canadian strike committee at Douglas headed by Archie Wilson was ordered to appear at Solidarity House, headquarters of the UAW in Detroit. There, in the Detroit office, the American president Leonard Woodcock and the American Executive Board ordered Canadian workers at Douglas back to work – with the declaration that they were, as of then, cut off from strike pay.

The argument has continued to rage as to whether the American President and Executive Board, in ordering an end to the strike and in interfering directly in the affairs of a Canadian local had acted on behalf of a majority of workers in that plant. The contention was that a minority of radicals in the local had obstructed the will of the majority, and that Detroit had come to the rescue of that majority.

Two succeeding elections in the local have answered that question. Five months after the strike, Archie Wilson was re-elected with a majority of 600 votes as Plant Chairman. One year after this first test, the President of the Local and his supporters who had backed the return-to-work movement against those who wanted the strike to continue, and who campaigned against the "useless strike," were roundly defeated by the group which had been in the leadership of the strike. The real sentiment of the majority is now beyond challenge, and the story of the American headquarters cancellation of a Canadian strike stands as a monument to domination by an American union of Canadian workers who allegedly enjoy "Canadian autonomy".

Another example of direct interference by the headquarters of a U.S. union in Canada is an event that occurred in 1966 in the Hamilton Local of the U.S.W.A. (Local 1005) in Stelco, the largest local in the Canadian steel industry with 11,000 members. A group known as the "Autonomy Group" were active in the union's affairs and were critical of their union leadership. At the time of a rise in union dues they argued that such increases had in the past been accompanied by a rise in the high salaries of top officers and staffers.

For this they were charged by Stewart Cook, International representative of the union. Although a trial committee of the local found them guilty, a meeting of the Local membership at which over 600 workers were present voted against the trial committee's recommendations and acquitted them. In spite of this, the Pittsburgh office of the U.S.W.A. suspended their constitutional rights for one year. During that time they were not even allowed to visit the Steelworkers Hall in Hamilton. Moreover, because the constitution provides that steelworkers must be union members in good standing for two years to run for office in the union, they were effectively barred from running for a period of four years.

The fact that these people were simultaneously the main advocates of greater control of their union in Canada may be coincidental. However, the boast of the u.s.w.a. leaders in Canada that their union enjoys full Canadian autonomy to decide all matters relating to the Canadian membership carried a hollow ring in the face of this high-handed decision of the Pittsburgh headquarters against the rights of Canadian workers to criticise a rise in dues and the allegation that such dues would boost officers' salaries. If that is autonomy, then Canadian workers need much more – full independence – to be masters in their own union house.

The question of international unions must be put in the context of Canada's hinterland status *vis-à-vis* the U.S., that is, in the context of American imperialism. Dependence creates costs for Canadian workers, in terms of fewer jobs and a lower standard of living, and thereby creates objective conditions that should favour national unions. Why, then, have international unions persisted? It is not enough to cite the activities of U.S. union leaders and their Canadian counterparts, real though their power is in blocking national unions. Certainly, the AFL-CIO and the CLC leadership have not stopped the QFL from relating in a radical way to the economics and politics of Quebec. Rather, we must recognize that the costs of dependence have not been crippling for English – Canadian workers, and Canadian unionists have generally done well, or at least well enough from their point of view. This results from Canada's historic special status within the American empire.

Special status can be used as a term to describe Canada's position within the American empire from 1945 to 1971. During most of this period, as the American economic empire expanded, Canada's economy expanded along with it. Special status was most evident in special arrangements – the military agreements of World War II, NORAD, and the Defence Sharing Agreements; the autopact; the exemption from the Interest Equalization Tax in 1963 and from balance of payments directives to direct investment firms in 1965 and

1968. When in the late 1960s America's economic hegemony was threatened by resurgent economies in Japan and Western Europe, the process of de-industrialization began in the Canadian economy. In 1971 Nixon's new economic policies marked the end of special status for Canada.

At the same time, our status as a resource supplier to the U.S. has not been ended, but enhanced, though it creates few jobs directly and can destroy many indirectly. Furthermore, the AFL-CIO unions, which had supported freer trade following World War II as part of the great consensus with the multinational corporations, have moved sharply protectionist. This is evident from their support for the Burke-Hartke bill, which would set quotas on U.S. imports of manufactured goods at their late 1960s level. When Canadian Steelworkers went to the international union's convention in Las Vegas in the fall of 1972, they encountered Buy American posters and were subjected to an address on the virtues of Burke-Hartke. The effect was consciousness-raising – in this case, national consciousness.

Overall, the apparent ending of special status puts independence for the Canadian economy more firmly on the agenda of our politics. It does the same for Canadian unionists. But it does not in itself end the search for special status. The first response of the Trudeau government after August 1971 was to go to Washington and plead for the restoration of special status. The then Secretary of the Treasury Connally sent the Ministers home with their tails between their legs, but you may be sure they haven't given up trying. Similarly, the heads of the Canadian sections of the international unions have argued that international unions are beneficial because they enable Canadian workers to lobby the American union leaders for special status.

Let me quote from the *Globe and Mail* of December 5, 1972:

> As part of their campaign for Canada's exemption (from Burke-Hartke), Canadian Labour Congress spokesmen visiting the United States have told U.S. unionists that Canada exports mostly job-creating raw materials to the United States.
>
> "We are creating jobs for them through this trade," a CLC official said recently. [That we can agree with! Then it gets nasty.] "We support the intention of this bill, which is to

curb cheap imports from 'slave-wage' countries like Japan and Taiwan," the officials said. "But Canada is not the same as those countries."

The CLC spokesman also said that because Canadian union members belong largely to international labour organizations, this enabled them to argue more successfully for Canadian exemption."

Nor is the campaign utterly misguided. *Time* magazine of December 11, 1972, reports: "During a Steelworkers' seminar in Niagara Falls, Ontario last month, International President I. W. Abel agreed to press for Canadian exemption from Burke-Hartke." And Leonard Woodcock of the UAW – a union which is not supporting Burke-Hartke – supports the rights of Canadian workers under the Autopact.

Whether the U.S. unions can get this for their Canadian brothers as part of the Nixon Administration's new love-affair with them remains to be seen. But even that is not the real point. Rather, what has to be understood is that such a strategy puts Canadian workers in the untenable position of asking for favours, and is bought at the price of evading the alternative strategy of independence – for the Canadian economy and for Canadian workers within their unions.

There is now a cleavage between the American union leadership and Canadian workers. It is not of the making of Canadian workers, but neither should it be seen as basically of the making of American workers. American workers do not run the United States, but the multi-national corporations do. The present split has been created by Nixonomics and the fact that the leadership of the American trade union movement supports Nixonomics.

Given the intransigence of the leadership of the CLC and the American unions in Canada, the near future is likely to see further break-aways of single locals and a concerted counter attempt by the internationals to smash the Confederation of Canadian Unions. But in the longer run, as the contradictions in the Canadian-American relationship increasingly manifest themselves, we might expect to see the breakaway of whole Canadian sections. The independent Canadian unions that will result will do much to increase anti-imperialist consciousness among working people and thereby transform Canadian politics.

Labour and Politics

We have seen that trade unions are indeed necessary for workers to improve their lot under capitalism; in fact, they are their most important institution. But we have also seen that "pure and simple" unionism is not sufficient, but must be supplemented by general political action. This is true under capitalism; it is doubly true if the intent is to abolish capitalism and create socialism.

Furthermore, we have noted that almost everywhere under industrial capitalism, we see not only trade unions but also labour parties – and even socialist parties. Canada is not an exeption, as witness the NDP and, at least historically, the Communist Party.

In fact, what we observe is a relationship between unions and political parties, where the more politically conscious unionists support social democratic or socialist parties, and where political parties of the left endeavour to create formal links with the labour movement.

Historically, in the 1930s and 1940s, members of the Communist Party and of the CCF played critical roles as union organizers and deserve much of the credit for moving Canada into the age of industrial unionism. As already noted, both parties had much to do with Canadian workers joining the internationals and the CIO. This is presumably related to the fact that neither party was able then – or even down to this day – to evolve a serious commitment to linking independence and socialism.

So far as present electoral politics are concerned, many workers still look to the NDP. Thus, the relevant question is whether the NDP understands the contradictions that presently face Canadian working people and is prepared to organize around them. The Cold War, the revelations about Stalin, and the Russian adventures in Eastern Europe destroyed the credibility of the Communist Party. The CCF survived, but in the face of the Diefenbaker landslide of 1958 merged with the CLC to form the NDP.

Affiliation of unions with the NDP might have seemed a good thing at the time. But recent history suggests that neither the trade union movement nor the NDP benefitted from the formalization of the ties. On the one hand, for many rank-and-file trade unionists voting for NDP candidates became a substitute for grass-roots political involvement within the unions. On the other hand, rank-and-file unionists failed to get involved in the affairs of the party to any significant degree; indeed, many voted Liberal or Conservative while their check-offs went to the NDP. As the party began to move toward a tough stand on independence and social-ism, a handful of Canadian leaders of the international unions choked off the process. In the long run, that is bound to be costly to the labour movement itself, for Canadian workers find that their labour party is not very different from the two existing capitalist parties and is intolerant of change.

But to find the NDP wanting is not to leave trade unions with nothing to do in the seventies in the area of general political action. In the face of the Nixonomics of resource exploitation and de-industrialization, a cleavage exists between American labour leadership and Canadian workers. Canadian unionists can define the interests of Canadian workers as a class. They can put forth general demands – like stopping the Mackenzie Valley pipeline. They can advocate independent political action outside the party system, such as common front activities by the CLC. They can move beyond the reformism of the NDP and play a major role in the creation of a new socialist party which truly represents the interests of the Canadian working class.

Notes

[1] *Canada Year Book*, 1972, pp. 866, 867.
[2] *Canada Year Book*, 1972, p. 866.
[3] Leo A. Johnson, "The development of class in Canada in the twentieth century," in Gary Teeple, ed., *Capitalism and the national question in Canada* (Toronto, 1972)
[4] John Crispo, *International Unionism: A Study in Canadian-American Relations* (Toronto, 1969)
[5] Charles Lipton, *The Trade Union Movement of Canada, 1827-1959* (Montreal, 1967)
[6] I. M. Abella, "Lament for a Union Movement," in Ian Lumsden, ed., *Close the 49th parallel etc: the Americanization of Canada* (Toronto, 1970), p. 89; see also his *Nationalism, Communism, and Canadian Labour: The CIO, the Communist party, and the Canadian Congress of Labour 1935-1956* (Toronto, 1973).

Populist and Socialist Movements in Canadian History
John Smart

Canada is and has been a society where economic and political power have been concentrated, rather than distributed on an egalitarian basis. This was true of the seigneurial system in New France, the agricultural and commercial societies of the English colonial period after 1763, and of modern Canada under industrial capitalism. Just as important – Canada is, and has been throughout its history, a colony[1] in successively the French, British, and American empires. Since people want control over their lives, though, our history is equally a history of people's movements aimed at redistributing power in their favour.

The rebellions of 1837 in Upper and Lower Canada, the Riel rebellions of 1870 and 1885 in Manitoba and Saskatchewan, the farmers' movements and their political parties after 1890, and the socialist and labour movements in the modern period all involved large numbers of Canadians in collective efforts along the same lines. Canadian historians have, by and large, been content to tell the basic facts about these events rather than going on to develop detailed and comprehensive analyses. Good books exist on all these events but there is no school of Canadian scholars devoting themselves to further study of these phenomena. In the case of socialist and labour movement history, it is only in the past five years that even the basic books have begun to appear.[2]

Few Canadian scholars have called themselves Marxists. We therefore lack the research and analyses in Canadian history which their point of view provides. As one member of the younger generation of Marxist scholars put it recently:

> ... there is little evidence on the Canadian left of the deep concern for factual accuracy, indigenous theoretical elabora-

tion, and insight into the unique circumstances of national class development which has characterized European Marxist thought. In most cases the little intellectual work that has been undertaken is devoted almost entirely to polemics rather than analysis. . . . As a result of these failures, political leadership of Canadian Marxists has been almost uniformly disastrous . . . generally and rightfully distrusted in Canada by the very classes whose interests it desires to serve.[3]

So most Canadian history has not been written by socialists. As our scholars become socialists and as our socialists become scholars this situation will change. These intellectual developments will, of course, not materialize unless the working people of the country are also moving to socialism and demanding that their history be written. From the historical accounts that do exist at present, it is clear that the important people's movements in Canada's past do not all share the same motivation or pattern of development.

The rebellions of the nineteenth century were aimed at achieving political independence and at breaking the log-jam of reactionary British policy. The *patriotes* and the followers of Mackenzie in Upper Canada in 1837 sought each other out and were able to agree to co-ordinate the timing of their uprisings because they shared a common problem – the imperial control of Great Britain, imposed through local élites chosen by Westminster. By the fall of 1837 the economy of the St. Lawrence-Great Lakes system was in serious crisis due to local crop failures and to a series of commercial disasters that started in London and reached Montreal and York, as well as the United States, very quickly.

The British government was unable to deal with these problems in the colonies and was unwilling to let the colonists deal with them themselves through their assemblies. In the case of Lower Canada, the governor took the initiative and moved against the *patriotes* before their organization for an uprising was complete. The rebellions in both Upper and Lower Canada were aborted, but the home government was forced to change its policies toward British North America. A one-man royal commission – Lord Durham – was sent out to investigate. His recommendation that the colonies be given "responsible government" was eventually taken up by the British government.

In the case of the Riel rebellions in the Northwest more than a generation later, the local population – Indian, white and Metis – united against the colonial status which Ottawa insisted upon imposing on the territory purchased from the Hudson's Bay Company in 1869. The Métis and Indians were also resisting the loss of their lands, and of their distinctive way of life, culture, and economy. They knew all these were threatened by Ottawa's plans for the settlement and development of the West.

The local population was not forgotten by Ottawa . . . it was purposely ignored. Control of the land and natural resources of the Northwest was seen by Ottawa as essential in order to finance the private railway company. This company would build the line to British Columbia and people the country with immigrants. The principle of local control could not be admitted. The Métis nation had existed at Red River since the eighteenth century and had developed a sophisticated economy and culture, including an educational system and ties with Quebec. It was natural that such a community would resist, and in 1869-70 it did so effectively. The representatives of the Canadian government were not allowed entry. A provisional government was set up, and its representatives went to Ottawa and negotiated provincial status for their part of Manitoba.

The only mistakes made by the Red River community in 1870 stemmed from *naiveté*. People there believed Ottawa's promises about amnesty for their national leader, Louis Riel, and a clean slate all round. Instead, the Canadian government and the British co-operated and a military expedition under Garnet Wolseley (one of the great imperialist soldiers of the nineteenth century) was sent to take possession of Red River. Provincial status was not withdrawn, but control of land and natural resources of the Canadian west was retained by Ottawa until 1929.

The Métis broke up and many moved to Saskatchewan, where a second, bloodier revolt was staged for the same reasons in 1885. The federal government responded in the same way except that, following the 1885 rebellion, really punitive measures were taken against the Indian population because they too had risen in conjunction with the Métis.[4]

The historical role consistently assigned to the west by the federal government in Ottawa has determined the character and persistence of western revolt.

The current indifference of the politicians and the courts to the claims of the native peoples of James Bay and the Mackenzie Valley for land rights and for protection of their environment and way of life, as threatened by giant government-sponsored projects in their areas, is clearly in the Canadian tradition.

The farmers' movements of the late nineteenth and early twentieth century were almost entirely populist in character. By that is meant that they were movements (and political parties) which purported to represent the rank and file of the people against "the big interests," but which did not go much beyond that analysis. They aimed at specific reforms in the economic and political systems. They called for a return to *laissez-faire*, free trade and fair competition, greater government control over large corporations and more progressive taxation policies.[5] These populist movements lacked a class analysis and did not differ much in their overall ideologies from those whom they were opposing, though they were class movements if one looks at who participated in them.

The extent to which these farmers' movements enjoyed electoral success is often forgotten. In 1894 the Patrons of Industry in Ontario elected 14 members to the Ontario legislature and briefly enjoyed the balance of power.[6] Between 1919 and 1923 the United Farmers of Ontario formed the government at Queen's Park with labour support. In 1921 the United Farmers of Alberta swept the province and remained in office until defeated by Social Credit in 1935. Manitoba farmers formed a government in 1922, though they later merged with the provincial Liberals. In Saskatchewan some farm leaders co-operated with the Liberal party and the farmers did not win office during the 1920s. In the 1921 federal election the Progressive Party – the national Farmers' party – won 65 seats, fifteen more than the Conservatives.

These were regional movements, and there were important differences. In Ontario the farmers in politics were generally more conservative and less effective. They felt, correctly, that agriculture and the rural way of life were being displaced from their dominant position in society, and they were right to resist the unpleasant changes in their lives which were being imposed on them. The farmers, though, worked out no alternative strategy of development for the province and spent too much time either harking back to a golden age or convincing themselves that they were still all-powerful. In the West, particularly in Alberta and Saskatchewan, the farmers' movements were much more creative and dynamic. In addition to experimenting with democratic reforms in their politics, the wheat farmers built their own union (the Farmers' Union of Canada), and a mechanism for marketing their crop co-operatively – the Wheat Pool.

Populism began to give way more and more to socialism among the western farmers during the 1920s.[7] Some lessons were learned in the tough fight the farmers experienced in building the Wheat Pool (against the opposition of government and the corporations) and from seeing that, once operative, the Pool "alleviated the situation but did not solve agrarian problems." That the farmers' governments elected early in the decade were unable or unwilling to effect very much change was also noted. In Saskatchewan the United Farmers of Canada, through its political arm, the Farmers' Political Association, co-operated with the Independent Labour Party to contest the provincial election of 1933 on a socialist platform. In 1931 a formal merger followed and the Farmer Labour Group was founded. It was this Group which formed the basis of the CCF in Saskatchewan and which participated in the Calgary and Regina Conventions of 1932-33 which founded the CCF.

It was changes in ideology, along with the depression, which allowed large numbers of western farmers to come together with urban socialists of the west and east, in and out of the labour movement, to form the CCF. This was the first dominant national organization on the left in Canadian history. The CCF only emerged after thirty or more years of experimentation. It revealed both strength and weakness among Canadian socialists and organized labour in their fight to find a viable political movement.[8] Other strategies and ideologies were tried by significant numbers of socialists and socialist workers before the democratic socialist federation of the CCF was achieved in 1933. Labourism – the election of independent labour candidates – was tried and discarded early. Syndicalism – contempt for electoral politics and parliamentary power in favour of reliance on the general strike and a single industrial union, swept western Canadian labour after World War I, carried by the One Big Union movement. On a program formulated at the Western Labour Conference in Calgary in March, 1919, syndicalists carried out a referendum on the OBU among western unionists. They succeeded in getting a number of locals to disaffiliate from their local labour councils, which were branches of the Trades and Labour Congress, the centre of the international unions in Canada. The OBU movement lasted about a year. The TLC counter-attacked strongly in the West to maintain its organization. There were clear cases of government and judicial discrimination against OBU unions in favour of the less militant TLC. The Winnipeg General Strike was at least partly a result of the OBU fervour. OBU sentiments lasted longer among Winnipeg labour unions than anywhere else.

Marxism and advocates of Marxist and Communist political parties existed throughout the period, but it did not emerge as a national political movement nor as a significant force in the trade unions. Why not? Before 1917 the Marxists in Canada tended to be pure and doctrinaire, cut off from the working class struggles of the time and largely concentrated among east European ethnic groups. 1917 was a key date. As Robin says:

> The Russian revolution and the establishment of the Third International had a profound effect.... Bolshevism meant Socialism now, the bold translation of revolutionary propaganda and theory into practice.... Hitherto divided by their own pet orthodoxies, radical socialists were agreed that a new unity of the far left should be built on the basis of common support for the principles and strategy of the Bolshevik revolution... the international communist movement rather than the Canadian Labour Party was foremost in the mind of the far left.[9]

Canadian Communists did a lot of good work that has its place in the history of socialism in Canada, in the years after the party was formed in 1921. The CP played an important role in organizing the unemployed[10] in the 1930s and in organizing industrial workers into industrial unions.[11] Communists were often the most vocal advocates of civil rights and spoke out usefully against political repression. Communists were also in many cases indefatigable organizers and educators, bringing many Canadians to have a basic understanding of socialism, capitalism and communism.

What prevented the CP from realizing its full potential was the same thing that gave the Communist movement its original stimulus – dependence on events in the Soviet Union. The belief that the U.S.S.R. represented the advancing wave of successful international socialism prevented Canadian Communists from seeing that much that happened in the Soviet Union after the mid-1930s had nothing to do with the growth of socialism – only with the growth of Stalinism and the Soviet empire. This was particularly true after 1945.

By 1945 the CP in Canada had changed its position, in line with Soviet policy changes so often that it was finished as a movement in Canada. (In the federal election of that year, the LPP publicly supported Mackenzie King and the Liberals against the CCF.)

Unfortunately, its quick-change policy harmed more than the CP as an organization. The CP's opportunistic flip-flops over whether to support Canadian unions or right-wing international unions hurt the whole movement for independent Canadian unions. During the 1920s Communists worked in both the Canadian Labour Party and the all-Canadian Congress of Labour in ways which harmed both organizations without doing the CP any good. In 1935 under instructions from Moscow the CP in Canada disbanded its all-Canadian labour centre, the Workers' Unity League. As Abella says:

> Thus, on orders from Moscow, the most militant national union in Canada unilaterally disbanded and turned over its entire membership to the American-controlled Trades and Labour Congress. It was a blow from which the national union movement was not to recover.[12]

So it is not surprising that the only mass social democratic movement and party which did emerge during the Great Depression was not Marxist in its ideology, nor was it organized by Communists. What exactly was the CCF? The CCF was a federation of farmers, labour and urban socialists brought together principally through the agency of J. S. Woodsworth. Woodsworth had a special personal moral force based on his career as a clergyman in north Winnipeg, a worker, labour organizer, writer,[13] and member of Parliament since 1921. Martin Robin calls him the first labour man elected to Parliament who did not either sell out or quit.

Looked at from the point of view of European socialist parties, the CCF was only semi-socialist. The Regina Manifesto pledged the CCF to eradicate capitalism, but the document was based on an assumed rather than stated class analysis. No strategy was enunciated for restructuring society. Tensions among right, centre, and left, and between socialists and social democrats, were present in the party from the start. The Saskatchewan CCF had a large number of members who were strong socialists and who were dedicated to building a democratic socialist movement in Canada. The Ontario CCF had a significant number of members with the same point of view. Up to 1945 there was a right versus left struggle in the CCF but there was generally right-wing control in the national party. After 1945 the left lost out entirely and the movement aspect of the CCF was almost completely lost.

In my view a socialist movement is decentralized and contains a high proportion of activists to members. A movement turns people on to the idea of their own power and responsibility as individual members of the collective. In a movement the members control the politics and strategy of the movement and they know they deserve to because of the work they do. They create the movement and they see the movement as creating the kind of society they want to live in. In a socialist movement specific people are chosen to do specific tasks but the members decide the political content of what is done; the power of political decision-making is not delegated.

The traditional political party is the opposite of a socialist movement. There is a low percentage of activists among the membership. The membership is content to choose representatives who do make important political decisions and to whom much power is delegated. A party is always strong on unity and discipline. A socialist movement is strong on dedication and commitment.

Walter Young's book on the CCF, *Anatomy of a Party*, begins "Socialists belong to movements, capitalists support parties." It goes on to chronicle the ways in which the CCF as a movement was killed by the CCFers, who wanted a winning political party. Young insists on posing the two aspects as necessarily opposite and at war by definition whereas the two are complementary in a parliamentary system. But the movement should be primary and dominant.

What happened with the CCF, both nationally and in the Ontario and Saskatchewan provincial parties, was that the adherents of the CCF as a movement failed to keep control of the leadership and failed to replenish the leadership by developing new people who believed in the CCF as a movement. Young says "The success of the CCF as measured by its effect on the political life of Canada is really the success of the CCF as a movement." The CCF achieved power in only one province – Saskatchewan. Here the idea of the CCF as a movement was strong, with many party members believing that the CCF would have its greatest effect by posing an alternative view of Canadian society – socialism – and educating people to it.

Power in the CCF gradually became centralized in the national office of the party at Ottawa and in the parliamentary leadership. From the start it was assumed that executive bodies in the CCF had the right to initiate party policy, subject to approval by the party convention. The Regina Manifesto itself was drafted by an executive set up by the Calgary conference of 1932 and the national CCF council, through the life of the CCF, was responsible for nearly every major resolution passed by CCF national conventions. The executive officers quickly became a separate body in the party, meeting frequently at the national headquarters in Ottawa from which they were able to supervise the whole party and to monopolize communications within the national party. Woodsworth was at first opposed to the creation of a central party headquarters with full-time paid officials at Ottawa, but he was overborne, and threatened with a number of resignations unless he capitulated. He wrote in 1938 to M. J. Coldwell;

> Then again there is the whole question of centralization. I recognize a good deal can be done at Ottawa, but at this stage of development it seems to me most of our energy put into a central office is apt to draw from the various localities where money and energy are much needed.

To which Coldwell replied:

> You fear that our movement may become too centralized. I am not afraid of that. Indeed, we are in the same position as the Dominion itself, with loosely associated units duplicating and multiplying activities that ought to be national in scope.... Unless the movement shows that it is really in earnest I personally do not choose to remain as its national chairman.....

Step-by-step, centralization and leadership control were achieved.

205

In 1934 the national officers of the CCF suspended the constitution of the Ontario party, and in fact reorganized it totally, because a number of Ontario CCFers were wobbly on the relation between the CCF and other left groups. In 1938 what Young calls "the original confederational structure of the CCF" was abandoned in favour of a structure which set up a national CCF with provincial sections. In 1940 the national convention resolved that disputes between provincial and national bodies were to be resolved in favour of the national body. In 1944 David Lewis, national secretary of the CCF, advised T. C. Douglas, the new CCF Premier of Saskatchewan, as to who should be hired or fired in the establishment of the first CCF government in Saskatchewan. In the years after 1945, the CCF executive and council, by convention resolution, acquired more and more control over and responsibility for disciplining of provincial organizations, membership and the content of CCF election platforms.

In 1956 the CCF national Convention passed the Winnipeg Declaration as a substitute for the Regina Manifesto of 1933. The Winnipeg document was drafted by a four-man committee selected by the national executive. One gets the essential flavour of the two documents and of how much the CCF had changed over 33 years by comparing their final paragraphs. The Regina Manifesto ends:

> No CCF government will rest content until it has eradicated capitalism and put into operation the full programme of socialized planning which will lead to the establishment in Canada of the Co-operative Commonwealth.

Winnipeg says:

> The CCF will not rest content until every person in this land and in all other lands is able to enjoy equality and freedom, a sense of human dignity, and an opportunity to live a rich and meaningful life as a citizen of a free and peaceful world. This is the Co-operative Commonwealth which the CCF invited the people of Canada to build with imagination and pride.

The membership of the CCF allowed its organization to be taken away from it and killed. Even in Saskatchewan the membership went along with the idea that it was right to modify the CCF programme in order to appeal to a wider audience among the electorate. The CCF in Saskatchewan dropped its radical socialism (notably its position in favour of nationalization of the land) before 1940 for electoral reasons. It remained a socialist party but failed to recognize the limitations of parliamentary socialism. As a result, during its 20 years in office the CCF government grew increasingly distant from the rank-and-file, "and this spelled doom to an organization which had to depend upon grass roots activity to offset the economic power of its opponents and a hostile mass media."[14]

The payoff came in Saskatchewan in the period (1962) when the CCF government had great difficulty withstanding the on-slaught of the medical profession and business establishment in the province against medicare because it had not educated the people to see medicare and the CCF government as things operating in their own interest. In 1964 the CCF was defeated.

The CCF membership also failed to build structural defences for themselves against the inexorable pressures of leadership control and centralization. Here they were partly misled by their own idea that socialism could only be achieved by a united centralized party and a united centralized federal government.

The other factor which always affected and finally decided the character of the CCF (and of the NDP after it) was the role played by organized labour. Here three processes ran together. Union leaders in English Canada over the past 50 years have spent most of the time which they did not devote to organizing and adminis-tering unions and negotiating contracts, to battling over three related problems – whether unions shall have a "business" orienta-tion; whether labour's political arm should have a socialist or a social democratic programme; and whether their unions should be independent Canadian unions or affiliated to the American unions.

By the 1950s the character of the labour movement in English Canada was largely set in a business union framework, strongly affiliated to U.S. unions, and looking for a social democratic party to support. Out of this set of ideas the major industrial unions created the Canadian Labour Congress (1956) and the New Democratic Party (1961). The final outcome of the three battles was clearer and clearer after 1945 but during the first years of the CCF the outcome was in doubt.

A good deal of clarification of the battle lines came during the struggles of the 1920s. In 1929 when the first Western Conference of the Labour Political Parties met at Regina (with Woodsworth and M. J. Coldwell among the delegates) the organizers of the conference must surely have known whom to invite and whom not to invite. Since the purpose of the meeting was to "correlate the activities of the several labour political parties in Western Canada," it made sense to them to leave out the hard-line Marxists and Communists in favour of delegates and organizations who could be expected to co-operate on the basis of a shared philosophy. The fourth conference of the Labour Political Parties took place in Calgary in 1932 – a joint meeting with the farmers' groups to found the CCF.

Unions as such played little part in the creation of the CCF in 1932-3. The 1933 CCF constitution made no provision for the affiliation of national trade unions "as much the result of the hostility of the rural delegates toward labour unions as anything else." Aaron Mosher of the Canadian Brotherhood of Railway Employees was the only leading unionist from central Canada who attended the Calgary and Regina conventions. Key figures in the CCF from the start (certainly including David Lewis after he become National Secretary in 1936) did seek an organic link between the CCF leadership and the leadership of the principal unions. At the 1937 national convention, a resolution was passed approving the principle of trade union affiliation.

It was no accident that this resolution came forward just when industrial union organizing in English Canada was hitting its stride under Communist, not CCF, leadership.

> ... Everywhere there is the demand for union organizers, everywhere there is the cry "Labour Party," everywhere there is a new attitude, a new public opinion, and everywhere the CCF is almost totally ineffective.[16]

So the CCF leader in Ontario wrote to David Lewis in April, 1937.

The CP, on the other hand, was only too effective from the CCF point of view in its union-organizing work. The most recent commentator on the Communists' role in the building of industrial unionism in Canada calls their contribution "invaluable ... the large CIO unions, Steel, Auto, Electric, Woodworkers, Mine-Mill, and Textile, were organized at the beginning by Communists and were all, at one time or another in their history, dominated by the party."[17]

The CP's ground-floor position in the new unions was attacked from two sides from the start. CCF unionists opposed the Communists inside their unions as political and ideological rivals. The American Federation of Labour put pressure on the Trades and Labour Congress to expel the Canadian CIO unions from the TLC, and this was done in 1939. The CCFers in the CIO unions immediately began successful negotiations with Mosher's All Canadian Congress of Labour and the founding convention of the new Canadian Congress of Labour was held in Toronto in September, 1940. At this convention the CCFers swept the leadership positions and a resolution condemning communism, nazism, and fascism was passed.[18] David Lewis attended the convention as an advisor to the ACCL.

Some damage done to the Communists was self-inflicted. As the Soviet Union moved from united front against fascism to the Hitler-Stalin pact, through to an all-out effort to win the war after Germany attacked Russia, so too did the CP move. In the unions and the country at large during World War II, the CP often cared more about preventing the CCF from gaining support than it did about anything else. In the Ontario election of 1945 and the federal election the same year, the CP carefully organized its candidates and activities so as to do the greatest possible damage to the CCF. The opening of the Cold War after 1945 opened the CP up fully to general attack. By 1951 the CCL had rid itself of its three major left-wing affiliates – Mine-Mill, the International Woodworkers of America, and the United Electrical Workers. Communist influence in the Steel and Autoworkers was also under control. Conformity of views on the role of unions finally allowed the CCL and the TLC to merge into the Canadian Labour Congress in 1956. A related phenomenon – the CCF party also moved distinctly right-wards after 1945. The CCF, in convention and in Parliament, was generally accepting of the U.S. position in foreign affairs and criticized the growth of the Russian empire without paying much attention to the growth of the U.S. empire or to its penetration into Canada. Domination of the party by right wingers in and out of the labour movement was easily extended, particularly in Ontario. The momentum of the movement of the 1930s and early 1940s was largely lost.

On such a basis was the NDP formed in the years following the election of 1958. The precise steps taken in developing the New Party – the twin resolutions from the CLC Convention of April, 1958, and the CCF Convention of August, 1958, are set out in Stanley Knowles' 1961 publication, *The New Party*. Knowles presents the NDP as the culmination of all that the CCF and the labour movement had been attempting for over 20 years, "the creation of a broadly based people's political movement, embracing the CCF, the labour movement, farm organizations, professional people and other liberally minded persons interested in basic social reform through our parliamentary system."[19]

Knowles describes the NDP correctly as a social democratic party rather than a socialist movement. Page references to "Socialism, democratic" in the index of Knowles' book turn out in some cases to be references to pages where only the term "social democratic" appears – an interesting confusion. In Chapter 7, "Programs", Knowles offers the following comments on democratic socialism and its role and definition in the New Party:

> ... It is clear that the New Party, in drafting its program, is drawing heavily on the principles of democratic socialism. Let it be remembered that democratic socialism is not a condition but a process. Indeed, it is an endless process, a social direction rather than a static or final goal. The objectives of that process are greater equality, social justice, economic as well as political freedom and dignity for all. It is the objectives that count and these objectives determine the extent to which democratic socialists advocate public ownership or other ways of enlarging the public sector of our conomy. . . . a united effort is (to be) made to forge the kind of political instrument Canada needs to go forward in the nineteen-sixties.[20]

And on that basis the NDP did go forward in the 1960s – sad to say. The party became more and more an electoral machine, which debated nothing fundamentally and became more and more irrelevant to the real problems of Canadian society. The hottest debates in the national NDP were over matters of foreign policy. Socialists in English Canada either did or did not do some election work for the NDP, but spent the majority of their time quiescent or working in the labour, student or peace movements.

The NDP's electoral strategy itself came to look bankrupt. The hopes created by the fairly dramatic increases of the federal election of 1965 and the Ontario election of 1967 were blasted by the Trudeau election of 1968. What was disturbing about the 1968 result was not that NDP seats and votes went down but that the Liberal party and continental capitalism 'had shown themselves resilient enough to bounce back and co-opt the saleable parts of the NDP programme and wrap them more attractively.

At the same time, George Grant's *Lament for a Nation* and the 1968 *Report of the Task Force on Foreign Ownership and the Structure of Canadian Industry* had shown what was happening to the Canadian economy and political culture. And there was zero response from the NDP, which we had all been regarding as the party of the left. In this situation, it is not surprising that a new formation came together in the NDP.

In the Spring of 1969 a group of socialists who were members of the NDP met in Toronto to write a major paper to be submitted to the NDP Convention in October of that year. The Waffle Manifesto, which was released to the press on September 4, 1969, had a remarkable reception in the party and in the press. Among individual party members, it was received with great enthusiasm – far surpassing the expectations of those originally responsible for it. The press, editorially, generally criticized it heavily but they treated it more seriously than they had any other document produced by the left in Canada since the Regina Manifesto.

In 1972 the Ontario Waffle was expelled from the NDP. Given the domination of the trade union bureaucracy in the party, neither the attack on the Waffle nor its success should have been surprising. In November, 1971, the Ontario Waffle labour caucus was for the first time a vocal and organized force at the Ontario Federation of Labour convention. The previous month, the Ontario party, under its new leader, Stephen Lewis, had suffered serious losses in a provincial election where great gains were expected. NDP candidates who had been part of the Waffle did significantly better than the party generally, though none was elected. With a federal election on the horizon, there were excellent tactical reasons for the union and parliamentary leadership of the NDP to move against the Waffle and they did so. The non-union membership of the NDP in the constituencies was strongly opposed to the purge, but unable to organize itself or to overcome thirty years of CCF/NDP history.

Notes

[1] One of the points made by critics of the Waffle Manifesto in 1969 was that it used "alien" terms like empire and colony to describe the United States and Canada. In reality, these terms have been used and understood by every generation of Canadians except this one.

[2] It has been a late but very good harvest. See Irving Abella, *Nationalism, Communism and Canadian Labour,* Toronto, 1973; Gad Horowitz, *Canadian Labour in Politics,* Toronto, 1968; Charles Lipton, *Trade Unionism in Canada,* Montreal, 1969; Paul Phillips, *No Power Greater:* A Century of Labour in B.C.; Martin Robin, *Tadical Politics and Canadian Labour,* Toronto, Kingston, 1968; Walter Young, *The Anatomy of a Party: The National C.C.F. 1932-61,* Toronto, 1969.

[3] Leo Johnson, "The development of class in Canada in the twentieth century," p. 143-4, in G. Teeple (ed.) *Capitalism and the National Question in Canada,* Toronto 1972. Johnson's article is a step in the right direction. For an example of polemics replacing analysis, see Gary Teeple's attack on the CCF-NDP and the Waffle in the same volume "Liberals in a hurry."

[4] For a full account of the rebellions, see G. F. Stanley, *Birth of Western Canada* or J. K. Howard, *Strange Empire.* W. L. Morton, *Manitoba: a history,* has an excellent account of the Red River rebellion and the history of the Métis. *An Unauthorized History of the RCMP,* chaps. 1-2, Caroline and Lorne Brown, Toronto, 1973, tells the story of the federal police in the Northwest up to 1900.

[5] For a stimulating and detailed account of the farmers' movements in the west, see Lorne Brown's "The progressive tradition in Saskatchewan," *Our Generation,* vol. 6, No. 4, Spring – June, 1969.

[6] See John Smart's "The Patrons of Industry in Ontario," unpublished MA thesis, Carleton University, 1969, and Sam Shortt's "Social Change and political crisis in rural Ontario: the Patrons of Industry, 1889-1896" in *Oliver Mowat's Ontario,* D. Swainson (ed.), Toronto, 1972.

[7] L. Brown, "The progressive tradition . . . " (cited n.5), p.36, has a good account of how the farmers and the urban socialists in Saskatchewan came together in the same organization around the same platform..

[8] The story of that experimentation is very well told by Martin Robin, *Radical Politics in Canadian Labour,* Kingston, 1968, to which I am indebted for much of the analysis which follows.

[9] Robin, p. 145 – 6.

[10] See R. Liversedge, *Recollections of the On to Ottawa Trek* CUL 1973.

[11] See the early chapters of I. Abella, *Nationalism, Communism and Canadian Labour,* Toronto, 1973.

[12] Abella, p.4.

[13] In Woodsworth's writings one sees the work of one of the earliest Canadian sociologists – shrewd, sensitive and politically conscious. Two of his books, *My Neighbour and Strangers within Our Gates* have recently been republished in paperback by University of Toronto Press in The Social History of Canada series.

[14] L. Brown, "The progressive tradition. . . . "

[15] Young, *op. cit.,* p. 76

[16] I. Abella *Nationalism, Communism and Canadian Labour* Toronto 1972, p. 24.

[17] Abella, *ibid.,* p. 221-2.

[18] Abella, *ibid.,* p. 51.

[19] Stanley Knowles, *The New Party,* Toronto: 1961, p. 33.

[20] *Ibid.,* p. 94.

Canadian Culture and the Liberal Ideology
Robin Mathews

Death and Revolution

They say we are nothing.
They say if you look into faces here
You see motor cars and television sets.
In the eyes, they say, you can see fear,
A fear that crouches,
A fear that fawns on power.
Or they say you see a mixture,
In the eyes, of greed and Jansenism.
This people, they say, wants to possess things.
All this people wants is comfort
And the material lie.
What have Canadians ever done, they say to me,
But sell themselves. . . .

I look into faces here.
I see unnumbered reaches like the prairie sky,
Empty, lonely, longing for the hands that will come.
Or I see eyes full of darkness
Like the black, high moment of night
Just before the beginning of coming day,
Or I see eyes that look beyond the watcher
To the other side. . . .

I see faces
here
Grown beautiful as ravaged trees
Are beautiful—
With the fact of their survival

The terrible beauty of survival.

And I see all around them
At their roots
Green shoots
Reaching up into the sharp air
Like the flames of revolution.

Some of us are economists, political or other. Some of us know something of Canadian culture and Canadian literature. But almost all of us think or have thought of ourselves as "liberal" with a small "l". In fact, most of us think of ourselves as *liberal* people, people with *liberal ideas.* And we think of the word *liberal* as generally meaning "progressive," "liberationist"; or, at its most mild, we think of the word as meaning at least something tending to fairly strong reformism.

But let me say as an opener that until we destroy the idea of the liberal ideology in Canada, there can be no independence; there can be no genuine growth of the roots and traditions of Canadian society that are presently being rubbed out; and, for those who believe in Socialism as the answer, there can be no genuine Socialism.

That is a troublesome fact. But it is the more significant because it is troublesome, since there are many aspects of the liberal ideology that are or seem appealing, humane, and enno-bling. But we are always asked to accept a package – all of the liberal ideology or none of it. And so we must take it apart – the liberal ideology – as it operates in Canada. I am going to begin with that aspect of culture because it relates to every other aspect and because I am sure there is no more important aspect that needs examination at this time in our history.

The liberal ideology, as we know it in Canada, is very largely a product, first, of British Imperialism and now of U.S. Imperial-ism. The human product, in human terms, of the liberal ideology is the Robber Baron of free enterprise and the cop-out hippie/yippie of the so-called counter culture. At what appear to be the ends of the spectrum are different manifestations of the liberal anarchist individualist who is essentially self-regarding, essentially anti-community. The liberal ideology supports all manifestations of liberal anarchist individualism, whether that of the rich free enterpriser who manipulates community for his own profit or the so-called *disengaged* rejecter of community who denies it. The liberal ideology teaches, invites, encourages the Canadian to think of himself or herself as responsible to self, to his or her own *personal development.* It teaches the Canadian to scorn history, to reject communal values unless they are the values of a fragmented experimental, a-historical little ephemeral society of contemporar-ies.

The liberal ideology, in brief, is an ideology which fragments social response, for it asserts the primacy of the individual and the individual's "rights." It creates the wholly self-regarding individual and the despotic social order. The liberal ideology creates the liberal anarchist individual. The liberal anarchist individual takes his own experience as the measure of value; and in a position of authority he shapes a despotism circumscribed by his own limitations. In liberal capitalist democracy, the liberal ideology is the basis of so-called "free enterprise," in which all people are said to have an equal right to compete freely for positions in which they may exploit their fellows. In liberal imperialist democracy the situation is simply taken a step or two farther.

The best example I can use of that kind of condition, as a symbol is to be found in *Huckleberry Finn*. I use a U.S. text consciously, because the liberal ideology as we have it in Canada is very much a superimposition from the U.S.A. If you will look at the writers in Canada who claim to be "North American" writers, you will see most of them create liberal anarchist individualist heroes and claim influence from major U.S. writers who create the same kind of heroes.

At the end of *Huckleberry Finn,* Huck is invited to accept some terms of the community: he is, that is, asked to wash behind his ears and go to church on Sunday. Instead, he chooses to "light out for the territory," the place where the U.S. has dominance but where there is no law, no traditional or historical community demands. There Huck will be free to make his own law – the ideal condition for the free enterpriser and the cop-out hippie/yippie.

As Frederick Jackson Turner, the great U.S. theorist of the Frontier Thesis in U.S. history put it, Huck would be able to take the scalp with the Indians. Canadians who have talked about the Frontier Thesis of development of Canada, by the way, have overlooked something that Frederick Jackson Turner says at the early part of this century about the U.S. Frontier. He writes in one of his works that the U.S., having got to the Pacific coast and having filled up the territorial United States, must now begin thinking in terms of "democracy and empire." Yes. The liberal ideology in Canada is a product of imperialism and supports imperialism.

Frederick Jackson Turner outlines a theory of U.S. expansionism in which the U.S. individual progressively throws off the shackles of the past and tradition and "Europe" and creates the U.S. character in a return (which Turner thinks is Romantic) to savagery and to what he thinks is fundamental human nature – but which is, in fact, the nature of the imperialist.

In Canada we have a strain of little Huck Finns – the Canadians who have accepted the liberal ideology, who have become alienated from their own community, and who have celebrated one or other manifestation of the liberal anarchist individualist as hero. One thinks immediately of Mordecai Richler who has told us that success is New York, Canada is second-rate, and to care about the Canadian nation and to do something about caring will lead us all into concentration camps. On various fictive levels his heroes are the ultimate liberal anarchist individualists in Canadian literature.

When we turn from the little Canadian Huck Finns, we find a tradition, a truly compelling tradition that rejects the individualist anarchist liberal as hero; and that rejects, therefore, the liberal ideology out of which he comes. What is more, we find that rejection in a good deal of immigrant lierture, the literature we are told to expect is full of alienated people who will have naturally gravitated to an individualist and anarchist position because of their feelings of strangeness and rejection.

Among the writers who reject the liberal individualist position and who build novels with specific concern about the choice between the individual and the community, the list is almost endless. But listen to the names of some of them: Susanna Moodie, Sara Jeanette Duncan, Hugh MacLennan, Philip Grove, Dorothy Dumbrill, Louis Hemon, Adele Wiseman, Robertson Davies, John Richardson, W. O. Mitchell, Ralph Connor, even, I believe, Margaret Laurence, as well as Nellie McClung and Laura Goodman Salverson to name two more Prairie writers.

There has been a major strain in Canadian literature and in Canadian society that rejects the product of the liberal ideology. Why? Because many Canadians have known that the liberal ideology means the destruction of Canada. The empire expands when its individual exploiters go out into the less powerful world and establish personal wealth and the power of their State. The colony survives and moves to independence when it resists the exploiter, unites as a community, lives for the good of all, and develops the only kind of struggle that can beat off the power of the imperialists – a unified struggle that by its very definition rejects the individualist anarchist liberal hero. Nineteenth-century Canadian conservatism had that quality to it, however much nineteenth-century conservatism may offend some Canadians now. Twentieth-century socialism and semi-left movements have tried to have that quality, but they have often failed, partly because of coercion, coercion from the liberal ideologists.

If the left weren't coerced by the liberal ideology, it would take stands from a humane and socialist point of view on more matters which the Canadian working people care about. The left would condemn a manifestation like Rochdale College in Toronto, for instance. If there have indeed been a dozen or eighteen suicides in the last three years in Rochdale, then there is a great evil dwelling there. Individualist anarchism taken to extremes, of course, creates an inhumane alienation which is soul- and body-destroying. Rochdale, the residents of which accept the present liberal anarchist ideas about drugs, is a running sore of liberal capitalist democracy. It has to have a high number of suicides.

Socialists who are truly serious about the good of the whole society and the possibility of men and women making *right* choices instead of choices they are pressed into by liberal capitalism, would have a position on drugs, for instance, that would leave the other political groups fifty years behind.

By the same token, Canadians who are seriously progressive would support women's liberation strongly, but would throw out most of the U.S. influence and U.S. women messing around in Canadian women's liberation. Liberation in the U.S. – liberation of anybody or anything – is the liberation of the individual within a society that possesses world predominance in power. Liberation in the U.S. involves the individual getting loose from a cruel imperial monolith, getting loose from it from within. Moreover, in the U.S.A., as we know from the Huck Finn syndrome, the most realized human being is the one most able to possess dictatorial powers in his or her own sphere. That is what the liberal ideology leads to, and in U.S. fiction that is the place of conflict over and over: the boy-man hero who must dominate or run away. Liberation in a dependency like Canada has, in contrast, got to be liberation with the people for the people and in a way that releases in the community the strength to survive and to throw off the imperial master while changing the structures that support the imperial predominance.

Everywhere I go in Canada to speak, I am told by Canadian women (who usually take me aside to tell me) that the women's movement is twisted by U.S. women, that the libraries are full of U.S. women's literature to the exclusion of English and even Canadian materials. The first supposedly Canadian women's liberation book, called *Women Unite*, put out by a group that calls itself the Canadian Women's Educational Press, possesses an article on Susanna Moodie, calling her a racist. It is the worst article ever written about Susanna Moodie, who fought with the anti-slavery movement in England decades before the U.S. moved to emancipate the slaves – which of course they still haven't done. Moreover, Susanna Moodie ghost-wrote a book for a young black woman to show the horrors of slavery.

The writers of the article in *Women Unite* treat her work from the point of view of the U.S. idea of the hero, which Moodie doesn't conform to and so for them she becomes a racist. She becomes repellent to them because she isn't an individualist anarchist liberal. She believes in responsibility to values, to ideas of the past and future, and so the writers reject her. When I looked into that publication by the Canadian Women's Educational Press, I discovered the article was written by two U.S. citizens who had been in Canada about two years.

When I went to Manitoba for a huge week-long festival of ideas a year or so ago, the person they had brought in at highest cost was a U.S. women's liberationist from New York. I heard the beginning of her speech in which she said that she didn't believe in any of "the shit about borders," echoing exactly the beliefs of the U.S. multi-national corporation. And she told the assembly just as I was leaving that "We might get two or three people into Congress, but that won't do very much good . . . ." I was convinced that it wouldn't do very much good for the women of Manitoba, who had been dealt the insult by the organizers of being given to understand that there was no Canadian woman who would be as relevant to them as a U.S. feminist from New York.

The colonization of Canadian thought and social/political movements has a direct bearing on the political economy of culture in this country. We must not confuse colonization with leadership. The people I have mentioned are not providing a necessary leadership, even if we believed ourselves so inferior that we needed to import U.S. leaders. No. The people I've been talking about superimpose the values of an alien imperialist country, and by doing so support the continued colonization of Canada. Many Canadians don't want to talk about the continuing colonization caused by U.S. immigrants because the Canadians are afraid they will be accused of not being *liberal*. Or else they are so colonized they believe that Canadian and U.S. intellectual history are the same. Or they are such fawning colonial sycophants they believe that everything that has happened in Canada is second-rate and the faster we accept the U.S. definition of reality, the better it will be for us.

But it is the liberal ideology which prepares them for all those positions. It insists that the ideas of mobility put forward by the imperial centre are "progressive." To resist those ideas is "reactionary." It insists that all history is going in one direction, led by the imperial centre. Inasmuch as the colonial country is like the imperial country, it is "advanced." Inasmuch as it is different, it is "underdeveloped." It insists that the ideas created for and propagated from the imperial centre are ideas of universal interest and importance. Inasmuch as the colonial country permits those ideas to be superimposed, and permits them to be superimposed by immigrants from the imperial country, the colonial country is "liberal." Inasmuch as it insists upon the integrity of its own ideas and people, it is, of course, "chauvinist," "narrowly nationalistic," "navel-gazing," and so on.

When did the liberal ideology arise, you might ask? When Britain was becoming the most powerful imperialist nation, various of her theorists began arguing for free trade which is the liberal ideology at work in Commerce, and others of her theorists began even to develop a philosophy based on the right of individualist exploitation. George Grant calls the philosophers in question the philosophers of greed. Duncan Campbell Scott calls the men in commerce who practiced the liberal ideology of individualist exploitation the white men-servants of greed.

Britain supported open ports and open minds. She could ship in her trade goods through the open ports and her ideas through what is now called "the free flow of ideas" but which is, in effect, the free flow of imperial propaganda. When Britain lost her

219

empire, she lost her liberal ideology. The West Indians, for instance, who were taught for a few generations to think of Britain as home, where all free men could go, began to get a little money and to go *home.* They got something of a shock at their "welcome."

For a century the cry was that an Englishman can go anywhere in the world. Oxford and Cambridge poured out colonial administrators and sent them abroad to teach the British way of life. Suddenly all that changed. But their imperial propaganda worked for a long time. I am old enough to have observed Englishmen with B.A. degrees being hired before Canadians with M.A. degrees because an Englishman was by definition superior. Not only did we get British teapots and afghans, and engines and guns. We got British ideas and all the propaganda that supports empire. The propaganda that supports empire made the colonials want British teapots and afghans and engines and guns instead of wanting to make their own for themselves. Imperial propaganda serves to make colonials want to stay colonials.

The U.S. empire is not new or recent, alas. It began in 1776. Presently the U.S.A. operates the same liberal ideology in support of its empire that the British used. In 1886, for instance, nineteen years after Confederation, Henry George, an influential U.S. political economist wrote in *Protection and Free Trade* that "The spirit of free trade is that of fraternity and peace." On the same page, however, he tells his U.S. audience that "Free trade would give us again mastery of the ocean which protection has deprived us of...." And then on the next page, speaking of free trade which he has said is the spirit of "fraternity and peace," he writes:

We may annex Canada to all intents and purposes whenever we throw down the tariff wall we have built around ourselves. We need not ask for reciprocity; if we abolish our customhouses and call off our baggage searchers and Bible confiscators, Canada would not and could not maintain hers. This would make the two countries practically one. Whether the Canadians chose to maintain a separate Parliament and pay a British lordling for keeping up a mock court at Rideau Hall, need not in the slightest concern us. The intimate relations that would come of unrestricted commerce would soon obliterate the boundary line....

That argument for the liberal ideology goes on. If we are not bringing in John Connally to make it to the Empire Club, fittingly enough, we are bringing in Harry Johnson, the continental economist, to make it at some university. And if those two men are busy, there is always a member of the Liberal cabinet to make the argument for them.

But of course it is not an argument for free trade at all, it is an apology for imperial control. It isn't an argument for the equal sharing of the continent in balanced production and competition. It is an argument for the right of U.S. branch plants to organize and direct Canadian production to suit the needs of the U.S.A. It is not an even, however undesirable, argument for half the unions on the continent to be U.S.-run from U.S. offices with U.S. priorities, and the other half to be Canadian, run from Canadian offices with Canadian priorities. It means that the Canadian worker will be bent to U.S. needs and sacrificed whenever that is considered desirable by U.S. people. What is true for imperial propaganda about free trade is also true for culture. The ideas and arts of the colony are not even taken into the centre to modify its existence; the ideas and the arts of the imperium are conveyed to the colony to be set up as the criterion of excellence.

Cultural invasion is integral with and indistinguishable from economic invasion. That is a simple fact. It is economically profitable to take over Canadian publishing, film-making, advertising, magazine production, the creation and distribution of educational aids, Canadian hockey, Canadian movie houses. They are profitable activities, and so by taking them over for economic gain they are also transformed culturally. Take one example from the list: for decades the U.S.-owned monopoly on Canadian movie houses has done everything in its power to prevent Canadian films from being shown. The reasons are obvious at every level of analysis. Maintaining strict control of Canadian movie houses assures profitability, cultural hegemony, and the continuation of imperial power. In a 1928 editorial, the *New York Times* boasted that the sun never sets on the U.S. movie. Before that, remember, we were told that the sun never sets on the British Empire. The cultural hegemony and the continuation of imperial power are supported by so-called liberals who insist that to interfere in the monopoly domination of Canadian expression by aliens would be to limit free expression, to deny Canadians the right to free

221

choice, to suppress individual liberty and *the free flow of ideas*. The imperialists and their docile disciples always claim that interference with the propaganda system of empire is an interference with the free flow of ideas.

It is not just a matter of profit, obviously, the takeover of cultural and non-cultural institutions. It is a question of the values that will be purveyed, the purposes for which the institutions will be operated. It is a question of the direction that the energies of the Canadian people will take: to serve the profit of alien owners, or to serve the ideals of community among and for Canadians. I suppose if Walter Gordon or Eddie Goodman or Mel Hurtig were to own a national chain of movie houses, Canadian films might find they had a real friend. But the nationalist capitalists are rare, as anyone must know who reads the financial papers in this country. Besides, capitalism *is* acting artificially when it is not totally devoted to profit-making. The fundamental intention of capitalism is to maximize profits and to accumulate the power that will make the maximization of profit possible and stable. And so for anyone who has genuine regard for the whole community of Canadians, there is no doubt that capitalism has to go. Imperialism is a form of global capitalism, put simply, and so the struggle against the U.S. empire is a struggle against capitalist injustice. The struggle against capitalism in Canada has to be, moreover, a struggle against U.S. imperialism, since the U.S. owns and controls so much of the Canadian economy and culture. And, finally, it has to be a struggle against the liberal ideology which is the philosophical basis – the apologetics – for both capitalism and imperialism in our time.

The liberal ideology makes a way for the imperialist power. But you may fairly ask if the liberal ideology does not call for free and open discussion out of which the best ideas will surface and prevail? Doesn't the liberal ideology call for the absolute sanctity of the individual? Is it not the liberal ideology that has created Human Rights Commissions and the paraphernalia of individual freedom? The answer is a modified "Yes", only a modified "Yes."

We must take the idea of individual freedom and the liberal ideology very carefully in hand if we are not going to fall back into the phony myths about them in Canada. Apart from the occasions (the Winnipeg Strike is a good example) when individual freedom and human rights have been conspired against by the state, we must examine liberal ideas as they are applied to a "boundaryless ideal." Canada is unique. It is not only unique in its identity and intellectual history, but it is uniquely on the North American continent with the most powerful imperial nation in history along its nearly four thousand miles of border. Unique, too, is the fact that two hundred million U.S. people speak the same language as sixteen millions of the Canadians. Canada is in the unique position of having that imperial nation own or control more of its economy than is the case with any other technologically advanced country in the world. Put bluntly, two hundred million people could supply all the managers, all the teachers, all the artists, all the policy-makers for the sixteen million people without noticing a significant strain. If we accept the liberal ideology of empires that ideas and people should move without obstruction, then what are the rights of the Canadian people lying along a border with two hundred million people of the most powerful imperial nation in history?

What are the rights of non-Canadians who move into Canada, take jobs, especially culturally important ones, when we know as a simple, unique fact that the U.S. could fill all the culturally sensitive jobs in Canada and feel no strain in its workforce? In fact, it would have a personnel safety valve which empires always want – to ship out qualified personnel when there's a glut at home and to suck them back when there's a need at home. In fact all the talk about U.S. generosity to Canadian talent is so much hogwash. The U.S. has always measured very carefully what it would take – and has only taken what its economy needed. It has never openly embraced incoming Canadians if there was a chance U.S. citizens would have their jobs threatened as a result. At this very moment U.S. laws are more stringent than Canadian laws on the flow of talented personnel between the countries. Even if the U.S. was generous, genuinely generous, sixteen million people could not throw up the personnel to fill all the culturally sensitive jobs in a country of two hundred million. Canada is never a threat to the U.S. in those ways, and the U.S. knows it. The U.S. is always a threat to Canada in those ways, and Canadian governments try never to admit it, quite apart from the role U.S. immigrants play as cultural imperialists.

Step back a little more and ask what is the role of liberal

ideology in ideas and people for an imperial nation. The empire, basing its argument upon the liberal ideology, asserts that each individual ought to have the right to move freely (as ought ideas) in the world, without obstruction. It is upon that basis that many U.S. professors in Canada ask not to be considered as "American professors" but just as "human beings." The liberal ideology, too, asks them to be considered simply as "human beings." If history is non-existent and community secondary, then a U.S. professor is not a culturally conditioned entity; he is "just a human being."

The result of such a policy has many effects. There is a subtle communication of the values of the imperial centre when it takes over the cultural institutions as a part of economic takeover. Moreover, personnel effect a considerable influence. If we accept Marshall McLuhan's statement that the medium is the message, and I think we can without a lot of discussion, then the teacher, the arts administrator, the artist, the branch-plant manager and communicating media will convey, consciously and unconsciously, the message of empire. Even the radical dissident from U.S. life communicates radical dissidence as it is understood in liberal anarchist individualist U.S. society. The U.S. immigrant is always, in some blind portion of his or her being, a cultural imperialist.

When we began our work on the de-Canadianization of the universities, I met a young man who had been a book representative for a U.S. firm. At a convention in New York City he asked two questions. The first he asked was why that U.S. firm didn't publish more Canadian material. The answer was that if the material wouldn't sell in the U.S. the firm wasn't interested in it. Secondly, he asked if the firm wasn't a little uneasy about all the U.S. material they were pumping into Canadian universities. The answer was that they were not uneasy because there were enough U.S. professors working in Canadian universities to assure the firm that they could sell all the U.S. material they wanted to get into Canadian universities. Half of the U.S. professors referred to probably didn't know even what Canadian material existed and didn't think for a moment that they were playing the role of cultural imperialists by ordering books as if they were in the U.S.A.

More subtly, imperial powers know that the more they can argue for individual and so-called "human rights", for the falseness of boundaries, for the horrors of nationalism, the greater mobility there will be for people in the world. But what people? Who will be the most mobile? We know the answer, though we seldom think of it. The most highly organized educational systems are in the imperial centres. The richest and therefore the most mobile populations are in the imperial centres. For the U.S. to argue for individual and human rights and for the free flow of talent and ideas is for the U.S. to argue for the spread of its own trained population around the world and for the unobstructed predominance of U.S. ideas, however good or bad, "neutral" or "imperialist" they may be. Knowing that, all the African nations, for instance, take foreign scholars for two, three, and four year terms of appointment, on the clear understanding that when Africans are ready, the foreigners will be phased out and the major cultural positions will return to Africans. Only in Canada do we take hordes of representatives from the Imperial centre and allow them lifelong jobs and power over the Canadian educational and cultural institutions.

The liberal ideology in ideas goes deeper than that. To explain how, I am going to quote from an article by Ron Lambert in the Fall 1972 issue of *This Magazine is About Schools*. He writes:

> The systematic devaluing of the Canadian fact is to be found in the ideology of liberalism. Modern liberalism comprises a set of values requiring the creation of conditions favouring the free access of American power, commerce, definitions, and assumptions throughout the world. While belief in the free and open marketplace of commodities has dissipated, liberals continue to cling to a belief in an open marketplace of images and ideas unconstrained by economic resources, technological superiority, organizational factors, social status and interpersonal relations. The effect of the liberal ideology is to provide the psychological underpinning which renders colonial people susceptible to the highly efficient cultural delivery systems of the American empire. Specifically, liberals regard with suspicion boundaries of any kind. . . . Nationalism is illiberal, too, when it signifies a high valuation by a people of their *own* experiences, and a determination to comprehend them.

Ron Lambert points out in his article, too, that the Canadians who were asking for a fair representation of Canadian materials at

Waterloo University were asked to consider their proposals in relation to the rise of the Nazis in the 1930s! That is a familiar suggestion. Since the liberal ideology is in fact an instrument of U.S. imperialism, to resist it is to face every kind of coercion and slander.

The reaction to resistance against the U.S. empire on the cultural level – and especially where resistance seems to offend the apparently sacred idea of the liberal ideology – is furious on the part of the imperialists and their docile Canadian disciples. In October of 1970 at a Carleton University Teach-In, the head of the Canadian Association of University Teachers Gordin Kaplan, who had taken citizenship a few months before declared that the concern for Canadianization in the universities "smacks of fascism" and he pointed out that French laws dealing with the question of French faculty in France were passed during the Nazi occupation.

In a brief to the Ontario Select Committee on Economic and Cultural Nationalism presented recently by the leaders of ten, mostly U.S., advertising agencies, the desire to preserve Canadian advertising for Canadian agencies was attacked. The U.S. advertisers wrote:

> Some advertisers who wish to appoint a specific agency will sometimes not do so for fear of unfavourable publicity that will accrue because the agency is not Canadian-owned. This smacks of economic and political terrorism.

The response to Canadians who desire the reasonable flowering of their own culture and economy, when that flowering impinges upon U.S. expansionism, is a strident defence of the liberal ideology in terms that describe the Canadians as fascists and terrorists.

Canadian literature parallels and comments upon that situation in Canadian life. Over and over again Canadian writers have rejected the liberal anarchist hero who is the creature of the liberal ideology. Canadian writers have created, instead, in a major traditional theme, the hero in community. And so Canadian literature is sprinkled with the hero as preacher, teacher, community builder, or one whose battle between individualism and community ends with an affirmation of community. For decades now we have, however, had our critics casting scorn upon those writers, for the critics have been seduced into the U.S. liberal anarchist and individualist pose. Why the writers should return again and again to a traditional theme related to Canadian survival, while the critics attack them and support the ideology of the imperial power might provide an interesting study for someone interested in the sociology of colonialism. For now, I simply want to look at a couple of examples of Canadian writers in action.

In *Barometer Rising* by Hugh MacLennan there is a character called Colonel Wain. His family, originally British, has been five generations in Canada. But he still longs, like a good colonial, to be in England. And he says that everything in *this* damn country is second rate. Colonel Wain is a kind of WASP, military Mordecai Richler. The resemblances are numerous and surprising. The generation after Colonel Wain is determined to have its self-respect, and MacLennan releases it into a possible future. Colonel Wain, however, is discovered near the close of the novel in a blown-out house, in the snow, naked, with his mistress, dead.

We have been faced with the systematic devaluation of the Canadian fact, as Ron Lambert says, but we have had in our writers an insistence upon the legitimacy of this place, a declaration of the significance of Canadian ideas and tensions. In Sara Jeanette Duncan's *The Imperialist*, (1906), the young hero is a man who believes in the myth of British superiority and the idea of Imperial Unity. He discovers that Britain and the British want to use Canada and not be bothered by its needs. He discovers that the lure of the U.S. dollar is stronger for many business people than the desire to build a good community. Ironically, an English immigrant steals his girl and climbs economically doing it. After a political candidacy which teaches him the game of politics in Canada and a sharp insight into the historical forces at work in the major power struggles in this country, he is almost broken, and he considers going to the United States. But he turns back to Canada, almost by an accident; he is chastened; he is wiser; he is a little cowed. But he has learned lessons in survival and lessons about struggle. And he doesn't give up or light out for the territory.

We have been faced as Canadians with the systematic devaluing of the Canadian fact as a result of the liberal ideology. Many of our critics have invited us to see the conservative nineteenth century as something we should be ashamed of. We have been asked by leading critics, for instance, to have contempt for

Susanna Moodie because she came to Canada from an intelligent and well-educated class. She had a sense of community responsibility, however conservative. The U.S. writers I wrote of earlier are only the worst writers about Susanna Moodie. Northrop Frye and Doug Jones are almost as bad. They reject Moodie, and in their rush to accept U.S. individualist anarchist terms of the hero, they deny the Canadian past and are ashamed of it.

Susanna Moodie's book, *Roughing It In The Bush*, is a great work. It is the first in a tradition of immigrant works that include many of our fine novels. It contains some values we reject or are amused at – but what nineteenth-century work doesn't? Some of the best insights and values in Canadian life are in that book, the story of a woman who braved the bush, often alone with small children, finally working in the fields side by side with her husband, facing fire and sickness alone, and coming, with the feelings of ambiguity that only the bush people can know, to love the land and to call herself Canadian. Of course, Susanna Moodie presents what has come to be known as a WASP view of settling. But you can read the Ukrainian, Jewish, Hungarian, Icelandic, and Belgian views too. They are there, novels in the tradition, and they all relate importantly – in their rejection of the liberal anarchist hero or their acceptance of responsible community – to Moodie's work.

What we must do if we are to read our literature right is to come to terms with our history. We must recognize the struggle for community, our colonial condition that has lasted too long, the conservative values that shaped much of our beginnings – for good and ill. But we mustn't be ashamed of those beginnings, of that history. We must sort the good from the bad, learn what we can build on, and why we must reject some aspects as we grow into new forms, new concepts of love and justice. We must come to know what is the greatness of Susanna Moodie, of Philip Grove, of Hugh MacLennan, of Adele Wiseman and others, not to mention any of the poets. But we will not do those things as long as we permit the liberal ideology to rule our thinking.

Margaret Atwood has allowed the liberal ideology to rule her thinking in her book, *Survival*. As a result she cannot help herself from putting down Canadian literature at every turn. The liberal critic is finally the critic who says: "Well, we better read it because it is ours." Because of the liberal ideology, the concept of the hero as liberal individual anarchist, Atwood must dismiss and reject much of Canadian literature: its communal sense, its insistence on history, its admission that community shapes character as well as vice versa, its self-sacrificing hero. Because the liberal critic rejects those things, he or she is forced to say: "Well, we better read it because it is ours." But those who find out what the literature is about, what its genuine struggle is, what its deepest tensions are, come to see that Canadian literature is a great literature with great individual works. They say, "You'd better read Canadian literature or miss the most important literature you can ever lay your hands on."

The critics with a liberal ideology in Canadian literature see Canadians as losers without identity, the perpetual victims of someone's exploitation. They don't see the hard stoicism of Canadian characters in fiction. They don't see the terrible strength that is born in the struggle to survive and to make possible the survival of community. They don't see the heroism of a certain resignation that is the resignation into responsibility and service, for those are the qualities of fools – when you accept the hero as individual anarchist liberal. Margaret Atwood is trapped into that position. Like the colonial critics, she describes only half of Canadian life and literature.

Of characters in two films she says: "They are born losers . . . it's pure Canadian from sea to sea." (p.34). A little later she says, "Could it be that Canadians have a will to lose which is as strong and pervasive as the American's will to win?" (p.35) And she goes on that, "There is a sense in Canadian literature that the true and only season here is winter. . . . " (p.49) "Canadian writers as whole" she says, "do not trust nature . . . ." (p.49) She tells us that "The Canadian experience for immigrants seems programmed for failure." (p.158) She says "The Canadian way of death is death by accident." (p.166).

And so on. All that is not only untrue, it is criticism that is peculiarly colonial-minded in its perception of Canadian experience. Margaret Atwood leaves out of consideration too many major writers, most of whom make her theories fall into tatters. She doesn't write in any serious way of Richardson, Mair, Haliburton, Duncan, Grove, MacLennan, Hemon, Ringuet, D. C. Scott, F. R. Scott, Dorothy Livesay, Anne Marriott, W. O. Mitchell, Robertson Davies, Isabella Valency Crawford, Abraham

Klein, and others. Those major writers make statements which would make much of her book unable to stand up.

Moreover, Margaret Atwood includes and analyses writers who can be seen as deeply inflicted with a sense of colonial helplessness and sterility or who have disappeared almost completely into a kind of liberal individual anarchist retreat and unease. She includes from that group George Grant, Northrop Frye, Douglas LePan, Doug Jones, Eli Mandel, Dennis Lee, George Bowering, Anne Hébert, St. Denys Garneau, Bill Bissett, and others. Many of those people are said to be torn, and tormented victims. Grant wrote *Lament for a Nation.* Douglas LePan wrote "A Country Without A Mythology." George Bowering says he is a "Canadian surrounded by strangers," a fact that he learned from his U.S. professor! Northrop Frye says we want to get our writers into the position of the "individual separated in standards and attitudes from the community." Frye is saying that we want to separate the writer from the people so that he can alienate and write individualist anarchist stuff. George Bowering calls himself "a failed American." The implication is that a failed American makes a successful Canadian. Alas, alas, that is very much the over-riding sense of Margaret Atwood's *Survival.*

We can see where the feeling comes from. In the beginning was the liberal ideology, instrument of empires. Those empires sucked the blood of Canada for more than a hundred years, saying always that excellence is elsewhere, know-how must be brought in, and no one must impede the imperialist' right to use the country however and whenever they want. Canadians who attempt to stop the oppression and abuse of their country, Canadians who wish to end the contempt and the scorn that is heaped upon Canada and its people must be, they say, racists, fascists, chauvinists, xenophobes, anti-semites.

In the beginning was the liberal ideology, instrument of imperialism. It helped condition young Canadians to the fact that the brand names of most of the products around them would be foreign, that the books they would read would be foreign, that the artists they would enjoy would be foreign, that the films they would see would be foreign. If there are only three Canadian magazines on a magazine rack in the nearby drug store carrying three hundred magazines, we are invited by the liberal ideologists to think that we are witnessing the free flow of ideas.

Some of those evils are changing now, and only just in time. But we still are coerced by the liberal ideology. We still think we have to put Mordecai Richler on every platform in the country. We still are afraid to say that U.S. influence is often not leadership in progress but imperialist destruction of Canadian life and values, whether in union organization, education, women's liberation, or so-called "radical" politics. We are afraid to reject destructive domination and forge our own struggle. But we are beginning. And when we settle the question of the liberal ideology for once and for all, when we realize we can have love, justice, self-respect, self-determination, and a liberated people without the imperialist handbook of liberal domination, then the progressive forces will begin to win. Then there will be a genuine movement of the Canadian people, for they will have found their cultural roots, the legitimacy of their deepest feelings, and they will be able to express themselves on any issue of significance to their lives and the lives of their children without being cursed as reactionary, parochial, second-rate, and irrelevant.

The liberation of the Canadian people is not the discovering of an alien way of seeing reality. It is the legitimizing of the best of Canadian thought and action. It is a cultural revelation which will engender a cultural revolution, a struggle not separate from the economic struggle but one with it.

Margaret Atwood's book is an attempt to effect that cultural revelation, but it fails in its task. And that is to be expected, for history hasn't placed us quite yet where we can communicate the joy and tragedy of our imaginative experience and see through to the point at which we will have a population fully participating as makers of the society in its life and direction. But the day is not far off. On that day the war will be over, the war with the liberal ideology and all it implies. The rest will be a mopping-up operation. For when the people can tell itself that it knows what its experience truly is, then the people can be master of its own soul. When we are individually and collectively masters of our own souls, we will find we need only take a short step to becoming masters in our own house.

Quebec in the Canadian Federal State
Jim Laxer

The logic of Confederation was to establish an enlarged market within which the Canadian bourgeoisie could flourish. For the bourgeoisie to carry out its commercial plans, it was necessary to create a more formidable state system in British North America that could float loans in Britain, for the construction of a transcontinental railway system.

But to carry out a fundamental rearrangement of the state structure in British North America, the bourgeoisie and its political allies had to determine a place for French Canada within the new state system.

At the time of Confederation, French Canadians were overwhelmingly small farmers, although a relatively small class of French Canadian urban labourers had come into existence. Few French Canadians were members of the upper strata of the Canadian bourgeoisie. Instead the French Canadian elites were tied in a junior partnership to the predominant Anglo-Canadian bourgeoisie. Politicians like George Etienne Cartier, the leader of the French Canadian *bleu*, or Conservative party which was at that time the largest single bloc in Canadian politics, formed a link between the Anglo-Canadian bourgeoisie and the Roman Catholic hierarchy in Quebec and the independent professionals; the lawyers, notaries, doctors, and journalists who dominated Quebec politics.

As a colonial people French Canadians had lived in the legislative union of the province of Canada between 1841 and 1867 that had tied Upper and Lower Canada together. In the generation following the defeat of the Rebellion of 1837, French Canadian politics had been dominated by politicians who, like Lafontaine and Cartier, were willing to be junior partners to the English. This was so especially after the defeat of the European Revolutions of 1848 when the church moved in a sharply conservative direction. The period of Confederation was the high point of the power of the ultramontane wing of the church which attempted to establish a theocracy in Quebec. The Church set itself up as the guarantor of French Canadian survival. But it systematically sided with the English masters against all popular movements, including popular nationalist movements in French Canada.

The hierarchy of the church had been mortally afraid that the Rebellions of 1837 would mean that the ideas of the accursed French and American revolutions would follow them to Quebec. Following the rebellion, the church systematically fought whatever elements of *rouge* liberalism still existed in Quebec. By the 1860s, they had managed to stamp out the remnants of the Papineau tradition almost entirely.

The legislative union of 1841 had been designed as a vehicle for the assimilation of French Canada. It had failed in this purpose for a number of reasons. French Canadian numerical superiority in 1841 had resulted in the establishment of a legislative union between Upper and Lower Canada in which the two sections of the province had equal representation in the assembly. Designed as a way of keeping the French Canadian majority in check, this system backfired in the 1850s when the English population of what is now Ontario moved ahead of the French population of what is now Quebec. From the mid 1850s on, one of the demands of politicians in Canada West was for representation by population in the assembly as a means of submerging the French of Canada East. Naturally, even colonial politicians like Cartier were unwilling to go along with a simple legislative union in which French Canadians would have no guarantees of their national rights.

In the representation-by-population fight of George Brown, we can see an early version of the One-Canada position, which holds that in Canada democracy is a matter of individual rights and does not involve rights for the national collectivities that make up Canada.

But because Quebec was central to the design of commercial empire of the Anglo-Canadian bourgeoisie, it could not simply be subjected to the assimilationist programme of George Brown.

Instead the program of the Great Coalition of 1864 was

evolved to settle the relationship between French Canadians and the rest of British North America. The Great Coalition, which included both the English and French Conservatives led by Macdonald and Cartier and the Reformers led by George Brown, excluded only the liberal *rouges* of French Canada.

The program of the Great Coalition which was substantially enacted in the British North America Act provided for the following position for French Canada within the Canadian federal state.

The French language was to be recognized as official in the legislature and courts of the province of Quebec and in the parliament and courts of the federal government. Quebec was to retain the French civil code instead of operating under English common law as did the other provinces. Above all, French Canadians got federalism, the recreation of the province of Quebec, a province in which they were to form a very large majority of the population. At the time of Confederation it was expected that the provinces were to be unimportant creations. Macdonald called them mere "local" governments.[2] All the real financial powers and authority over critical matters like railways lay in the hands of the federal government. Furthermore, the BNA Act which Dorion, a leader of the Quebec *rouges*, called the most illiberal constitution in the world,[3] gave an absolute power to the federal government to disallow any piece of provincial legislation within one year of its passage. Canada's financial capitalists were determined not to allow the provinces, seen as colonies modelled after the view of colonies held by the British imperial government, to interfere with the grand design of their national policy.

And so at the time of Confederation, the federal arena was regarded as the critical one for French Canadians in terms of their national survival. Cartier pledged to French Canadians that as long as there was a solid bloc of French Canadian MPs from Quebec no federal government would ever dare to take actions which fundamentally violated the collective views of French Canadians on critical national matters.[4] Thus, according to the architects of Confederation, French Canadians were to retain their position in Canada through the workings of the federal system and through their power in both national parties, the Conservatives and Liberals at Ottawa.

The first phase of post-Confederation French Canadian nationalism which spans the period from 1867 to 1917 can be seen as the response of French Canadian society to the workings of the Confederation system. French Canadian nationalism then developed around issues primarily in federal politics: the issue of French Canadian minority educational rights outside Quebec, the matter of whether the Canadian west was to be English speaking or bilingual and the question of Canadian participation in the defence of the British empire.

Within the logic of the National Policy, the place of French Canadians in the Canadian west was inexorably determined between 1869 and the mid-1890's. The Riel Rebellion of 1869 – 70 upset the plans of the Macdonald government for a smooth acquisiton of the territories of the Hudson Bay Company. Because there was no railway between central Canada and the prairies at the time, Riel was able to force the federal government to make concessions to the already-existing population of the west, made up of Indians, French and English-speaking Métis, and a small number of settlers from Ontario and the British Isles. The federal government was forced by the rebellion to create the province of Manitoba in 1870 and to establish for it French language and educational rights as existed for the province of Quebec. But the steady flow of Ontario immigrants to Manitoba between 1870 and 1890 undid the original status of Manitoba as a bilingual province. By 1890, with anti-French racial feeling running high in English Canada (fomented by the Orange lodge, the Protestant Protective Association, the Imperial Federation League and the rhetoric of Dalton McCarthy), the government of Manitoba abolished French as an official language of the province and removed tax support from the separate Catholic and French language school system. The issue of Manitoba schools was to break the Conservative party in the 1890s and to make way for the election of Laurier in 1896.

The second Riel rebellion of 1885 took place in circumstances less auspicious for the Métis than did the first. The CPR had largely been built by then and the rebellion provided an opportunity for the railway to demonstrate its utility to the dominion. It moved troops promptly to the spot and in return was awarded a further government subsidy. French Canadians who looked on the Métis as racial inferiors did not object to the sending of troops to crush Riel. In fact, French Canadians signed up as part of the Canadian militia that crushed the rebellion. It was the aftermath of the rebellion and the hanging of Riel that sparked the building of a massive nationalist response in French Canada. When it became clear that the Macdonald government would treat the French-speaking leaders of the rebellion much more harshly than the English-speaking leaders, French Canada came to see Riel as a native son and saw his defeat as the crushing of French Canada in the west. Riel's hanging led to a demonstration of 50,000 French Canadians at the Champ de Mars in Montreal.[5] The revolutionary symbols, the tricolor and the Marseillaise appeared briefly in Quebec for the first time since 1837. The church hierarchy was filled with fear at the reappearance of popular nationalism. But whatever militancy there was dissipated into the vacuous politics of Honoré Mercier and his provincial *Parti National*, which spent its time serving the interests of the church and involving itself in railway scandals.[6]

By the mid 1890s it was clear that western Canada was to be a preserve of English Canadian national expansion. The idea that the federal government would be the protector of minority educational rights died with the Manitoba Schools Question in the 1890s.

Laurier federalism has remained dominant ever since. Its emergence meant that from that time forward French Canadians would define their rights more and more in terms of Quebec provincial rights. The arrangement of 1867 was already coming undone.

The issue which led to the formation of a French Canadian nationalist movement, the direct predecessor of today's movement, was that of Canada's participation in the wars of the British empire. In October 1899, under pressure from colonial secretary Joseph Chamberlain and under the pressure of militarist and Anglo-Saxon chauvinist groups like the Imperial Federation League, the government of Wilfrid Laurier decided to send 1,000 Canadian troops to fight in the South African war.[7] The war was opposed by the majority of French Canadians, who were more inclined to identify with the Boers in South Africa than with the British imperialists. Henri Bourassa, the young Liberal member of parliament for Labelle riding, resigned his seat in protest against the sending of Canadian troops.[8] The struggle against participation in the Boer War made Bourassa the leader of a renewed nationalist movement in French Canada. The movement that grew up between 1900 and 1914 found its centre of gravity in the independent professionals of French Canada. Its activities and ideas struck a responsive chord in the province's classical colleges and among the lower orders of the clergy.

The Bourassa nationalist movement was a defensive, conservative movement. It sought to maintain what it saw as the compact or agreement made between English and French Canada in Confederation. Bourassa asserted that in 1867 English Canadians had entered into a compact with French Canadians under which Canada would not participate in the wars of the empire except for the defence of Canadian soil.[9] Bourassa made his claims for French Canada in terms of British precedent. He argued that the decentralized empire of the mid-19th century little Englanders and free traders was congenial to French Canada. He deplored the rise of a new protectionist, militarist imperialism in late 19th century Britain that threatened to undo Canadian self government.

Bourassa did not call for Canadian independence from the British empire. He called merely for the restoration of a decentralized empire and fought against the excesses of the empire in a period of inter-imperialist rivalry between Britain and such countries as France, Germany and the United States. Bourassa's complaint was that Canada as a self-governing colony of Britain had no rights in the area of foreign policy. Therefore it was the business of Britain to defend Canada and not the business of Canada to defend Britain.[10] As a political figure in colonial French Canada, Bourassa feared the three English speaking collectivities that surrounded Quebec: Britain, English Canada, and the United States. He wanted to retain the British connection as reinsurance against English Canadian control of Canada which might lead to the destruction of existing French Canadian rights. He favoured Confederation as a barrier against American domination of French Canada and he saw the United States as a useful prop against British militarist imperialism.

The impotence of Bourassa's politics stemmed from its base in a declining independent petit bourgeoisie in Quebec. As Quebec became urbanized and French Canadians flowed into the factories from the farms, as French Canadian small business faced competition from European immigrants, as the Anglo-Canadian and American lumbering, mining and electric power trusts moved in – the world of the independent petit-bourgeoisie became ever more insecure. Its programme involved such elements as rural colonization so that French Canadians could be directed away from

Montreal to the barren ground of small farms in areas like Rouyn-Noranda where French Canadians could retain their faith and their pastoral way of life at the cost of grinding poverty and incredible suffering. The Bourassa movement promoted the *caisse populaires* in Quebec as lending institutions that would help French Canadian farmers and small businessmen. It advocated the creation of nationalist and Catholic newspapers like *Le Devoir, L'Action Sociale* or *Le Droit* to combat the materialistic, protestant values of English speaking North America. In its latter days, it sponsored Catholic unionism in Quebec as an alternative to a unionism that was secular and believed in class struggle.[11]

The complete colonialism of French Canadian politics during this period can be seen from the fact that the political leaders of French Canada defined their politics in British terms. In the great debate between Laurier federalism and Bourassa nationalism, both protagonists defined their positions in British terms. For Laurier it was his speech in 1877 in Quebec City on political liberalism that set out his view of politics. In the speech he rejected the tradition of Papineau radicalism and the link with the revolutionary republicanism of Europe. He claimed that his liberalism was English liberalism of the variety of Bright and Fox and Cobden.[12] Later, as Prime Minister, while attending a colonial conference in London, he uttered the famous statement that for him the proudest moment of his life would be to see a French Canadian take his place in an imperial parliament at Westminster.[13] Later he was to spend the last years of his life as leader of the opposition engaged in the task of trying to persuade French Canadians to fight for the British empire in World War I.

For Bourassa, too, politics was defined in terms of convincing the English Canadians and the British to live up to commitments they had made decades before to French Canada. Bourassa was capable of stating that his anti-imperialism did not make him any the less British as a French Canadian within the empire. At the height of his career, Bourassa's strategy was to create a French-Canadian nationalist bloc in federal politics based on the model of the Irish nationalists in British politics. In 1911 he formed an alliance between the nationalists and the Conservative party, hoping to come out of the election holding the balance of power in Ottawa between the Liberals and Conservatives. His Conservative-Nationalist candidates won 27 out of 65 seats in Quebec, but they did not achieve their purpose. The Conservatives came out of the elections with a majority which did not need the support of Nationalist MPs. And it was this Conservative government that was to lead Canada into World War I and conscription.

Conscription in 1917 revealed clearly that English Canada was prepared to use its majority position to force French Canadians to knuckle under on a life and death issue. Even though Quebec elected 62 out of 65 MPs opposed to conscription in 1917, an English Canadian federal government made up of Conservatives and pro-conscription Liberals was able to impose its will on Quebec. Faced with conscription, over 90 per cent of French Canadians called up sought exemption. Thousands went into hiding, many in the north woods of Quebec where the police and the military were afraid to go to confront them in their armed camps. In 1917 riots broke out in Quebec City, riots which were quelled when a regiment of Toronto troops was sent into the city.

The nationalism of Bourassa died with conscription in 1917. Never since that date have Quebec nationalists seen Ottawa as the focus of their politics.

The second phase of Quebec nationalism begins with Conscription and lasts until World War II. This second phase, sometimes described as Laurentianism, was based on the same class forces as underlay the Bourassa movement.

This time the leading figure in the movement was Abbé Lionel Groulx, a professor of History at the University of Montreal. Groulx did not define the Quebec interest in terms of compacts with the English as Bourassa had. Instead he created a mystical corporatist nationalist creed that sought its inspiration in New France before the Conquest. As in corporatist movements in inter-war Europe, inspiration was sought in historical epochs far removed from modern industrial society. What some movements sought from the Goths, the ancient Romans or the Gauls, Abbé Groulx sought from pristine New France.

He was the founder of the myth of Dollard des Ormeaux. We all know who Dollard was – he was the man who with a handful of comrades in the mid 17th century fought off an invading army of Iroquois with such audacity that in giving their lives Dollard and his friends saved New France. Groulx writing in 1919, turned Dollard into a Christ figure of French Canada, a man who had given his life for the Church and for New France.

For Groulx, the tale of Dollard was meant to have important

contemporary significance. Dollard, if he were alive today, would lead French Canada, said Groulx. He would lead French Canada out of its sense of inferiority toward the English. He would be the leader, the *chef* of the French Canadian people and along with other members of an elite he would guide French Canadians back to the values of their faith and their race.[14]

For Groulx these values were to be found in his view of what New France had been: a religious society that rejected the commercialism of the Protestant English, a society of large families organized into parishes with each household headed by the stern but just father. It was a society that according to Groulx was so pure and devout, that between 1608 and the conquest in 1759 only one illegitimate birth had occurred. For Groulx also, New France had produced a pure French race with the world's highest birth rate and with no intermarriage with the Indians. French Canadians were descended from carefully selected gentlewomen of devout character.[15]

It is amusing to contrast this view with the view in Bergeron's history of Quebec in which French Canadians are seen as the descendants of criminals and prostitutes. Dollard is pictured as merchant exploiter of the Indians and the Conquest is seen as decapitating a developing merchant capitalist society.

For Groulx though, the idyll of New France was to instil values in French Canadians in the 1920s. It was the desperate cry of a dying class of independent professionals who wanted to forget the urban industrial society dominated by foreign capitalists that was rising around them.

The right wing nationalism of Groulx declined in the late 1920s during a period of relative prosperity, but revived during the desperate times of the Depression in the thirties.

The thirties led to the formation of a new force in Quebec politics: the Union Nationale. The Union Nationale was born as an alliance between a group of liberal reform intellectuals called *Action Libérale Nationale* and the Quebec Conservatives led by Maurice Duplessis. *Action Libérale Nationale* developed a programme of social reform including such items as maximum hours and minimum-wage legislation, social welfare and unemployment insurance. The programme was developed out of the ideas of reform Catholicism in Europe, an attempt to evolve an alternative to socialism. The deal between the ALN and Duplessis was that the new party, the *Union Nationale* would adopt the ALN reform programme, but that Duplessis would provide the leadership and the organization. Duplessis, of course, quickly took control of the party and following the election of 1936 changed its political direction to suit his own purposes.[17]

The Duplessis government embodied many of the aspects of the nationalism of Abbé Groulx. Duplessis engaged in a symbolic defence of Quebec against foreign influences that involved Quebec in a long staged battle with the federal government at Ottawa. Duplessis during his time in office unveiled a provincial flag for the province, passed the Padlock Law that allowed the provincial government to close down the premises of alien organizations like the Communist Party and Jehovah's Witnesses. He refused to accept money from the federal government in the 1950s for assistance to higher education or as part of the Trans-Canada highway programme. Following World War ii, Duplessis held up the return of the Polish art treasures held during wartime for Poland in Quebec, to the Communist government of Poland. In the early fifties, the Duplessis government answered the federal government's Rowell-Sirois Report on federal-provincial relations with its own Tremblay Report which outlined a provincial rights position for the province of Quebec.

But beneath the façade of Duplessis' Quebec first policy, lay the reality of a government that placed advertisements in New York newspapers inviting American capitalists to come to Quebec to exploit the cheap labour of the French Canadians. Not only did Duplessis employ a persistent anti-Red witchhunt to hold back the consciousness of Quebec workers, but his variety of nationalism had as one of its components, Catholic unionism.

Catholic unionism made its appearance in Quebec in the first decade of the century. The roots of trade unionism in Quebec actually go back to the early decades of the 19th century. Quebec had been an important site for the organizing of the Knights of Labour, an early variant of industrial unionism, in the 1880s.[18]

Catholic unionism was devised, beginning in Europe, as the church's answer to the secular and militant class conscious organizations of workers. By the end of the 19th century, the church, faced with the reality of syndicalism and socialism changed its position of opposition to all workers' organizations. It accepted the right of workers to organize but only in Catholic unions which had as their goal the overall harmony of society and which did not adhere to policies of class conflict.

In 1921 40,000 Quebec workers who had been organized into Catholic unions were brought together in a Catholic trade union federation, the CTCC. Each local in the CTCC had a clerical advisor who had a great deal of authority over bargaining between the union and the employer. The CTCC was based on the philosophy that unions should avoid strikes and should appeal to the Christian sense of the employer.

It is not difficult to imagine the field day employers enjoyed in the early years of Catholic unionism in Quebec. Their existence was, in part, responsible for Duplessis' ability to advertise the cheap labour of the province to American corporations.

But even Quebec under Duplessis, during the period which Pierre Vallières called "the great darkness' was changing. World War II led to rapid and intensified urbanization and industrialization in the province. A new secular leadership was beginning to emerge within the Catholic trade union movement.

In 1949 the Asbestos strike revealed that the Quebec working class had reached a new level of organization and consciousness. When the workers ignored Duplessis' labour legislation and went on strike against the Johns Manville company in Asbestos, support was massive from workers around the province. For once the Catholic unions, the Trades and Labour Congress unions in Quebec and the Canadian Congress of Labour unions temporarily overcame their bitter rivalry and supported the Asbestos strikers. Amazingly, Archbishop Charbonneau took the side of the strikers and one Sunday churches across Quebec took up a collection for the striking workers. But the power of Duplessis' goon squads and provincial police prevailed in the end, and the long and bitter struggle was lost. The provincial government, appalled at the church's support of the workers, dispatched its labour minister to Rome to discuss the archbishop's behaviour with ecclesiastical authorities. Archbishop Charbonneau's efforts were rewarded by his almost immediate retirement. He was exiled to a retreat in British Columbia.[21]

By the mid-fifties the Catholic trade union movement had evolved into a fully secular organization with the creation of the Confederation of National Trade Unions (CNTU). From the position of company unions signing sweetheart contracts, the movement had cast off its clerical garb and had emerged as Quebec's most militant and most national trade union central.

At the same time as the Quebec people had been making the

transition from the church and the farm to the factory and the trade union, a new middle class had been emerging in Quebec. Unlike the independent professional petit-bourgeoisie that had dominated the previous two phases of French Canadian nationalism, the new middle class held positions in the civil service and in business. It was made up of top civil servants and French-Canadian junior executives in the corporations. Both groups mushroomed in size in post war Quebec and both felt that they were being held back in Duplessis' Quebec. The civil servants looked to the higher salaries enjoyed by their counterparts in neighbouring Ontario. French Canadian junior executives or would-be executives who were graduating in Quebec were becoming impatient to remove the barriers to the advancement of French Canadians in the corporations in Montreal. The fact was that French Canadians consistently obtained fewer promotions and received lower pay in the corporations than did their English speaking counterparts with the same level of education.

Within the cast-iron system of Duplessis with its electoral corruption and blatant patronage, the new middle class began organizing for power at the provincial level.

In 1960 the provincial Liberals under Jean Lesage brought the new middle class to office with the support of the other great emerging force, the Quebec proletariat. The Quiet Revolution of the early sixties saw the arrival of the new middle class. English Canadians breathed a sigh of relief, believing that Quebec had finally entered the 20th century, with a decent, clean liberal reform government. It was briefly assumed that the old problems caused by Quebec's odd identity were solved at last. All Canada could settle down to enjoy the comforts of branch-plant liberalism.

But English Canada's nirvana was short lived. The Quiet Revolution quadrupled Quebec's educational budget in several years. It brought demands for federal subsidies to build the highways that had been long delayed. It led to the nationalization of the power companies into Hydro Québec through the floating of a loan on the New York money market. All this led to a severe crisis in federal-provincial tax sharing arrangements. It turned out that simply accommodating the arrival of Quebec's new middle class would seriously strain federal-provincial relations.

The nationalist campaign of the new middle class which sought the removal of barriers to Québecois advancement within the

Canada Ltd.

corporate structures shook Confederation far more than had the earlier nationalist movements.

But the 1960 coalition which had involved Lesage, Lévesque and Trudeau as well as most of the labour leaders of Quebec began to break apart quickly.

One wing of the new middle class supported a position of stronger nationalism edging toward endorsement of independence for Quebec. Federalists like Trudeau undertook their intellectual denunciations of the thrust toward independence. In his book, *Federalism and the French Canadians*, Trudeau accused the independentists of fearing the rational international world of the multi-national corporations which was emerging. He warned contemptuously that French Canada was unprepared for democracy and dismissed the independence struggle as a retreat to the wigwam and as a new treason of the intellectuals. Echoing the opposition of the trade union leadership of the early sixties to separatism, Trudeau said an independent Quebec would involve a cut in living standards for the working class while benefitting the middle class.[22] His logic led him to oppose Canadian as well as Quebec nationalism and Lévesque was flirting tantalizingly with the separatists, Quebec's economy, it could not consistently oppose the control of Wall Street over Bay Street.

While Trudeau was preparing the intellectual defences for federalism and Lévesque was flirting tantalizingly with the separatists, the separatist party the *Rassemblement pour L'Independence Nationale* (RIN) with a mere 900 members proved the electoral possibilities for independence by winning 210,000 votes in the 1966 election.

In 1967, René Lévesque made his ultimatum to the Quebec Liberal Party by challenging it to accept a programme calling for virtual sovereignty for Quebec. His programme having been rejected by the Quebec Liberal majority, Levèsque led his followers out of the Liberal party and into a transitional organization called the *Mouvement Souveraineté Association* (MSA) which was to prepare for the creation of a new independentist party.

The wing of the new middle class that favoured independence got its respectable political vehicle in 1968 with the creation of the *Parti Québecois*, which swallowed up the two existing independence parties, the RIN and the *Ralliement Nationale*.

Lévesque's PQ, in fact, called for Canadian status for Quebec within the American empire. For the PQ the problem was not imperialism but the illogic of dealing with the real power centres of New York and Washington through the back door at Ottawa. The PQ made it clear that it welcomed foreign investment in Quebec and in the 1970 election the party's literature featured a statement by David Rockefeller to the effect that he did not care whether Quebec separated or not, provided that it welcomed foreign investment.

Calling for a common market with the rest of Canada to calm his more squeamish potential supporters, Lévesque insisted that the struggle for independence meant only a battle over sovereignty with Ottawa, with hands off the foreign corporations. The most recent convention of the PQ, held early in 1973, reconfirms its character as a party of the new middle class, seeking Quebec independence to further the aspirations of this class to be branch-plant managers and to be dominant in the state structure of the new Quebec.

In 1970, the PQ won 24 per cent of the popular vote in the Quebec provincial election, though electing only 7 members to the National Assembly. Six of the party's seven seats were located in the east end of Montreal, the great metropolitan bastion of the French Canadian working class. The party, by then, boasted a membership of about 80,000. That is more than the Canada-wide membership of the NDP.

By the time the PQ had been founded and had fought its first election, the French Canadian saviours of federalism had arrived in Ottawa. In 1968, Trudeau won office as a French Canadian who was pledged to a hard line position in keeping Quebec under control. He had made it clear that he regarded Quebec as having no rights going beyond those of any other province. English Canadians were relieved at having found a French Canadian federalist who was on record as complaining about the quality of French spoken in Quebec, who was prepared to sit through a rock-pelting for federalism at the 1968 St. Jean Baptiste day parade. He was a man who made it clear that if Quebec seceded, he would not return to his native province but would instead settle in New York.

Naturally, the large corporations of the continent preferred the Trudeau position to the Lévesque position, although in neither case were their basic interests threatened.

But while the federalist and new middle-class independentist options were being prepared, Quebec society continued to undergo basic changes.

The early sixties in Quebec saw an almost cataclysmic rise in anti-clericalism among masses of young urban Québecois. The passage of Bill 60 meant the end of the church monopoly in the province's educational system. During the decade, the church was faced with an insoluble recruiting problem in replenishing the ranks of the clergy, which literally began to age and to die off.

Radical militancy was on the rise among Quebec's workers during the sixties. The radical unionism of the Montreal wing of the CNTU under Michael Chartrand, the militant movement of Montreal taxi drivers, and the long, grueling struggle of the Lapalme drivers were a few cases.

Also during the decade, a small terrorist movement usually known as the FLQ began sporadic incidents of violent, symbolic opposition to federalism. In October 1970, the kidnappings carried out by the FLQ led to the invocation of the War Measures Act by the Trudeau government. Without entering into a lengthy discussion of the crisis of October 1970 we can point to a few of its important features. Trudeau, Bourassa and Drapeau saw one aspect of the crisis as an opportunity for silencing their political opponents in Quebec, in the trade union movement, in the PQ, in the citizens' action committees which had led to the formation of the radical municipal party in Montreal, the Front d'Action Politique (FRAP). The crisis was seized as a chance to heighten the readiness of the state apparatus for dealing with the populace.

To understand the strategy of the FLQ, read Pierre Vallières' book, *White Niggers of America*.[23] Vallières describes his life as the son of a worker in the Angus Shops of the CPR in Montreal. The misery and the sense of hopelessness of the working class of Quebec in the fifties is depicted in the book.

But it is clear that Vallières, even as an FLQ ideologist, retains his sense of hopelessness about the working class. The workers can only be moved from their inert helplessness and unconsciousness in his view through the inspiration of the symbolic violence of a few who strike back at the system. That was the road to revolution outlined by Vallières in the 1960s.

But the War Measures Act crisis led Vallières to change his

position. In 1972 he published a new book, *Choose*,[24] in which he renounced his earlier advocacy of terrorism, arguing that all the FLQ did was to mobilize the state without mobilizing the workers. He then goes on to endorse the electoral strategy and political programme of René Lévesque and the PQ, maintaining that all Quebec independentists should work together for political independence, after which they can decide what kind of social order an independent Quebec should have. Above all, he warns against independent political action by the working class of Quebec, advising the workers to stick with the leadership of René Lévèsque. The interesting thing is that Vallières, in turning from terrorism to PQ electoralism, retains the same basically incorrect understanding of the working class. His politics remain individualist in both the adventurist and the opportunist manifestation.

The crisis of October 1970 led to a temporary shocked numbness in Quebec politics. But the following October, it was not the FLQ handful, but masses of Quebec workers who arrived as a new political force on the stage of Quebec politics.

The epochal strike against *La Presse* centred on the question of who should control the content of the paper. The journalists wanted to replace Power Corporation with its anti-socialist and anti-independence position. But the strike did more, it brought about a new alliance of Quebec trade unionists. The new alliance was symbolized when Louis Laberge, president of the Quebec Federation of Labour (QFL) who until then had been an international unionist with an undistinguished record of business unionism, announced that he would lead a demonstration to the *La Presse* building in defiance of the city police.

In the months following the *La Presse* strike, the Common Front among public employees represented by the QFL, the CNTU and the Quebec Teachers' Corporation came into existence. In the spring of 1972 the historic general strike of 200,000 Quebec public employees took place.

The three trade union centrals that entered the Common Front also issued manifestoes. The manifestoes were the first full evidence of the Quebec working class entering politics in its own name. Quebec workers had been the foot soldiers for the Papineau rebellion in 1837, for the Catholic unions, for the Quiet Revolution in 1960 and for René Lévesque in 1970. Now the mainstream of the trade union movement issued manifestoes which broadly favoured the independence of Quebec and the destruction of capitalism.

The QFL manifesto, entitled *The State is Our Exploiter*, detailed the way in which the state is used as a coercive force on behalf of the capitalist system. It showed how the whole rationale of the state is to hold down the working class both through its coercive instruments and by redirecting the taxes paid by workers into grants to the corporations.[25]

The CNTU manifesto, entitled *Its Up to Us*, to which Vallières takes greatest exception in *Choose*, sees American imperialism as the main enemy. The manifesto analyses Quebec's economy as a hinterland economy based on the extraction and export of resources and on light manufacturing. Quebec is an under-industrialized hinterland of Ontario and the United States, it says. The manifesto points to the structural problems of a Quebec economy which has such an enormous service sector in relation to the amount of manufacturing done in the province. It points out that over 50 per cent of all construction in Quebec is now being undertaken by state expenditures. It shows how the state is trying desperately to cover over the structural weaknesses of Quebec's hinterland economy.[26]

With the Common Front and the Manifestoes, it was clear that a significant working-class, anti-imperialist struggle for an independent Quebec was being born.

For English Canadians who are concerned with building an anti-imperialist socialist independence movement in English Canada, the struggle in Quebec is enormously significant. In it lies the hope that English Canadians and Québecois will no longer be victimized by a federal system which has simply handed both parts of the country over to the American corporations. Let us hope that an anti-imperialist alliance is possible. Perhaps the simultaneous proposals for the Mackenzie Valley Pipeline and the James Bay Hydro Project, both of which will turn the northern half of this continent into even more of a resource hinterland of the United States, give us the opportunity to begin to create an anti-imperialist alliance.

Notes

[1] Donald Creighton, *The Road to Confederation*, (Toronto, 1964), p. 44.

[2] Donald Creighton, *Canada's First Century*, (Toronto, 1970), p. 10.

[3] Mason Wade, *The French Canadians*, (Toronto, 1956), p. 324.

[4] *Ibid.*, p. 362.

[5] *Ibid.*, p. 417.

[6] *Ibid.*, p. 429.

[7] James Laxer, *French-Canadian Newspapers and Imperial Defence 1899-1914*, (unpublished M. A. thesis, Queen's University, 1967), p. 27.

[8] *Ibid.*, p. 35.

[9] *Ibid.*, p. 36.

[10] *Ibid.*, p. 177.

[11] Henri Bourassa, *Syndicats Nationaux ou Internationaux*, (Montreal, 1919), p. 16.

[12] for an understanding of Laurier's views, read O. D. Skelton, *Life and Letters of Sir Wilfrid Laurier*, (Toronto, 1965), v. 1, 11.

[13] Mason Wade, *op. cit.*, p. 474.

[14] Abbé Lionel Groulx, "If Dollard Were Alive Today," in Ramsay Cook (ed.), *French-Canadian Nationalism*, (Toronto, 1969), p. 195.

[15] for his views on New France, read: Abbé Lionel Groulx, *Nôtre Maître, le Passé*, (Montreal, 1921).

[16] Léandre Bergeron, *The History of Quebec*, (Toronto, 1971).

[17] for a full treatment of this subject, read, Herbert Quinn, *The Union Nationale*, (Toronto 1963).

[18] Charles Lipton, *The Trade Union Movement of Canada 1827-1959*, (Montreal, 1967), p. 68.

[19] *Ibid.*, p. 225.

[20] Pierre Vallières, *White Niggers of America*, (Toronto, 1971), p. 121.

[21] Léandre Bergeron, *op. cit.*, p. 197.

[22] To understand his ideas, read, Pierre E. Trudeau, *Federalism and the French Canadians*, (Toronto, 1968).

[23] Pierre Vallières, *op. cit.*

[24] Pierre Vallières, *Choose*, (Toronto, 1972),

[25] Daniel Drache (ed.), *Quebec – Only the Beginning*, (Toronto, 1972), p. 158.

[26] *Ibid.*, p. 27.

Contradictions and Alternatives in Canada's Future
Mel Watkins

The process of capitalist development proceeds dialectically, on the one hand constantly revolutionizing production, on the other hand creating conditions antagonistic to capitalism itself. The resulting contradictions, to the extent that they are fundamental, necessarily contain the *possibility* for the radical transformation of capitalism and the creation of its alternative, socialism.

Now the record of the advanced capitalist countries demonstrates the remarkable resiliency of capitalism, that is, its ability successively to transcend particular contradictions. The likelihood that this will not indefinitely be the case depends not on the mere waiting for the contradictions to deepen and to ripen, but on the articulation of the socialist alternative, on the development of socialist strategies around particular contradictions, and on the building of a socialist movement as a force in being.

It follows that a necessary first step for socialists in Canada is the identification of the contradictions inherent in contemporary Canadian capitalism. That is, of course, what we have been endeavouring to do in these essays. We have spoken of the struggle between labour and capital, which is the primary contradiction of capitalism; of Canada as a resource hinterland in the context of American imperialism, which is the most important of the immediate contradictions of Canadian capitalism; of the *Québecois* as a specially-exploited people within Canada, now struggling for national self-determination; of the double exploitation of women as underpaid workers outside the home and unpaid workers within the home; of the growing fiscal crisis of the state. We have endeavoured to expose the liberal ideology as a set of beliefs that can only perpetuate domination and inequality. We have appealed to the history of dissent and protest of the Canadian people to show that there is a tradition of struggle in this country, but we have argued that its presently dominant institutional forms – the trade union movement under American union control, and the New Democratic Party – increasingly fail us.

In this chapter I shall organize the argument around a book, now eight years old, which has been tremendously influential – George Grant's *Lament for a Nation.*[1] The occasion for the book was the rise and fall of Diefenbaker, but for Grant the implications were profound:

> To lament is to cry out at the death or the dying of some-thing loved. This lament mourns the end of Canada as a sovereign state. . . . Lamenting for Canada is inevitably asso-ciated with the tragedy of Diefenbaker. His inability to gov-ern is linked with the inability of this country to be sovereign. . . . Diefenbaker's confusions and inconsistencies are . . . to be seen as essential to the Canadian fate. . . . The 1957 election was the Canadian people's last gasp of nationalism. Diefen-baker's government was the strident swan-song of that hope. (pp. 2, 4, 5).

Grant's argument with respect to independence consists of three propositions:

1. **Canada is dominated by American corporate capitalism particularly since 1940.**

The United States is "the world's most powerful empire to date." Its ruling classes are "those that control the private governments (that is, the corporations) and those that control the public government which co-ordinates the activities of these corporations. . . . Our ruling class is composed of the same groups as that of the United States, with the specific difference that the Canadian ruling class looks across the border for its final authority in both politics and culture." (pp. 8, 9) Again, "the dominant classes in Canada see them-selves at one with the continent on all essential matters." "Dominant classes get the kind of government they want"; Canada has become "a branch plant of American capitalism" (p. 41) and "foreign capital is able to determine possible gov-ernments by incarnating itself as an indigenous ruling class." (p. 43)

The major culprit for Grant, as later for Donald Creighton in

251

his *Canada's First Century*,[2] is the Liberal Party which "for twenty years before its defeat in 1957 . . . had been pursuing policies that led inexorably to the disappearance of Canada." (p. 4) Its major accomplishment was to move Canada from the British to the American Empire. "From 1940 to 1957, the ruling class of this country was radically reshaped. In 1939, the United Kingdom still seemed a powerful force, and the men who ruled Canada were a part of the old Atlantic Triangle. They turned almost as much to Great Britain as to the United States, economically, culturally and politically. After 1940, the ruling class found its centre of gravity in the United States." (pp. 9-10)

2. An independent capitalist Canada is an impossibility.

Grant calls this option "Gaullism" and conceives of it as the planning and control of investment by the elites "so as to stop the tendency of capitalism to become international." For him "Macdonald's 'National Policy' was of the Gaullist kind." (p. 46) But Grant makes it clear that what is at issue, is the nature of the capitalist class itself: "After 1940 it was not in the interests of the economically powerful to be nationalists. Most of them made more money by being the representatives of American capitalism and setting up the branch plants. No class in Canada more welcomed the American managers than the established wealthy of Montreal and Toronto, who had once seen themselves the pillars of Canada. Nor should this be surprising. Capitalism is, after all, a way of life based on the principle that the most important activity is profit-making. That activity led the wealthy in the direction of continentalism. They lost nothing essential to the principle of their lives in losing their country." (p. 47) Grant recognizes that "Much of English-speaking conservatism was simply a loyalty based on the flow of trade, and therefore destined to change when that flow changed" (p. 69) – an admission that some of his left critics who see him as mired in nostalgia have ignored – and he concludes that "no small country can depend for its existence on the loyalty of its capitalists." (p. 69)

3. The only possibility for Canadian independence is socialism, but socialism is impossible.

To have argued not only the first two propositions but also

the first half of this proposition in 1965 was a formidable achievement. "If Canada was to survive, the cornerstone of its existence was the Great Lakes region. The population in that area was rushing toward cultural and economic integration with the United States. Any hope for a Canadian nation demanded some reversal of the process, and this could only be achieved through concentrated use of Ottawa's planning and control. After 1940, nationalism had to go hand in hand with some measure of socialism. Only nationalism could provide the political incentive for planning; only planning could restrain the victory of continentalism." (p. 15) But, says Grant, "No such combination was possible, and therefore our nation was bound to disappear." (p. 15)

Why? "To have anticipated a socialist Ontario was to hope rather than to predict. Certainly its leadership could not have come from the good-natured utopians who led our socialist parties. They had no understanding of the dependence of socialism and nationalism in the Canadian setting. Their confused optimism is seen in the fact that they have generally acted as if they were 'left-wing' allies of the Liberal party. Socialist leadership in Canada has been largely a pleasant remnant of the British nineteenth century – the Protestant tabernacle turned liberal. Such a doctrine was too flaccid to provide any basis for independence." (p. 75)

To reject the only two routes to independence was a bitter experience for someone who loved his country, though Grant refused to completely abandon hope. In 1967 he wrote: "Nothing here written implies that the increasingly difficult job of preserving what is left of Canadian sovereignty is not worth the efforts of practical men."[3] But as Abraham Rotstein has observed, "It is a dim candle to light the way."[4]

The later Grant has become obsessed with the horrors of the technological society. He sees technology as obliterating all traditions and national identities. For him Marshall McLuhan's shiny global village is filled with darkness.

But, you ask, what of the second half of the third proposition? Is socialism possible? Is Grant's lament, in fact, only a "Lament for a Bourgeois Nation"? Let us try to get at this question by re-examining each of Grant's propositions in the perspective of 1973.

Independentism

There is no doubt as to the dominance of American corporate capitalism in Canada, and of its increase in recent decades as an aspect of Canada's "special status" within the American Empire down to August 15, 1971. But the important fact since Grant wrote is the beginning of the weakening of U.S. world hegemony and, closely related thereto, the apparent end of special status for Canada.

While it is clear that the last chapter has yet to be written of the American War in Indochina, it is evident that American imperialism has suffered a major defeat and that U.S. military supremacy *vis-à-vis* the Third World has been seriously undermined. That is hardly a small matter, for the open door for the American-based, multi-national corporation has always hinged ultimately on force of arms. At the same time, the deteriorating position of the U.S. dollar is clear evidence of the erosion of U.S. economic hegemony, and its replacement by a new era of inter-imperialist rivalry amongst capitalist blocs.

The extent of U.S. balance of trade difficulties which underlie the monetary crisis has compelled the U.S. to demand trade concessions from its major trading partners and, as an aspect thereof, to end Canada's "special status." To date, this has taken the form of no further exemptions for Canada, but it promises in due course to lead to the rolling back of exemptions and concessions previously granted.

In the nature of dependency, Canadian dependence on the U.S. is costly for Canada. Foreign ownership of the resource industries has meant the outward drain of potential jobs as well as profits. Our manufacturing sector has been high-cost, with a high propensity to import and a limited capacity to export, because it is mainly foreign-owned. But in recent decades these costs have been masked by benefits arising from special status. It follows that the loss of "special status" now leaves us simply with the costs. This is bound to have pervasive consequences, exactly because at the same time Canada's role as a resource supplier to the U.S., particularly in the energy field, is being greatly intensified. Simultaneously our already weak manufacturing sector is being undermined, both overtly by U.S. policy and covertly by mechanisms such as an overvalued Canadian dollar and rising energy costs – set in motion by highly capital-intensive resource development for the U.S. market.

The result of all this is to create a major contradiction in the Canadian political economy. The emergence of trading blocks, notably of the enlarged European Common Market, creates a dilemma for Canada. Since Canada is already closely tied to the U.S., the logic of blocs suggests closer formal integration into a North American Common Market. This is what both John Connally, former Secretary of the Treasury and advisor to Nixon, and Senator Hartke, of Hartke-Burke fame, have pointed out to us recently.

Such bluntness sends shivers up Ottawa's spine. Even our most continentalist Cabinet Ministers, such as Sharp, take pains to deny this option; the one lesson of history the Liberals have learned is the 1911 Reciprocity election, where the people were actually allowed to vote on the question of continentalism and decisively rejected it.

But to rule out integration is to leave as the only alternative an independent industrial strategy; and that is a nettle the Liberals have not, and cannot, firmly grasp. The result is, at best, drift and ad hoccery; at worst, silent surrender into complete continentalism. This country has not formally signed a continental energy deal, and Donald Macdonald has even learned to say that he is opposed to it. But Canadian exports of oil and gas to the U.S. have risen significantly in the first part of 1973, and that is presumably what a continental energy deal is really all about. The U.S. has not formally abrogated the auto pact, but there is evidence of significant cutbacks in new investment in automotive plants in Canada, particularly by Ford. This strategy can effectively abrogate the pact in terms of jobs for Canadians.

The closest our political leaders have come to articulating a way out of this contradiction is to suggest, as Senator Lamontagne has done, that we use our resources, which the U.S. wants, as a bargaining weapon to maintain special status and stop Nixonomics from de-industrializing us. But there are two problems with that solution. The first is that it is unlikely that the U.S. can afford to be so benign to us, precisely because we are its major trading partner. The second is that selling off resources necessarily brings into play the full range of de-industrializing mechanisms, that is, the contradiction re-asserts itself. There is no avoiding the fact that since the United States is the problem, it cannot be the solution.

Indeed, the contradictions involved here are already leading to manifestations of resistance within Canada. Just beneath the surface there lies a gut feeling that selling off non-renewable resources is a bartering away of one's birthright, and it can turn into a rage against the con men. Diefenbaker emerged out of the resource mania of the '50's associated with Korean War stockpiling, the Paley Report, and the pipeline fiasco; next time we should try to do better.

The opposition to American domination is picking up momentum. An opinion poll taken in the Spring of 1973 showed that far more Canadians are in favour of nationalizing the energy resource industry than are in favour of leaving it in the hands of the U.S.-based corporations. Workers in the manufacturing sector are now becoming aware of the causes of de-industrialization. There is a growing opposition to such manifestations of U.S. imperialism as the Mackenzie Valley pipeline and the James Bay Scheme.

Bourgeois Nationalism

By denying the possibility of an independent capitalist Canada, in effect Grant wrote off the Committee for an Independent Canada before it happened. Was he premature in that regard? The intellectual guru of the CIC is Abraham Rotstein; let us examine the quality of his analysis.

He begins well: "It takes only the briefest acquaintance with the realities of the Canadian scene to appreciate that the middle class in this country has been the spearhead of the great sell-out. No other business class in an advanced industrial society has presided so gracefully over its own liquidation." (p. 24) But thereafter the argument lacks conviction. Rotstein rules out both known methods of repatriation: buying back for Canadian capitalists, because it is too expensive; and public ownership, because the majority of Canadians are not ready for nationalization. Those who advocate the latter are warned that they are adding "needless risks" to the task of saving Canada, and are thereby assuming "a grave responsibility." Instead, says Rotstein, because the nationalist movement is weak "It must, in my view, mobilize all classes and segments of society in order to be successful." And around what concrete demand should they be mobilized? Rotstein proceeds to conjure up something called "functional socialism," based on the premise that property consists not only of titles but also of functions; and that, rather than worry about the former, the government should usurp the latter as it sees fit, on a one-by-one basis.

Now both in terms of a political process and a political program, this is seriously deficient analysis. Take first the process of achieving independence; the relevant questions, which Rotstein never really poses, are: What is the nature of the Canadian capitalist class? What is the nature of the multi-national corporation? Is national economic independence attainable in the twentieth century?

Tom Naylor has given a convincing answer to the first question, and it is not helpful to Rotstein's cause. The Canadian capitalist class is a financial bourgeoisie which does not control industrial production in Canada. Hence, bankers are the most powerful section of the Canadian bourgeoisie. They make money financing the foreign take-over of Canada, and joining international consortia the better to rip off the Third World. They are explicitly anti-nationalist.

Naylor's argument comes out of a powerful strand of Marxist writing which has been elaborated by Paul Baran[5] with respect to developing countries in general, and by Andre Gunder Frank[6] for Latin America in particular. Baran argues that imperialism has worked to strengthen mercantile capitalism in the underdeveloped countries. Naylor has demonstrated how both British finance imperialism and American corporate imperialism have done exactly that in the Canadian case. Frank asserts, on the basis of concrete studies of Chile and Brazil, that "The contemporary structure of capitalism . . . does not provide for the autonomous development of a national bourgeoisie independent enough to lead (or often even to take an active part in) a real national liberation movement or progressive enough to destroy the capitalist structure of underdevelopment at home."

The basic reason is the nature of the multi-national corporation, about which we now know a good deal, and its tendency to emasculate the national bourgeoisie. Paul Sweezy and Harry Magdoff, put it this way: "While multi-national corporations do not, as so often claimed, internationalize their managements, they do *dena*-tionalize a section of the native bourgeoisies in the countries they penetrate. This of course weakens these native bourgeoisies. . . ."[7]
Stephen Hymer[8] makes the point metaphorically and graphically when he describes the corporation as a pyramid or vertical hierarchy, with a narrow power centre at the top and a broad base of powerless workers at the bottom, and when he pictures its multi-national operations as the spatial shifting of the pyramid, but with the top remain-

ing firmly anchored in the metropole. In Hymer's world, the best a hinterland country can do is to shift some part of the middle of the pyramid.

These arguments cut deep, for they mean that the very existence of a national industrial bourgeoisie in dependent countries runs against the grain of this century. Capitalism today is imperialism. The name of the game, if you are a capitalist, is not independent capitalism, but being a centre for multi-national capital, or having your "fair share" of the multi-national corporations. The point seems to be grasped by Alistair Gillespie, our new Minister of Industry, Trade and Commerce who, having left the Committee for an Independent Canada, now favours making Canada a viable base for multi-national corporations.

We can agree that Canada is not well-endowed with its own multi-nationals at the moment. But will the strategy of getting more multi-national corporations be successful? Gillespie appears not to have read Arthur Cordell's study for the Science Council of Canada. On the basis of detailed interviews with the officers of our present multi-national corporations, it concludes: "The interviews suggest that, located next to such a vast market concentration [as the United States], Canada faces a possibly inexorable 'iron law' which might be as follows: *when a company in a relatively small country expands its international operations into a significantly larger market it finds, over time, that it pays to locate not only production but support and managerial functions in the larger offshore market area.*' The Canadian policy-maker who urges the use of public tax funds to support the establishment of Canadian-based multi-national corporations must carefully assess this built-in tendency."[9]

Nor should we be surprised that, if the name of the game is multi-national capitalism, it is a most difficult game to play. The viable centres of multi-national capitalism are presently the United States, Western Europe and Japan. As we move into a new era of inter-imperialist rivalry, we should be struck by the fact that this is the same list of participants who played the last round of that game in the pre-World War I era. The reality is that no new centre has emerged in this century within the capitalist world. The only country to join the magic circle of major industrialized countries has been the U.S.S.R., and it has been by rejecting the capitalist road.

In sum, the notion peddled about by the CIC that Canada can become a viable independent capitalist country has little to support it by way of either analysis or historical evidence. What, then, is the CIC really all about? The answer is to be found by considering its programatic demands.

Functional socialism in the abstract means in the concrete the screening mechanism of the Gray Report. Now both in the abstract and the concrete, these new-fangled words mean something very old-fashioned, called government regulation of private enterprise. We have something of a track record in this regard in this country – in whose interest have we regulated the CPR and Bell Canada? The notion that the Canadian government could regulate two-thirds of the giant and medium-sized corporations in this country – for that is what foreign ownership is really all about – is ludicrous. At best, there could be some marginal increase in net benefits, if the Nixon Administration were willing. In fact, it is not, being already on record as opposed to Canada's use of a screening mechanism which might harm U.S. interests.

There is a moral of some importance to be drawn here. Stripped down to its essence, functional socialism is simply social democracy. Rotstein got the idea from Adler-Karlson,[10] a Swedish social democrat. The hallmark of the social democratic mode of analysis is that it can perceive neither class itself nor the state as a class institution. Rather, it conjures up the bourgeois state as a neutral entity able to operate in the "public interest" or, in this case, in the "national interest." It pulls rabbits out of hats and gives them improbable names like "Canada Development Corporation," and "screening mechanism"; the former then joins the consortium to build the Mackenzie Valley pipeline. Predictably, they fail to run very well and are easily domesticated by the imperialists.

The social democratic analysis assumes that corporations that would not tolerate nationalization would nevertheless sit idly by while governments usurped their rights. It imagines that giant foreign-based multi-national corporations and metropolitan governments would let hinterland governments significantly affect the behaviour of their subsidiaries and demand no benefit in return. All of this, despite the knowledge that foreign-based companies in this country do not even pay taxes at the same rate as Canadian companies.

It turns out to be no accident, then, that the CIC and the NDP have the same position on foreign ownership, that both endorse the Gray Report recommendation. Such a strategy, to the extent that it would be effective at all, is not about independence but is rather about tidying up after the multi-national corporation, of trying to get more benefits and fewer costs from dependence. It's like having a referee at a rape.

Or, as Cy Gonick has argued, in a most convincing exposure of bourgeois nationalism, it's all just a debate between two schools of continentalists. The difference between the Walter Gordons and the Pierre-Elliot Trudeaus is that Gordon is an activist and Trudeau a passivist:

> Both schools accept the need for continentalism. Neither envisions Canada as being anything but a regional economy within the continental North American economy. And both agree that the multi-national corporation is here to stay, and that it is an agency for progress. The activists . . . complain loudly about the economic problems which emerge between Canada and the United States. . . . [T]hey advocate policies to strengthen Canada's bargaining position within the continental system – to win for Canadians a greater share of the continental pie. . . . The passivists fear the proposals. They downgrade economic difficulties with the United States. . . . [T]hey are 'misunderstandings' due to 'a breakdown of communication.' They argue, in effect, that the marginal gains to be made by tinkering with the continentalist mechanism will be more than offset by retaliatory measures by the Americans, or simply by the hostile environment it will create.

The analysis is wholly applicable to the Gray Report; significantly, its supporters are wont to argue that its implementation would strengthen Canada's bargaining position.

Neither the CIC nor the NDP are serious about independence. In the 1970's, this is no small matter. It is difficult to work out an energy policy without recognizing that W. O. Twaits of Imperial Oil is perhaps the most influential man in this country. In the spring of 1973, Eric Kierans described Donald Macdonald, Canada's energy minister, as W. O. Twaits' "executive assistant." It is difficult to work out an industrial strategy in the absence of a foreign ownership policy. The policy presently under debate in the House of Commons fails to come within a country mile of implementing even the Gray Report. It leaves untouched the existing activities of corporations when most of our industry just happens to be foreign-owned and is in trouble exactly because of that.

Independence and Socialism

Grant's linking of independence and socialism was shortly to be restated by Jim Laxer with a different and more hopeful twist:

> Continental integration has become so pervasive that those who value an independent Canada and those who reject the values of corporate capitalism are beginning to share a common agenda. Canadian nationalists are starting to realize that only large-scale government intervention in the economy can win back control of this country for Canadians; socialists are more and more aware that we cannot build a better society if Canada does not possess sovereign power. It is in the interest of North American capitalists to weaken the Canadian state and to limit it to the passive function of maintaining a peaceful and secure climate for investment. In contrast, it is in the interest of Canadian socialists to resist any decline in our national sovereignty. . . . [12]

This perspective provided the basis for the 1969 Waffle Manifesto "For an Independent Socialist Canada," and for its call for public ownership as the positive alternative to the multi-national corporation.

What are the prospects that the Canadian working class will support the call for socialism and independence?

Now, the major interest of the working class has been in the bread-and-butter issues of jobs and a rising standard of living, and is likely to remain so. Broadly speaking, there has been an increase in the standard of living in the postwar period, particularly for most sectors of the working class in southern Ontario. But the situation is now changing. Canada and the U.S. are now on a "collision course" in the search for jobs – and this dramatic language is not mine, but that of the highly respectable, if not downright reactionary, Canadian-American Committee. In the nature of inter-imperialist rivalry, the working classes in all capitalist countries will find their income squeezed, the better to permit their capitalists to compete, while the Canadian working class will face de-industrialization, tending further to erode the real standard of living. Indeed, this is already happening. Manufacturing employment has stabilized in recent years, while inflation has eaten away gains in money wages.

Some, though not all, of the slack in jobs has been taken up by the expansion of the service sector, and particularly of the public sector. Canada already has, as a per cent of the labour force, the largest service sector of any of the industrialized capitalist countries. In the nature of the case, the ability of that sector to expand is clearly limited by the size of the actual productive sectors – resources and manufacturing. The ability of the state to act as employer of last resort is severely constrained by its current fiscal crisis consequent on escalating costs of servicing and tidying up after corporate capitalism while, again, tax revenues are limited by the size and growth of the actual productive sector.

In sum, then, the Canadian working class faces in the '70's pressures unprecedented in the postwar period in terms of the ability of the system to continue to deliver. The loss of its "privileges" creates a new potential for militancy and, to the extent the connection is made with the exigencies of dependent status, there is a new potential for an anti-imperialist movement.

There are two further serious problems with which Canadians must come to terms.

Firstly, the survival of Canada is threatened not only by the external threat of the U.S., but by the internal crisis of relations between Quebec and English Canada. If, on the one hand, one assumes that the Quebecois have the capacity and the right to determine their own destiny, while, on the other hand, one takes note of the extent of English Canadian support for Trudeau's implementation of the War Measures Act in 1970 – though it was clear at the time that his intent was to use the FLQ crisis as an opportunity to discredit independentism – then the urgent necessity is for English Canadians to come to terms with what is really going on in this country. Indeed, the issue of Quebec – or "national unity", as the Kings and the Trudeaus call it – has the capacity to divert us indefinitely from seeing the United States as the real threat to our survival. The English-Canadian ruling class dominates Quebec on behalf of American capital. English Canada must break that chain, both for the benefit of Quebec and of itself. If English Canada wants independence from the U.S., it can only get it if it is willing to give up its dominance over Quebec.

Developments in Quebec itself, while indicating no lessening in independentist sentiment, do show both an increasing recognition by the left that the ultimate enemy is U.S. imperialism, not English Canadian dependent capitalism, and an unprecedented capacity for labour militance and receptivity to socialist analysis. The base for a bi-national alliance of socialists in English Canada and Quebec remains precarious, but developments are clearly moving in the direction of improving that possibility. The possibility of working out radically new confederal arrangements depends to a great extent on the efforts of English Canadian socialists in the causes of independence from the U.S. and the right of Quebec to self-determination. And just as the NDP has failed to lead the independence struggle, so too it has failed, and abjectly, to defend the democratic rights of the Québecois; indeed, on this critical issue, no real difference exists between David Lewis and Pierre Elliot Trudeau.

Secondly, the Americanization of Canada has facilitated the balkanization of Canada and, hence, its further Americanization. It is an instructive, though depressing, fact that the major consequence for our politics to date of the American energy crisis appears to be the feud between Alberta and Ontario, of which Ottawa, which might be thought to represent the national interest, washes its hands. It may be an iron law for hinterland countries that no matter what the imperialists are doing, what never changes is their imperative to divide and conquer. In Canada, the heart of this tension flows from the law of uneven development, from the grossly uneven distribution of industry which results from the centralizing tendency of corporate capitalism in general and foreign-controlled corporate capitalism in particular. Only a socialist strategy committed to evening out development has the potential to reduce these tensions and permit of the creation of English Canada as a viable nation.

The disintegration of Canada appears to be inevitable to many Canadians only in the absence of a socialist analysis which shows that this disintegration is abetted by the nature of Canadian corporate capitalism.

A socialist strategy for independence necessarily focuses on the two major and classical institutions for working class action – the trade unions as the largest, all-encompassing working class organization, and a socialist party which is the organizing centre for those advanced workers who espouse and struggle for a socialist program. To understand the role of these two organizations it is essential to analyze them in their unity and interdependence but also in their contradiction and "difference."

Trade unions are organizations which include all workers in a given industry or institution and potentially include all of the six million Canadians who work for a wage or salary. They include the whole spectrum of views of working people from right to left – but who achieve unity on a minimum program on which major opinion is possible at a given time. Unions must inevitably include all workers, and short of a witch-hunt mentality such as that which existed during McCarthyism and which forbade "Communists" from holding union office, most Canadian unions do not currently exclude whole sections of workers for their views. (Although, as noted in the chapter on the Trade Union Movement, a whole group of militant unionists were excluded from full membership in Local 1005 of the United Steelworkers of America (Stelco, Hamilton) as recently as 1966 by action of the Pittsburgh International Office for their advocacy of greater autonomy in the union and for their criticism of office holders.) This is not to suggest that unions in Canada – either American or Canadian-based have achieved even minimally acceptable levels of democracy, but that most do have the constitutional basis for a potential challenge to any particular leadership or set of policies.

The particular problem of American domination, of course, puts additional limitations and strains on the potential for democracy. But there is the possibility that if a majority of steel or auto workers in Canada opted for a fully independent Canadian union, they could find the legitimate ways, starting with the existing union structure, to establish a United Steel Workers of Canada or a United Auto Workers of Canada. This would no doubt require an organized group or caucus of Canadian workers within their own union determined to fight for such a structural reorganization of their union into a Canadian union. The possibility depends on the freedom of such a group to campaign for independent Canadian unions within the existing American unions in Canada. Should that freedom be challenged, thus blocking the democratic right of Canadian workers to change the constitution of their union, the fat will truly be in the fire. The consequences – weakening of the trade union movement through internecine war or local break-aways – would be the responsibility of those who limited the freedom of Canadian trade unionists.

A socialist party is indispensable for the successful struggle for an independent socialist Canada. For how else can a full socialist program for action on a mass public basis and through the parliamentary arena be made a living reality to millions of Canadian working people? A socialist party not only provides an anti-imperialist and socialist analysis, and a clear view of the socialist goal and how it is to be obtained. It constantly unifies the economic and political struggles, providing leadership in the first place to trade unionists and also to the unorganized workers. It points to the interests of the working class as a whole, as compared to the more narrow interests of a particular section. It provides the organizational power for cohesive and concerted action at particular pressure points in the struggle and thus unifies the working class for maximum impact on the political and economic fronts. A socialist party is also a kind of school for socialist leadership and activitists, who learn from struggle and study about everything from the contradictions in the political economy to the nature and problems of culture in a dependent capitalist country.

Trade unions express the natural, spontaneous consciousness and feelings of workers as they confront the boss at the local level or even at the national level, whereas socialists try to raise the consciousness to full class, or socialist consciousness. Socialists demonstrate the links between all the fragmented, separate struggles to show that they are part of one strategic struggle of labour against capitalist exploitation.

There is obviously an (organic) link between trade union organization and socialist organization. Socialists can enhance the fighting spirit and capacity of the unions and provide them with the best activists; while the unions are the mass base for the socialist political activity and education through which workers become politically active. There is always a tension between the objectives of the socialist movement and the immediate practice of the trade union movement. But this is a tension which can lead to creative development within both of these indispensable sections of a healthy labour movement.

It is evident that without a mass democratic socialist party there can be no transformation to an independent socialist Canada. The strategic question for socialists is how such a party can be achieved.

The prospect of establishing the necessary socialist party in Canada by internal transformation of the NDP is demonstrably improbable. For several years the Waffle operated on a strategy of trying to transform the NDP from a basically reform liberal parliamentary party into a democratic socialist party which would combine mass extra-parliamentary activism with parliamentary politics. This strategy achieved limited success in producing a greater understanding of the need for independence and socialism. It brought together two or three thousand socialists who saw the need for the development of a party adequate to creating independence and socialism. It laid the basis for independent organizations of Wafflers in Ontario and Saskatchewan and of smaller groups in Manitoba, Alberta and B.C.

But this strategy ran its course when the right-wing leadership of the Ontario NDP combined with the top trade union officialdom to expel the Waffle as an organized group. This clearly demonstrated the power of the top union leaders, who feared that analagous movements in their own organizations would soon topple them from power. But more important than the open revelation of their determined opposition to an anti-imperialist policy was the revelation of the main source of power in the Ontario and Federal NDP. From the beginning, but more recently through structual changes in the NDP constitution, the top trade union leaders have been able to exercise decisive power. Union affiliates in Ontario can now literally dominate either the Ontario Convention or the Provincial Council and even the Federal Convention, as seen in the election of David Lewis in April 1971. The key to domination of the Ontario NDP by the top union leaders is to be found in the small locals, which may not be able to afford to send delegates to conventions or Councils, and who turn their credentials over to their regional or national office. In effect, the small locals, most of which are relatively apolitical, are dominated by the international representatives in their unions. They serve effectively as "rotten boroughs" whose delegates are picked by the top leadership of the union. Typically the delegates are not even members of the local they supposedly represent. It is clear that the union leadership now dominates the NDP.

Has this gone beyond the point of ever establishing potential control by the rank and file of the NDP? The only possibility for re-opening the NDP as a potential arena for real socialist politics would be a radical transformation of the unions themselves. Such a radical transformation, in the nature of the case, would begin in the large locals and among the rank and file activists and middle-level leadership. Since the NDP is linke ' to the very top of the union structure, the NDP is tied to precisely those elements of the union structure which will resist a transformation until it has gone a considerable distance. In sum, then, the NDP can at best follow such a transformation. It cannot lead it.

Yet, the need for an anti-imperialist policy is now even more pressing than in 1969. As a transitional form, the Ontario Waffle Movement for an Independent Socialist Canada can continue to press for a program and organize actions for independence – such as on public ownership of energy resource industries and on a fully Canadian car industry under public ownership. But a transitional form is only transitional.

A New Socialist Party
We need a socialist party which will engage in all aspects of political struggle with all the means available to it. In the context of advance capitalism and liberal democratic institutions, the means include parliamentary activity, but the important point is that under no circumstance should politics be confined thereto. Direct political action with the labour movement and unceasing educational work to expose the class bias of liberal ideology are critical matters.

There are many who recognize the need for a socialist party that will relate to the concerns and the culture of working people, and evolve itself out of those concerns and be a manifestation of that culture. For my part, I can only state my strong conviction that to do that will be to discover and unleash a powerful will among English Canadian working people for the survival of this country. It is ultimately for that reason that I would argue that anti-imperialism, the day-to-day experience of being a Canadian, is the cutting edge of socialist politics. The anti-nationalist bias of the liberal ideology may well be a surface phenomenon; there is a tradition of anti-Americanism in Canada that traditional politicians have touched for irresponsible purposes, but which socialists can redirect to the radical transformation of Canada outside the

American Empire. And, as previously suggested, it is within that context, and only within that context, that English Canadians are likely to abandon their historic propensity to put down the Québecois.

We need a socialist party that would have a correct conception of the nature of the state under capitalism and under socialism. The state in a capitalist society is a capitalist state. Therefore, simply to take control of the state can never be sufficient, for the state must be radically transformed as part and parcel of the transformation of capitalism.

This is not to deny that control of the state in a hinterland area is a necessary means to expropriate the multi-national corporation and replace foreign private ownership with Canadian public ownership. Nor, again, is it to deny the relevance of the electoral route as one arrow in the bow. Rather, the achievement of office must be used to help take power away from the owners of the means of production, the capitalists, and pass it to the producers themselves, the workers.

To do this would be to release the creative energies of the people. We could then begin to move to that humane and democratic society where the working people themselves, will directly control the conditions under which they work. Then work, rather than being the oppression that it now is, would become an expression of our humanity.

Notes

[1] George Grant, *Lament for a Nation: The Defeat of Canadian Nationalism* (Toronto, 1965).
[2] Donald Creighton, *Canada's First Century* (Toronto, 1970).
[3] George Grant, *Technology and Empire* (Toronto, 1969).
[4] Abraham Rotstein, *The Precarious Homestead* (Toronto, 1973), p. 246.
[5] Paul Baran, *The Political Economy of Growth* (New York, 1957).
[6] Andre Gunder Frank, *Capitalism and Underdevelopment in Latin America* (New York, 1969)
[7] Paul Sweezy and Harry Magdoff, "Notes on the Multinational Corporation," *Monthly Review*, October, 1969, p. 6.
[8] Stephen Hymer, "Partners in Development," *New Statements*, Vol. 1, No. 1, 1971.
[9] Arthur J. Cordell, *The Multinational Firm, Foreign Direct Investment, and Canadian Science Policy*, Science Council of Canada, Special Study No. 22, (Ottawa, 1972).
[10] Gunnar Adler-Karlsson, *Reclaiming the Canadian Economy: A Swedish Approach through Functional Socialism* (Toronto, 1970)

[11] C. W. Gonick, "Foreign Ownership and Political Decay" in Ian Lumsden, ed., *Close the 49th parallel: the Americanization of Canada* (Toronto, 1970), pp. 49-50.

[12] James Laxer, "The Americanization of the Canadian student movement," in Lumsden, ed., *Close the 49th parallel*, p. 276; an earlier version had appeared in *Canadian Dimension.*

Acknowledgements

This book arose from a twelve-evening course of lectures and discussion groups sponsored by the Toronto Educational Committee of the Ontario Waffle Movement for an Independent Socialist Canada, between January and April, 1973. Over 300 people enrolled for the entire course, and hundreds of others paid to attend one or more evenings. The high rate of attendance throughout the course attested to the sustaining interest of the lectures. The registration forms indicated a goodly proportion of trade unionists, civil servants, office workers, elementary and secondary school teachers, undergraduate and graduate students and some twenty teachers in universities and colleges. Many of those who returned questionnaires evaluating the course remarked on its uniqueness – in that it combined a scrutiny of economics with political and cultural issues, a logic which is built into this volume.

The main inspiration for the book came, therefore, from the remarkable response of the public to the Waffle series, and from the lecturers who strived to achieve excellence in the face of such unexpectedly wide public interest. The editorial board members for this book who made a special contribution were Julia Bass, the educational committee chairman, James Littleton, whose work in preparing the book was invaluable, and Bela Egyed who spent several weeks in intensive editorial work. People who served as discussion leaders of the twelve groups contributed substantially, not only to the discussion groups themselves but to the evaluation process which entered into the revision of the lectures into chapters and of an integrated book on the political economy of Canada.

The editor warmly acknowledges their invaluable help. The authors worked co-operatively and with unusual speed in preparing the manuscripts. The editor and authors are grateful for the contribution made to the production of this book by Shirley Petgrave and Diane Hyndman who typed the manuscripts. While in agreement with most of the views expressed in this volume, I do not take responsibility for all of them. Ultimately the work of each author will be judged on its own merits.